SPIES

in the
Continental Capital

Also by the Author

Invisible Ink: Spycraft of the American Revolution
Rebellion in the Ranks: Mutinies of the American Revolution

SPIES

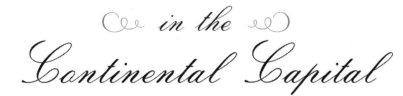

in the

Continental Capital

Espionage Across Pennsylvania
During the
American Revolution

JOHN A. NAGY

WESTHOLME
Yardley

Westholme Publishing, LLC

904 Edgewood Road

Yardley, Pennsylvania 19067

ISBN: 978-1-59416-133-9

Printed in the United States of America.

Book Club Edition

To Ida Marie Nagy, Jennifer Ann Nagy, and Lisa Marie Nagy
with appreciative thanks for all your encouragement,
help, and patience,
and to the memories of
my father, John Nagy, and my mother, Angela Nagy,
for always having been there for me.

CONTENTS

INTRODUCTION

This Pennsylvania spy story begins in 1763, when the French and Indian War ended, and it continues through to the end of the American Revolutionary War. Although the French lost most of their territory in North America as a result of the war, they did not give up the idea of reclaiming that territory and even more during their next war with their traditional rival, England. It did not take the French long to send spies to America to determine the attitudes of the people, the military situation, and the possibilities that could be turned in their favor. One of the key places for French spying activity was the colony of Pennsylvania, since its frontier had been an important crossroads of French influence in North America.

This book will discuss those individuals who were residents of the commonwealth of Pennsylvania and operated as spies for the French, British, or Americans, as well as the nonresident spies who operated within Pennsylvania, particularly in and around Philadelphia. Note that individuals on the frontier may have been called spies in period documents and memoirs, but when their activities are closely examined, many turn out to have simply been scouts doing reconnaissance. Such scouts are not included in this book. Although some of the techniques used by spies will be discussed, a more detailed study of the subject is found in my book *Invisible Ink: Spycraft of the American Revolution.*

Some spies were motivated by loyalty to their side while others were in it simply for the money. Some people played both sides to ensure they would be with the winner. Because Philadelphia was the largest city in North America, was occupied by the British during the war, and was home to the Continental Congress for long stretches, much of the espionage activity in Pennsylvania was centered in that great city.

One of the difficulties encountered in writing a history of spies in Pennsylvania is that the papers of General William Howe, commander in chief of British forces from October 10, 1775, to May

18, 1778, were destroyed when a family seat at Westport, Ireland, burned in the early nineteenth century. Therefore, information on British headquarters operations under his command has to be drawn from other sources. It is hoped that in the future, additional manuscripts will be found that provide more clues to identify more spies operating for the British in Pennsylvania and other colonies in America. Another problem is that much of the previous scholarship on spies during the American Revolution has focused on New England and the New York metropolitan area. An exception is the Benedict Arnold conspiracy, in which the American general offered to turn over the fortifications at West Point to the British, which was initiated from Philadelphia. Much of the information on Pennsylvania spies has never been consolidated.

Over time some spy stories get embellished, and it can be difficult to distinguish fact from fiction. It is the purpose of this book to reveal what we actually know about some of these spies. For example, Robert Walsh first published the Lydia Darragh story in the *American Quarterly Review* in 1827, based upon information given him by friends of the Darraghs.[1] Could the tale of this famous American spy be true? Until now, no documents had been found from 1777 to indicate that the Darraghs were the source of any military intelligence. Did the friends of the Darraghs remember all their incidents correctly, having recalled something that happened nearly fifty years earlier? Most likely they did make some errors, but they would have gotten the protagonist correct. The article *Lydia Darragh: One of the Heroines of the Revolution,* by Henry Darrach (no relation to Lydia Darragh), read before the City History Society of Philadelphia on November 10, 1915, is often overlooked in the discussions of the Darragh story. He makes a strong case that she could have been, and probably was, a spy.

One of two main arguments against the Darragh story has been that she could not have gotten through the American and British lines north of the city. But Charles Marshall wrote in his diary that his father, Christopher Marshall, said, "Lydia Darra[g]h came out through the British defensive lines on May 6, 1778 from occupied Philadelphia."[2] The Marshalls were intimately acquainted with the Darraghs; thirty-eight–year-old Christopher Marshall Jr. called her "Aunt Lydia Darragh."[3] Also, Adjutant General Major Carl

Leopold Bauermeister of the Hessian forces wrote on December 16, 1777, that on December 3, 1777, "the highways from Philadelphia to Germantown and Frankford, and the road to Trenton by way of Jenkintown, are open to anyone. Some Philadelphians have been appointed to give passes to loyalists, who are then permitted to pass the pickets. When returning, these people always bring foodstuffs with them. The rebel light dragoons frequently carry the women's packages on their horses as far as their vedettes.[4] From these people we receive most of the news about the rebels."[5] The British were interested in women going into the American territory and bringing back intelligence; therefore, Lydia Darragh would not have had any problem passing through lines to get into and out of Philadelphia.

The other argument against the story being true has been that according to the story, the older Darragh son was a Continental lieutenant, but no Lieutenant Darragh had been found among lists of the American forces. Charles Darragh, son of Lydia Darragh, was mentioned in her will as being in the army.[6] Charles was a former clerk to Commodore Thomas Seymour of the Pennsylvania navy. I discovered that in February 1777, he was promoted from ensign to lieutenant in the 2nd Pennsylvania Regiment of the Continental Line.[7] A 2nd Pennsylvania Regiment court-martial was held on April 21, 1778, with Captain Peter Gosner as president and Lieutenant Charles Darragh part of the board of officers hearing the case.[8] Charles Darragh left the service on July 1, 1778, less than two weeks after the British evacuated Philadelphia.[9] With Philadelphia back in American control, there was no longer any need to maintain secret communications with his parents. With the two main arguments against the Darragh operation removed, the probability of the core of the story being true are greatly raised.

One of the embellishments to the story was that the Darraghs were expelled from a Quaker meeting for their espionage activities. This was not the case. Lydia attended the Free Quakers Meeting (their meetinghouse still stands opposite the new Visitors' Center on Independence Mall), and before that, the old Arch Street Meeting. She and William, her husband, are interred in the old burial ground for that meeting (which is no longer standing), in what is now the parking lot behind the present meetinghouse at

Fourth and Arch streets. Her spying activities were not generally known at the time. She was read out (disowned) when most of those who had been Free Quakers or who were active militarily were being disowned by their respective meetings. Her disownment is recorded in October 1782 for not attending meeting and for "joining with a number of persons, associated under a pretense of religious duty, so far as to attend their Meeting."[10] Another embellishment is that she was the first to warn of the British attack on Philadelphia. This is not true, as her intelligence would have only confirmed what General George Washington, commander in chief of the Continental Army, already knew from other sources.

Although no one in 184 years had found a Darragh spy report, I decided to give it another try and put to work what I had learned in nineteen years of studying American Revolutionary War espionage. I reasoned that the document would not be signed "Darragh," or it would have been found. Therefore, I would be looking for a letter with either a code name or initials. The document would have exited Philadelphia by way of Frankford, Pennsylvania, as Walsh's article said. In later tellings of the story, William Darragh is writing the messages. I decided to search for a letter from William rather than one from Lydia. All the versions of the story have them active in early December 1777. The 1827 story has the Darragh contact at Frankford being an American officer named Craig. So I started examining correspondence from that period, looking for something between William Darragh and Craig.

When I searched the George Washington papers at the Library of Congress, I found that Captain Charles Craig of the 4th Continental Dragoons was at Frankford on December 3.[11] In Craig's letters to Washington of November 20 and 28 from Frankford, he mentioned that he was getting intelligence from within Philadelphia.[12] I continued my search and there it was—a letter dated December 4, 1777, from Frankford attributed to a "W. D."— William Darragh—who had been in Philadelphia. It was a report on the British army's preparations in Philadelphia to attack the Continental Army.[13] I had found an elusive Darragh document.

American historians usually identify Julien Achard de Bonvouloir, a secret envoy sent by France to Congress, as a spy; therefore, his story is included in this book.

I have tried to identify as many Pennsylvania spies as possible and to determine what evidence is true and what may be fiction. Since spies did their best to cover their tracks we are often left with documentation that provides little more than an identity, an accusation, an arrest, or an execution. Therefore some of these accounts in the book appear simply as fragments from the past. Although the flow of newly discovered Revolutionary War documents has slowed, it has not ceased. It is hoped that this work will encourage others to begin or continue to strive to use new documents and analysis to identify those spies who remain unidentified or to add to what we know about the spies revealed in this book.

ONE

A Peace Treaty Is Signed, the War Begins

The battle between England and France for most of North America and the Caribbean ended with the signing of the Treaty of Paris on February 10, 1763. The treaty, ending the French and Indian War (known as the Seven Years' War in Europe), gave Britain all of New France in North America east of the Mississippi, other than New Orleans. France retained an archipelago of eight islands south of Newfoundland in the North Atlantic, with Miquelon-Langlade and Saint Pierre being the largest. The French turned over their claim to New Orleans and the lands west of the Mississippi to their ally Spain, as compensation for Spain's losing Florida to the British. As soon as the ink was dry on the treaty, France began to prepare for the next war with England.

In 1764, French Lieutenant Nicholas de Sarrebourse de Pontleroy de Beaulieu, in the navy of the Department of Rochefort was sent to visit the English colonies in North America to determine their capabilities in the next war.[1] Pontleroy was well acquainted with ship building, drawing, and piloting. Upon the completion of his assignment, he returned to England in 1766 and reported to a Mr. Durand, the chief clerk at the French embassy in London. Durand forwarded the report to Etienne François Duc de Choiseul, the French secretary of state for foreign affairs. The report said the colonies were too ambitious, rich, and aware of their strength to stay obedient to Great Britain. A revolution that resulted in American independence would be a disadvantage to France because these states produced everything they needed and would be a threat to French rule in the West Indies.[2]

One of Choiseul's agents in London reported that the Americans needed only weapons, a leader, and a belief in their self-reliance in order to obtain their independence from England. The agent recommended that France and Spain try to make that independence come about.[3]

In a dispatch dated October 19, 1766, the Count de Guerchy, France's ambassador at London, asked for letters and a passport for Pontleroy, using his family name of Beaulieu. His mission was to travel throughout the British colonies to gather intelligence posing as an Acadian wanderer.[4] Durand wrote to Choiseul that Pontleroy did not have a talent for writing but could draw the plans of the principal ports. To accomplish this, Pontleroy was to enter the service of an American merchant who would put him in command of a ship. Pontleroy would receive just his lieutenant's pay for this task. Choiseul agreed, and Pontleroy left for America.[5]

Johann de Kalb was a Bavarian who entered the French army in 1743. He was a major during the French and Indian War and was promoted to lieutenant colonel on May 19, 1761.[6] In April 20, 1767, Choiseul, on a recommendation from Count de Broglie and the Prince of Soubise (Charles de Rohan), wrote to de Kalb and told him he had been reappointed in the French army.[7] Lieutenant General Count de Broglie had been made a marshal of France by King Louis XV.[8] The Prince of Soubise was a companion of Louis XV's, and his great grandmother was Madame de Pompadour, governess of the royal children of France. Because de Broglie and the prince had Louis's confidence, Choiseul had to consider their suggestions for political reasons. Two days later, de Kalb was informed by a Mr. Dubois, the chief clerk of the Ministry of War, that his assignment had been changed. A Mr. Appony, private secretary to Choiseul, had been told to write up instructions on a secret mission to America. The first part of de Kalb's assignment was to go to Amsterdam to gather intelligence on England's American colonies and then to journey to America. Once in America he was to determine whether the colonists intended to try to withdraw from British rule. If rebellion was their intention, he

Johann de Kalb, a French spy, took lodging in 1768 with Mrs. Rachel Graydon at the "slate-roof house." The house was built circa 1684-1699 at the corner of Second Street and Norris Alley (later renamed Sansom Street) in Philadelphia. It was rented by William Penn for use as his city residence from 1699 to 1701. It was torn down in 1867. Now it is the site of Welcome Park. (*Watson, Annals of Philadelphia*)

was to determine if "they are in need of good engineers and artillery officers, or other individuals, and whether they should be supplied with them." He was also to determine the colonists' ability to procure war supplies and raise an army.[9]

On May 2, 1767, de Kalb was given his passport and one thousand two hundred French francs to cover his expenses. He was provided with letters of introduction to the French ambassadors at Brussels and The Hague, who would send his dispatches back to France. He sent his first report from The Hague on July 18, 1767 and a second letter on August 11.[10] Choiseul answered on August 19 with instructions for him to make "a speedy tour to America."[11] He left for London after writing an answer to Choiseul on August 28. On October 4, he sailed from the town of Gravesend on the Thames River in the merchantman *Hercules* with a Captain Hommet bound for Philadelphia. De Kalb instructed the French ministry to send his instructions in a cipher to his wife, Anna Elizabeth Emilie van Robais, who was at the family home outside of Paris, and she would then forward them to him.[12] He hoped this method would not arouse suspicion and his mission would remain secret.

De Kalb landed in Philadelphia on January 12, 1768.[13] He sent letters to Choiseul on January 15 and 20, 1768, from Philadelphia. He took lodging at Mrs. Rachel Graydon's, a slate-roof house at the corner of Second Street and Norris Alley in Philadelphia.[14] She had leased the property from the Norris family beginning in 1764. The house was built sometime before 1700 for Samuel Carpenter.[15] Its famous guests included William Penn and his family, and Brigadier General John Forbes in 1759.[16] Edward Hyde, Lord Cornbury, the royal governor of New York and New Jersey, dined in the house in 1702.

De Kalb completed his intelligence gathering in Philadelphia and by March 1768 was in Boston. While there, he reported that he did not believe that the Americans could be induced to accept foreign aid, because they felt the king would treat them fairly.[17] Because he was not receiving answers to his reports, de Kalb decided to return to France, where he landed in June 1768, after first traveling to Canada.

Julien Achard de Bonvouloir was sent by France as a secret envoy to Congress. He was born in 1749, and was lame from a childhood accident. He had served as a volunteer in the French army in the West Indies in the Regiment du Cap. His two brothers also went into military service. After contracting a disease, he left Saint Domingue (present-day Haiti) and traveled through the British colonies in 1774 and 1775. At age twenty-six, he went to London at the suggestion of Count de Broglie. He offered his services to French Ambassador Adrien-Louis de Bonnières Comte de Guines, proposing to go to America and use his sources of information in Philadelphia, New York, and Providence.[18] The ambassador recommended Bonvouloir's mission through Charles Gravier, the Comte de Vergennes, who was the French foreign minister to King Louis XVI. Vergennes responded on August 7 that the king had accepted the proposal.[19] Bonvouloir was given two hundred Louis a year as payment and for his living expenses. He was also given a predated lieutenant's commission so he could enter the Continental Army.

Bonvouloir was instructed to send his letters to a Mr. Guillebert in care of a Martin Froment, assistant to the mayor in Calais, France. Froment would give them to a Mr. Grandin, who would forward them to their destination. All the letters were to be addressed to a company in Antwerp, Belgium, and were to discuss business matters. Any secret information was to be written in milk that would be invisible when dried. The invisible writing would be made visible by the application of heat.[20] On September 8, 1775, Bonvouloir left London for Philadelphia.

After one hundred days on rough seas, Bonvouloir arrived in Philadelphia. He reported that during the trip, as the ship's food supply dwindled, the captain of the vessel reduced Bonvouloir's food rations to two worm-eaten biscuits, a bit of dried beef, and some foul water.[21] His cover was that he was an Antwerp merchant on private business. Bonvouloir knew that a Paris-born bookseller named Francis Daymon was Benjamin Franklin's part-time librarian for the Library Company of Philadelphia. Bonvouloir described Daymon as "a steady man and one of great use to me."[22] Bonvouloir contacted Daymon, who, as an intermediary, notified the Second Continental Congress that a foreigner was in Philadelphia with a secret message to communicate.

The Congress was meeting at the Pennsylvania State House, now known as Independence Hall. It had recognized the need for foreign intelligence and foreign alliances with a resolution on November 29, 1775, that created the Committee of Correspondence (soon renamed the Committee of Secret Correspondence). The committee members—who made up America's first foreign intelligence directorate—were Benjamin Franklin of Pennsylvania (chairman), Benjamin Harrison of Virginia, John Dickinson of Pennsylvania, and John Jay of New York.

The Congress decided to meet with "M. de B." because it was looking to Europe for aid. The committee was to obtain answers to the following questions:

1. Can he inform us what the disposition of the Court of France is toward the colonies of North America, whether it is favorable, and in what way we can be reliably assured of this? 2. Can we obtain two able engineers who are trustworthy and well-recommended, and what steps must we take to obtain them? 3. Can we have directly from France arms and other military supplies, in exchange for the products of our country, and be allowed free entrance and exit to

French ports? M. de B . . . may rest assured that if by means of his efforts we are favorably heard, we shall repose in him all the confidence that one can give a man of distinction whose goodwill toward us has not yet received a sure token of our gratitude.[23]

Bonvouloir claimed not to represent the French government but to have powerful friends in France. His answer to the first question was that the matter was too delicate for him to answer. He quickly sent a request to France for two engineers and assured the Americans that they would be supplied. (The committee earlier that month had also made a request for two engineers to Charles Dumas, who was working as an American spy in Holland.[24]) In answer to the question on exchanging products for arms and other military supplies and having access to French ports, Bonvouloir replied that it was a merchant-to-merchant matter and not an inconvenience to France. But he cautioned the Americans not to send all their shipments to the same French port.[25]

Bonvouloir met with Franklin, Jay, and Thomas Jefferson, whom he called the Privy Council. Jefferson was a Virginia-born lawyer, slave owner, and politician who previously served in the Virginia House of Burgesses. He was selected in June 1775 as one of the Virginia delegates to the Second Continental Congress. The meeting with Bonvouloir was held in the Library Company's space in the east room of the second floor of Carpenter's Hall.[26] Bonvouloir was apparently wearing a disguise at the time, because Jay, who was thirty-one, described the twenty-six-year-old foreigner as an elder lame man.

During their conversations, the Americans asked about sending emissaries to France. Bonvouloir told them that it would be hazardous, as "everything about London is known in France and about France in London."[27] While in Philadelphia, Bonvouloir meet with Franklin and members of the Committee of Secret Correspondence between December 18 and 27.[28] The meetings convinced Bonvouloir that Congress would decide on independence, which he included in his December 28 report to the Count de Guines. His report was carried by his courier to Nantes, France, in the brigantine *St. John*, which carried flour and other agricultural items.[29] The merchandise was going to Swiss-born American agent Jean Daniel Schweighauser at Nantes. The courier was told that he was to sink the papers in the sea if they were being pursued. Bonvouloir also sent two other letters with significantly less information, which, unknown to him, the Americans were also sending to France in two different ships. Bonvouloir's future correspondence went by way of Saint Domingue, where he had a trusted friend.

Carpenters' Hall was the site of the First Continental Congress in 1774. It was built between 1770 and 1774 by the Carpenters' Company, a craft guild. (*Lisa Nagy*)

Bonvouloir advised the Count de Guines that he had paid informants in other colonies who were supplying him with intelligence. He asked that some ten or twelve packets of merchandise be sent to him marked with his initials, "AB," to offset his costs.[30] While in Philadelphia, Bonvouloir used his initials as code for his secret correspondence, which was sent to his place of residence in France to make it appear as if someone was writing to him there.[31]

A year later, Bonvouloir, apparently still living in Philadelphia, was suspected of spying. On November 27, 1776, Congress ordered that the Board of War, in conjunction with a member of the Pennsylvania Council of Safety, seize Bonvouloir and his papers, and, after examining them, report to Congress.[32]

The British also had spies operating in the British colonies in North America.

Gilbert Barkly emigrated from Scotland to Philadelphia in 1755, and went into the mercantile trade. In 1757, he proposed fitting out a vessel at Philadelphia with wines, liquors, and other necessities to be shipped to New York for John Campbell, Fourth Earl of Loudoun, and commander in chief of British forces in North America.[33]

Barkly and John Hay started the firm Barkly and Hay in Canada on June 14, 1756.[34] In July 1762, Hay traveled to Philadelphia for an accounting of their business. They decided that Hay would go back to Canada and dissolve the firm. Hay sold goods at Montreal at auction, and a brew house, distillery, and stock at Quebec, but the proceeds and buildings were converted to Hay's personal accounts. Barkly, believing he had been swindled by his partner, traveled to Quebec in June 1764. He accused Hay of keeping two sets of books and wanted to see the real accounting books. While in Hay's house, Barkly's bookkeeper, George Richan, and Barkly's clerk, James Skinner, tried to recreate the business accounts from the notebooks Hay supplied. After six or seven weeks, all the business books disappeared from Barkly's room.[35] Hay claimed that Barkly had tried to defraud him and that action justified his seizing all the firm's books.

Barkly spent a number of years as a merchant in Philadelphia before returning to London in 1773. On May 26 that year, he wrote to the directors of the East India Company about establishing a branch in North America and offering to provide information on the teas that will sell in North America. He claimed his information would help end the widespread practice of smuggling tea. He recommended warehousing the tea in America and holding quarterly auctions, as was done in London, to allow the merchants to pay what they could afford. He claimed a third of the three million people in North America drank tea twice a day, resulting in a yearly consumption of 5,703,125 pounds of tea. Naturally, he offered himself as one of the managers in North America. He also stated that John Inglis of Philadelphia, who was his business partner, was "a man of probity, fortune, and respect."[36]

On June 5, 1773, Grey Cooper, who was a member of Parliament and secretary to the treasury, recommended Barkly to the East India Company and endorsed his information concerning the quantity of tea being consumed in America. Cooper suggested he serve the company should it establish an office there.[37] Having friends in high places got Barkly included in a meeting of eleven interested parties concerning the exporting of tea to American that was held at noon on July 1, 1773, at the five-bay, three-story East India House on Leadenhall Street, London.[38] Barkly claimed that with the current taxes, it would be cheaper for Americans to buy tea from the East India Company than from merchants who were selling smuggled tea.[39] On August 4, Barkly was told that he was selected as a factor, or agent, and was being shipped a consignment of chests of tea to Philadelphia.[40] Barkly left England on September 27, 1773, and arrived in Chester, Pennsylvania, on December 23 aboard the *Polly*, which was carrying a consignment of the dreaded tea.[41] Barkly disembarked from the ship and resigned his commission as soon as he was told of a meeting at the Pennsylvania State House against landing the tea. He returned to England.

In March 1775, the British prime minister, Lord North, sent Barkly back to America with the mission of providing intelligence on the proceedings of Congress. He arrived in Philadelphia in May. His reports were sent to Grey Cooper. Barkly reported on a visit he received June 19, 1775, from John Dickinson, a member of the Continental Congress who was an old acquaintance. He also reported on ship arrivals, the activities of Congress, and the design of the chevaux-de-frise defense structures in the Delaware River.[42] This was claimed to be the first use of chevaux-de-frise in a river; previously they were used as a land defense in Europe. Barkly sent a copy of the design via a Mr. Weir on October 5, 1775. Weir was to be set on shore at Falmouth, England, and then make his way over land to London. He was to personally deliver the letter with the design to Cooper and get reimbursed for his traveling expenses in England.

Weir was to board the brig *Black Prince* at Chester, Pennsylvania, where he arrived late in the evening and obtained lodging. Early the next morning, a detachment of light cavalry surrounded the building and was going to search it. Weir gave the papers to a man who shared his room and told him that Weir's and Barkly's lives depended on them not being discovered. The lodger got away with the papers, and Barkly had to pay him 210 pounds for their return and for his effort. Barkly also had to promise the lodger more money to keep him silent. Weir boarded the ship and returned to England. On November 30, Barkly also sent a copy of the design of the chevaux-de-frise to Royal Governor William Tryon of New York via Captain John Davidson on a packet boat.

On October 29, 1776, Barkly left Philadelphia and traveled overland to New York City. On his trip, he stopped in Trenton and dined with Lieutenant Colonel Thomas Elliott of the 6th Virginia Regiment, who was very loose with his information. Upon reaching New York, Barkly turned in to British General William Howe an intelligence report dated November 10, 1776, that included information on the defenses on the Delaware River. Howe appears to have ignored the report.[43] Barkly returned to Philadelphia when the British occupied the city. He sailed for London on the *Britannia* on December 12, 1777.[44]

Sometimes spies are of the homegrown variety, offering their services to the enemy.

On September 6, 1775, between eleven a.m. and noon, about thirty associators took Isaac Hunt from his home to the London Coffee House in Philadelphia.[45] (Since 1747, the term "associators" had been used in Pennsylvania to refer to volunteer militiamen. By 1775, it was universally accepted throughout all the colonies to mean those individuals who associated for defense against the British.) Because of Hunt's subversive actions, the associators placed him in a cart and, with drum beating, took him through the city's main streets. They stopped at different locations, and Hunt would beg forgiveness from the crowd. When they got to Dr. John Kearsley's house, which was on Front Street a little below High Street, Kearsley "threw open his window, snapped a pistol twice amongst the crowd, upon which they seized him, took his pistol, with another in his pocket from him, both of which were loaded with swan shot.[46] In the scuffle, he was wounded in the hand. Hunt was removed from the cart and Kearsley put in it. With the drum beating to the tune of "The Rogue's March," Kearsley was taken through the streets without a hat and with a disheveled wig. He was brought to the London Coffee House and taunted, then returned to his house and left there. During all this, the associators had to prevent an assembled mob from tarring and feathering him. When the associators left, the mob proceeded to break the windows in the house.[47]

The London Coffee House was opened for business in 1754 by William Bradford, and it became a popular meeting place to conduct business and auctions. It was torn down in 1883. (*Watson, Annals of Philadelphia*)

It wasn't long before Kearsley was in trouble again. Leonard Snowden, a Philadelphia Quaker brewer on Pemberton Street, wrote to England statements that were detrimental to the patriot movement. The letter was given to a female courier.[48] She had sewn them in a pocket on the lower part of one of her garments. The Continental Congress on October 6, 1775, forwarded information to the Pennsylvania Council of Safety concerning several individuals whose activities were considered adverse to the patriot movement. The Council of Safety had the Philadelphia Committee of Inspection and Observation, which checked for subversive activities and spies, look into the matter.[49] Christopher Carter, who was in partnership with a Mr. Spikeman on Market Street in Philadelphia, was intercepted at Chester, Pennsylvania, while attempting to get letters on board a ship leaving Pennsylvania. He had the letters in two parcels—one addressed to Thomas Corbyn and the other to a Mrs. McCalla. After he told officials that the sources of the letters were James Brooks, Kearsley, Reverend Mr. Jonathan Odell, and Snowden, he was released.[50]

On October 5, 1775, Brooks and Kearsley were arrested at Kearsley's house, and Snowden was arrested in the street near Kearsley's front door. The doctor's desk was sealed, and a guard was stationed at his door. By eleven p.m., the three men were confined at the State House until the next morning.[51]

In its meeting in Philadelphia on October 7, the Committee of Safety received a committee report that included a deposition from Christopher Carter and letters from Kearsley, Brooks, and Odell to various people, some of whom were in the British army and the

Committee of Safety considered hostile to the American cause. The documents included a plan for private correspondence and Kearsley and Brooks's plan for British troops to subdue America by invading Pennsylvania and other colonies. The Committee of Safety considered Kearsley, Snowden, and Brooks guilty of espionage but did not decide about Odell, who was a resident of New Jersey. The committee issued a warrant dated October 7, 1775, to Thomas Dewees, jailer for Philadelphia, to take Kearsley, Brooks, and Snowden into custody.[52] Odell, who was in Philadelphia at the time, was put on his honor not to leave the city.[53] The Committee for Inspection and Observation for the City and Liberties of Philadelphia had intercepted two letters Odell wrote to England and sent them to the Pennsylvania Committee of Safety. The Committee for Inspection and Observation was formed to ensure compliance of the nonimportation, consumption, and exportation of British goods. The Pennsylvania Committee of Safety sent the letters to the New Jersey Committee of Safety because Odell was the Anglican minister at Saint Mary's Church in Burlington, New Jersey, and Saint Andrews's Church in Mount Holly, New Jersey.[54]

On October 8, Carter was brought to Philadelphia along with a parcel of letters recovered from the *Black Prince*. He was taken to the same jail as Brooks, Kearsley, and Snowden.[55] The Committee of Safety issued a warrant, signed by Owen Biddle and Bernard Dougherty, to Dewees to keep Carter in a separate cell from the other three men.[56]

On the ninth, the Committee of Safety met at the Lodge Room at the Philosophical Society. The four prisoners were paraded with an armed guard of no less than fifty, with drums and fifes playing to and from their trial.[57] On the tenth, additional letters were produced that originated from Brooks and Kearsley.[58] Kearsley had called the Whigs—those who opposed British rule—"a pack of cowards" (those who favored the British were called Tories). A map of the Delaware River channels had been found among his papers recovered from the *Black Prince*.[59]

On the fourteenth, the Continental Congress decided that Brooks and Kearsley should be closely confined and their movements restricted.[60] The Committee of Safety appointed General Daniel Roberdeau of the Pennsylvania militia to determine who would get admittance to Brooks, Carter, Kearsley, and Snowden. It also required that he be present at any interviews.[61] On the eighteenth, the committee ruled on Carter, who had turned over the incriminating letters of Kearsley and Brooks, who had attempted "to procure British troops to invade this [Pennsylvania] and the other colonies in a hostile manner." The committee was unanimous in its belief that Carter was guilty of espionage. But it added that

having been represented to this Board, by the Committee of Inspection and Observation, that a deputation from their Body had promised-the said Carter protection from punishment, on condition of his delivering up the papers and giving information of the designs to be executed by him and the others concerned, which he has complied with; It is therefore, Resolved, that Christopher Carter's person be enlarged and set at liberty, on his giving security in the sum of five hundred pounds for his good behavior, and that he will not leave the province without license from the Assembly or Committee of Safety, nor be concerned in practices or Correspondence during his stay, that shall be inimical to the United Colonies.[62]

On the nineteenth, the Pennsylvania Committee of Safety wrote to the Committees of Safety of Lancaster and York counties to say it was sending Brooks and Kearsley to their respective jails. Kearsley was not going alone: he was allowed to take a servant and a clerk, Stephen Bayard, to his jail in York. Kearsley, to offset the expenses that had been incurred by the Pennsylvania Committee of Safety and that would be incurred in his removal to York, issued a pay order to Robert Morris to pay Abel James, Thomas Lawrence, William Pollard, and Captain John Wilcox.[63] Morris was a Philadelphia merchant, delegate to the Continental Congress, and signer of the Declaration of Independence. During the war, he worked to raise money to keep the Continental Army in the field. Jailer Dewees submitted to the Pennsylvania Committee of Safety a bill for liquor and provisions for the soldiers who had guarded Brooks and Kearsley while they were in Philadelphia.[64] He apparently revised the bill and included Snowden and the provisions supplied to the prisoners. The committee approved payment of fifty-three pounds, four shillings, one pence from Thomas Wharton Jr., a Philadelphia merchant and a member of the Pennsylvania Committee of Safety.[65]

Shortly before dawn on October 24, Brooks and Kearsley left Philadelphia, guarded as far as Lancaster by Captain Abraham Markoe and seven other members of the Philadelphia Light Horse.[66] When they arrived in Lancaster, about eighty miles west of Philadelphia, Brooks and Kearsley were placed in jail there. Kearsley was taken to York the next day.[67] At the end of 1776, he was moved to the jail at Carlisle.[68] He died there in 1777.[69] Brooks, with the help of Caleb Johnson, escaped from the Lancaster jail on the evening of October 3, 1777. Johnson was suspected of helping Brooks escape. He was arrested and held in jail until the end of December, when he was released.[70]

Brothers Arthur and William Lee went to England in 1766 due to business pursuits. William was a mercantile agent for the Colony of Virginia in London and served as the high sheriff of London in 1775. Arthur was a doctor and lawyer and served as an agent for the colony of Massachusetts. On April 3, 1775, William Lee advised Josiah Quincy Jr., who was an attorney from Massachusetts, that "besides the money £1,000, a man paid to several members in the New York Assembly previous to their meeting in January last, large sums have since been sent there and to some other Colonies to bribe particular men. Dr Smith in Philadelphia should be watched."[71] Dr. William Smith was the provost, or college president, and secretary to the board of trustees of the College of Philadelphia (now the University of Pennsylvania).[72] He was also an ordained Church of England clergyman, and a likely subject for suspected sympathy to the British. During the French and Indian War, Smith was jailed by the Pennsylvania provincial assembly for his printed attacks on the colony's military policies. Smith actually conducted his ethics classes from February to April 1758 from a jail at Third and Market streets. In a most unusual turn of events, he courted Rebecca Moore—the daughter of his jail mate, William Moore, a leading Philadelphia Anglican, judge, and a provincial assemblyman—and married her that year.[73]

William Lee also sent information on April 12, 1775, that, "It is said that £25,000 has been sent to General [Thomas] Gage [at Boston] for the purpose of bribery and that Major S____ is now gone to Philadelphia with money to bribe the Congress."[74] Unfortunately, Lee does not identify who in Congress was to receive the funds.

TWO

British Intrigues in Congress

The delegates to the First Continental Congress assembled at City Tavern in Philadelphia at ten o'clock on September 5, 1774. They walked over to Carpenter's Hall on Chestnut Street, and upon inspecting the building, the majority agreed that it was acceptable for their purpose. The Congress met from September 5 to October 26. Twelve of the thirteen colonies sent a total of fifty-six delegates; Georgia did not participate, as it remained loyal to the king. The delegates met behind closed doors, and its members pledged to keep their transactions secret.[1] Joseph Galloway, a graduate of the College of New Jersey (now Princeton University) and large landowner, was a member of the Congress and provided intelligence of its meetings to New Jersey Royal Governor William Franklin. Galloway was a member of the Pennsylvania House of Representatives from 1757 to 1775, where he served as speaker from 1766 to 1774. He signed the Nonimportation Agreement, in which the colonies agreed not to buy any imported British goods, but opposed independence for the colonies. Governor Franklin wrote to Lord Dartmouth on September 6, 1774, that he was sending him an "extract of two letters from a gentleman who is one of the delegates." Governor Franklin later identified the source of the letters as Joseph Galloway of Pennsylvania.[2]

Benjamin Franklin, while in London as a representative for several colonies, wrote to Galloway, "Permit me to hint to you that it is whispered here [in London] by ministerial people that yourself and Mr. Jay of New York, are friends to their measures, and give them private intelligence of the news of the popular or country part of America. I do not believe this; but I thought it a duty of friendship to acquaint you with the report."[3] William Lee, a mercantile agent of Virginia in England, said he heard rumors about John Jay, who was a delegate from New York, providing information to the British.[4] Jay wrote to the Reverend John Vardill, a British spy, in England on September 24, 1774. He advised that the pledge of secrecy prevented his commenting on the proceedings of Congress and that many people were aroused by the closing of Boston Harbor and the Canada bill, which allowed the French Canadians to practice their religion and continue using the French language. Jay favored maintaining a union with Britain.[5] No other correspondence has been found from the opening of the Continental Congress to Benjamin Franklin's letter that shows that Jay passed secret information to the British.

Galloway put forth a "Plan of Union" that called for an American parliament and reconciliation with England. Galloway wanted American commissioners with full negotiating powers to be sent to the British court. The other delegates did not think they should send commissioners to "dangle at the heels of a minister, and under go the scorn of Parliament."[6]

The British army and navy arrived off of Sandy Hook, New Jersey, in July 1776. They began landing troops on Staten Island, New York, for an attack on New York City. The Continental Congress had formed a committee to devise a plan to encourage Hessians and other foreigners to desert from the British army. The committee gave its report on August 14, 1776. Benjamin Franklin wrote to General Horatio Gates, adjutant general (or chief administrative officer) of the Continental Army, that "the Congress being advised that there was a probability that the Hessians might be induced to quit the British service by offers of land, came to two resolves for this purpose, which, being translated into German and printed, are sent to Staten Island, to be distributed, if practicable, among those people."[7] One of the resolutions that was passed and sent on August 16 by John Hancock, president of the Continental Congress, to George Washington, commander in chief of the Continental Army, said

that these states will receive all such foreigners who shall leave the armies of his Britannic majesty in America, and shall chuse to become members of any of these states; that they shall be protected in the free exercise of their respective religions, and be invested with the rights, privileges and immunities of natives, as established by the laws of these states; and, moreover, that this Congress will provide, for every such person, 50 Acres of unappropriated lands in some of these states, to be held by them and his heirs in absolute property.

Furthermore, they resolved that the committee "be directed to have it translated into German, and to take proper measures to have it communicated to the foreign troops. In the meanwhile, that this be kept secret."[8]

Lieutenant Colonel Harmon Zedwitz of the 1st New York Regiment was given the job of translating the resolutions into German. Later he wrote to Royal Governor William Tryon of New York, informing him of the resolutions and their planned distribution, and offering to serve as a British spy. But that letter was intercepted, and Zedwitz was court-martialed on August 25, with Brigadier General James Wadsworth of the Connecticut militia presiding. He was found guilty of "carrying on a treasonable correspondence with the enemy" and was sentenced to jail for the duration of the war.[9]

Christopher Ludwick was a German-born baker. He lived and conducted his business on Laetitia Court in Philadelphia, and was known as the "governor of Laetitia Court."[10] His mission was to infiltrate the Hessian camp on Staten Island disguised as a deserter and distribute the handbills prepared by Congress and aimed at encouraging desertion. On August 19, Joseph Reed, an aide-de-camp to General Washington who was at the Continental Army headquarters in New York, asked New Jersey Governor William Livingston for assistance in getting Ludwick to Staten Island. Reed noted that Ludwick was putting his life on the line in order to serve the interests of America. Ludwick then carried the handbills to Joshua Mercereau, who would assist in the operation.[11] John Mercereau, another member of the Mercereau spy ring, had previously gone on a spying mission to Staten Island on July 16.[12]

On August 23, Livingston wrote to Brigadier General Hugh Mercer, saying that Ludwick got to Staten Island safely on the evening of August 22, but returned disappointed.[13] General

City Tavern was built in 1773 by subscription and was a popular meeting place for delegates to the Continental Congress. It suffered a major fire in 1834 and was torn down in 1854. This historically accurate reconstruction was completed in 1976 at the location of the original tavern. (*Lisa Nagy*)

Mercer had served in the French and Indian War at Pittsburgh with George Washington. He had settled in Fredericksburg, Virginia, where he opened an apothecary.

On August 26, Washington wrote to the Congress, "The papers designed for the foreign troops, have been put into several channels, in order that they might be conveyed to them, and from the information I had yesterday, I have reason to believe many have fallen into their hands."[14] But he reported to Hancock on August 29, about Ludwick's lack of success: "As to the encouragement to the Hessian officers, I wish it may have the desired effect, perhaps it might have been better, had the offer been sooner made."[15] Some of the leaflets, which were dated August 14, did reach their objective, being received by members of Colonel Friedrich Wilhelm of Freiherr von Lossberg's brigades on Staten Island.[16]

In the fall of 1776, Joseph Galloway fled with a wagonload of his belongings to the British lines at New Brunswick, New Jersey, for protection. When General Howe arrived at Trenton in 1776, Galloway had constant communication with his friends in Pennsylvania.[17] He may have been the source of a letter written with an invisible part given to an American officer who had been sent to the British under a flag of truce. The officer was given an unsealed letter and asked to forward it to a gentleman in Philadelphia. Upon returning to the American lines, the officer submitted the letter to American army headquarters.

George Washington asked Lieutenant Colonel Tench Tilghman, his military secretary, to inspect the letter. Tilghman thought he recognized the handwriting, but the name was unknown to him. The contents of the letter were mysterious and unintelligible. Tilghman said, "This raised all our suspicions and we were determined to unravel it." By chance the letter was held near the fire and "new characters began to appear and . . . the whole sheet was fully written with some composition that appeared when warmed." Tilghman told his father, James, "it was from a gentleman nearly connected with our family and gave an account to his friends of the intentions of the enemy. The [Delaware] River was to be crossed upon the ice and the army marched directly to Philadelphia. When every house, which the owners had left, was to be given up to be plundered, and the gentleman pressed all his friends and acquaintance to remove in[land]."[18]

The Second Continental Congress met at the Pennsylvania State House beginning on May 10, 1775. James Duane was a delegate from New York to both the First and Second Continental Congresses. During the second Congress, he lodged at the home of John Patterson, a royal customs collector in Philadelphia.[19] Duane routinely left his memoranda on his table, bed, and chairs. Mrs. Patterson, observing the lack of security, gave Duane a trunk to store the documents. Duane's servant, James Brattle, who could read and write, was given a key to the trunk.

At the time of the American Revolution, Christopher Marshall was a retired chemist and pharmacist.[20] Paul Fooks was the French- and Spanish-language professor at the College of Philadelphia and a good friend of Marshall's.[21] At breakfast on January 9, 1776, Fooks's housekeeper visited Marshall. The housekeeper stated that Fooks's servant, Neal, had heard his sister, Rosanna Thompson, say that Brattle was employed by Royal Governor William Tryon of New York.[22] Brattle was to collect all the news of importance to the British he could find and send it to Tryon. On October 13, 1775, Tryon had taken refuge on the British warship *Duchess of Gordon* in New York Harbor.[23] Tryon had promised Brattle that he would be well rewarded and given some post in consequence. It was believed that Brattle wrote to Tryon on the day an American fleet sailed from Philadelphia, providing the number of vessels and other pertinent information.[24] The messages apparently went from Brattle to a barber in New York City named Leslie, and then to Tryon.[25]

Christopher Marshall then contacted some members of the Committee of Inspection and Observation—whose job was to identify spies and British sympathizers—at the London Coffee House. Joseph Dean, an importing merchant, accompanied Marshall, and they were unable to find out any more information about Brattle's activities.[26] Major John Bayard of the Pennsylvania militia joined Marshall and Dean, and the three of them went to the home of Joseph Reed, a leading Philadelphia politician. Reed was not home, so they went to a Committee of Safety meeting, and again, Reed was not there.[27] They finally located him at the Court House at Second and High Streets. Reed went with the others to the Hall and Seller's

Joseph Galloway was a Philadelphia lawyer who was a member of the Pennsylvania House of Representatives 1757–1775, and served as speaker 1766–1774. In 1774 he was a member of the Continental Congress and a volunteer spy for the British, reporting on Congressional activities. His letters were sent through New Jersey Royal Governor William Franklin. Galloway fled to the British in New Brunswick in December 1776.

Printing shop on Arch Street and picked up Richard Bache, son-in-law of Benjamin Franklin.[28] Then the group went to Bache's house and called his maid, Rosanna, also known as Rose Thompson, who was confused and denied the whole story. Next they went to the coffee house and consulted with Major John Cox, who went with them to the Pennsylvania State House, where they saw James Duane about noon and informed him of the rumor that Brattle was employed by Royal Governor Tryon and was sending him information on the activities in Congress. Duane requested the entourage proceed to his house. They deferred to Duane in the detection and punishment of Brattle. Duane proposed that they immediately seize him and search his papers.

At Patterson's house, they questioned James Brattle and then went upstairs. They searched Brattle's bedding, clothes, and pocketbook but did not find anything. The group, including Brattle, went to Fooks's house and examined Neal, who insisted he had told the truth. Now the crowd plus Neal went back to Duane's house and sent for Rosanna Thompson, who was Brattle's girlfriend. After hearing her brother Neal's statement, she reluctantly admitted that her brother had told the truth.[29] She said Brattle had frequently told her that his master, James Duane, and all the members of Congress would be hanged. Brattle had told her that a person had come to Philadelphia and arranged for him to provide intelligence of activities in Philadelphia to Royal Governor Tryon. As a reward he was promised he would be allowed to ship commodities on board a merchant ship operating between New York and Boston. Brattle had told her that he provided information to Tryon on American warships being prepared to sail and their dates of sailing from Philadelphia. He had sent this information in a letter to a barber named Leslie in New York City. He had asked Duane to send the letter with Duane's letters going to Colonel Abraham Brasher of New York troops. He told Duane the letter "enclosed or gave an account of money which he had received from Mr. [Thomas] Cushing, then delegate for Massachusetts, for Leslie." Brattle told her that one day while he was writing intelligence for Tryon, Duane had surprised him, and "he was so much frightened lest he might make a discovery; that it threw him into a fit of sickness."[30]

Brattle was interrogated again but continued to deny the allegations. Convinced of his guilt, they sent for a constable to take Brattle to jail. Then Duane remembered that they had not searched Brattle's blue suit, which might contain evidence. Bayard and Marshall waited in the parlor while Cox and Duane took Brattle upstairs, but nothing was found. Duane told Brattle that he was a rascal and that he wanted nothing further to do with him. He also said he wanted an accounting of money Brattle had received and expended for him. Brattle said he wanted to change his breeches and get the account papers, so he went into the next room to do so. Cox discovered a basket containing some documents on top of a wardrobe-like cabinet, called a clothes press, that was between two rooms in the hallway. Cox and Duane examined the documents, then went downstairs, where they expected to find Brattle with Bayard and Marshall, but Brattle was missing. They searched the house, then the stable and yard, but he had fled. One of the children of the family of the house said Brattle had gone out the door into the yard. Marshall suggested to Duane that he apply to a magistrate for a warrant, but the complaint was not a civil case so it was decided that the Committee of Safety should issue a writ to bring him to appear for a hearing. However, Brattle could not be located.[31] He made his way to New York, and Royal Governor Tryon sent him to England.[32]

The London papers had a different version of the discovery of James Brattle's espionage activities. They reported that in the spring of 1776, Brattle had searched Duane's minute book at night and sent the information to Tryon, his former employer. According to *Lloyd's Evening Post and British Chronicle*, Duane suspected that Brattle was the source of Tryon's intelligence, and Duane planted some false information. Brattle unknowingly sent the false information to Tryon. Upon receipt, Tryon realized the situation and informed Brattle to protect himself. Brattle fled immediately, and eventually sailed to England.[33]

Brattle had indeed been sending intelligence reports to Tryon. The governor received a letter written by Duane to Abraham Yates, president of the New York Provincial Congress, and dated November 9, 1775, at Philadelphia. It was annotated in an unknown hand.[34] On December 7, Tryon forwarded the letter to Lord Dartmouth.[35] Another correspondence, dated November 16, 1775, at Philadelphia, made its way to Tryon and then to England.[36] Royal Chief Justice William Smith of New York wrote in his memoirs that Brattle's letters were sent to the owner of a small tavern at the sign of the Tryon Arms on Broadway in New York City. The owner had previously been a servant of Tryon's and a friend of Brattle's. The tavern keeper delivered Brattle's letters to Tryon on the *Duchess of Gordon* in New York Harbor.[37]

Another of Brattle's transmissions was the information that Congress, on November 23, 1775, had appointed a committee that drew up plans for the shipment of trade goods for Indians from France to America and for congressional regulation of trade with the Ohio Indians. A copy of a letter from Silas Deane on November 28, 1775, to the New York Convention, which was setting up a state government, included "a plan for regulating trade with the Indians on the Ohio and for keeping them in peace with the Colonies." Tryon sent a copy of this letter to Lord Dartmouth.[38] Deane, born in Groton, Connecticut, was a lawyer who later became a merchant. He represented Connecticut in the Continental Congress and was sent as the United States' first foreign diplomat to France to get aid.

After Brattle's escape, James Duane wrote about him to his daughter Mary Duane (whom he called Polly): "I agree with you that James [Brattle] was a most ungrateful villain, and that his employers, whoever they were, ought to be detested by all honest men.[39] No man can guard against the infidelity of his domestics. I leave him to the pangs of his own conscience."[40] In a letter to Robert R. Livingston, a delegate from New York to the Continental Congress, Duane added to the sentence "which must one day prove their [Brattle's and Tryon's] punishment."[41] (Livingston was one of the committee of five who worked on drafting the Declaration of Independence.[42])

The incident in January 1776 concerning James Brattle had all the gossips working overtime, and in February the rumor was still suggesting that Duane was part of the conspiracy to deliver intelligence to the British.[43] The rationale behind the rumor was that Duane initially had hoped for concessions from the crown and reconciliation.

Despite the delegates to Congress having pledged to keep their transactions secret, Lord Dartmouth in England was able to get information on the transactions of Congress from another source: an unnamed clerk of a merchant in the neighborhood of French Church Street (also known as Pine Street) in New York City in December 1775.[44] He played the role of being against the crown and in agreement with the colonists. He met and gained the confidence of the treasurer of Congress. When the clerk was making a trip to England, the treasurer gave him a couple of letters to deliver, which the clerk promised to do. Upon arriving in England, the clerk placed the letters in a packet to Lord Dartmouth and entrusted them to the ship's captain to deliver.[45]

The Continental Congress on July 29, 1775, had resolved "that Michael Hillegas, and George Clymer, Esquires be, and they are hereby appointed, joint treasurers of the United Colonies: that the treasurers reside in Philadelphia, and that they shall give bond, with surety, for the faithful performance of their office, in the sum of 100,000 Dollars."[46] So the source of the information provided to the clerk could have been either Hillegas, a Philadelphia merchant and sugar refiner who had been treasurer of the Committee of Safety in 1774 and was treasurer of Congress until September 11, 1789, or Clymer, who resigned on August 6, 1776.

Samuel Wallis, who owned about seven thousand acres of land around Muncy on the north central Pennsylvania frontier, offered his services to the British as early as January 13, 1776. Colonel James Robertson of the 60th Regiment of Foot wrote to General Sir Henry Clinton and advised that

> Mr. Wallace [Wallis] is a merchant of great property and good understanding, is better qualified to procure money and supplies for an army than any other man in America. He would not expose his fortune or person by openly engaging in a business that would draw the mob upon him but if the secret was in no other hands than yours, I fancy he would be a merchant and a friend to government contrive means to get money or provisions for the troops, under various pretenses and disguises. The letter if you approve should be put into his hands by one you can confide in, otherwise it should be destroyed.[47]

On a letter Robertson wrote to Clinton the next day, there was a note in the handwriting of Major Duncan Drummond, an aide to Clinton, that said, "Hints from R[obertson], advises me seeing Wallace alone."[48]

In 1776, Wallis represented his county in the Pennsylvania Assembly, which met in Philadelphia. That put him at the center of the major political events of the day and made him an important source of intelligence for the British. Philadelphia merchant Joseph Stansbury, who during the British occupation of Philadelphia had been appointed to oversee the city's patrolling guards and was one of the managers of a public lottery, in 1779 confirmed that Wallis had been extremely helpful to General William Howe.[49]

On February 6, 1778, the United States and France signed a treaty creating a military alliance against Great Britain. The treaty required that neither country agree to a separate peace with the British, and that American independence be a condition of any peace agreement. The same day, the United States and France also signed the Treaty of Amity and Commerce, which promoted trade and commercial ties between the two countries.

After the British surrender at Saratoga on October 17, 1777, the British feared that a union between the colonies in rebellion and France would change the situation from a revolt to a world war. A war with France meant that all British colonies would be at risk. Lord North, the British prime minister, had Parliament pass the Taxation of the Colonies Act of 1778, which repealed the Tea Act of May 10, 1773. The Tea Act had been an attempt by Parliament to expand the British East India Company's monopoly on the tea trade in all British colonies. It resulted in a number of men dressed as Mohawk Indians dumping 342 chests of tea into Boston Harbor on December 16, 1773, and added fuel to the American revolutionary movement.

On February 22, 1778, the Earl of Carlisle was appointed head of a commission to seek reconciliation with the colonies in rebellion. King George III approved one thousand pounds for the commission, and on March 7, the Earl of Carlisle accepted the responsibility. Carlisle was a friend to both William Eden, who supported, and Charles James Fox, who opposed, the king's American policies. Carlisle could be seen as being in both political camps on this issue. The commission was composed of the Earl of Carlisle (Frederick Howard), William Eden, and Richard Jackson. Jackson was a member of Parliament from New Romney and had been a colonial agent for Connecticut. Once the treaty of alliance between France and the United States became public knowledge, Jackson refused to serve and was replaced by George Johnstone. Johnstone had been the royal governor of West Florida and a member of Parliament. Adam Ferguson, professor of moral philosophy at Edinburgh, was secretary to the commission.

General Washington advised Congress on April 25, 1778, "the report of the Commissioners coming, according to intelligence received yesterday by a person of Philadelphia, is confidently believed, and it is there thought, that they will very soon arrive.[50] They arrived in Philadelphia on June 4, and initially they stayed out of sight. The arrival of the Earl of Carlisle, Eden, and Johnstone at Philadelphia was announced publicly by General Clinton on the evening of June 9.[51] The Earl of Carlisle took over the residence of Samuel Powel, mayor of Philadelphia from 1775–1776, at 244 South Third Street for his use.[52]

The Earl of Carlisle took over the residence of Samuel Powel for his use in 1778. Samuel Powel was the last colonial mayor and the first mayor after the Revolutionary War. The Georgian-style house was built in 1765 by Charles Stedman and purchased by Samuel Powel in 1769. (*Lisa Nagy*)

On June 13, the commissioners sent proposals to the Continental Congress, which was meeting at York Town (now York), Pennsylvania. The commissioners offered everything but American independence, which is what Congress demanded. Their offer was two years too late.

Washington thanked Henry Laurens, president of the Continental Congress,

for your polite attention in forwarding for my perusal the late exhibitions of Gov[erno]r Johnstone and his brothers in Commission. That of the former is really a curious performance. He trys to convince you that he is not at all hurt by, or offended at, the interdiction of Congress. That he is not in a passion, while he exhibits a striking proof of his being cut to the quick, and actually biting his fingers in an agony of passion.[53]

Congress responded to the commission's proposals:

To their Excellencies the right Hon: the Earl of Carlisle William Eden Esq: George Johnstone, Esq: Commissioners from his Britannic Majesty. Philadelphia

I have received the letter from your Excellencies, of the 9th instant, with the enclosures, and laid them before Congress Nothing but an earnest desire to spare the farther effusion of human blood could have induced them to read a paper, containing expressions so disrespectful to his Most Christian Majesty the good and great ally of these States, or to consider propositions so derogatory to the honour of an Independent Nation.

The acts of the British Parliament, the commission from your Sovereign, and your letter, suppose the people of these States to be Subjects of the Crown of Great-Britain, and are founded on the idea of dependence, which is utterly inadmissible.

I am further directed to inform your Excellencies, that Congress are inclined to peace notwithstanding the unjust claims from which this war originated, and the savage manner in which it has been conducted. They will therefore be ready to enter upon the consideration of a treaty of peace and commerce, not inconsistent with treaties already subsisting when the King of Great-Britain shall demonstrate a sincere disposition for that purpose. The only solid proof of this disposition will be, an explicit acknowledgment of the independence of these States, or the withdrawing his fleets and armies. I have the honour to be,

Your Excellencies most obedient humble servant. Signed by order of the unanimous voice of Congress, Henry Laurens, President, York Town [Pennsylvania] June 17, 1778.[54]

George Johnstone was lodged at the home of Charles Stedman in Philadelphia. Stedman was the part-owner of the Tulpehocken forge, also known as the Charming forge, on the Tulpehocken Creek in Tulpehocken Township, twenty miles northwest of Reading, Pennsylvania. Stedman also was a substantial landowner, but he eventually fell upon hard times and, in 1774, was sent to debtor's prison. At Stedman's home in Philadelphia, Johnstone met Elizabeth Graeme Ferguson, who was related by marriage to Stedman, and Mrs. Ferguson's husband, who was related to Adam

Ferguson, secretary to the peace commission. Mrs. Ferguson had gotten permission to travel into Philadelphia to see her husband before he left for England. He was a British subject who had left Pennsylvania in 1774 for England and returned to Philadelphia while it was under British control.

Mrs. Ferguson visited Stedman's house on June 16. She met and conversed with Johnstone in the tea room for an hour. She told him she was going to send a letter to the Supreme Executive Council of Pennsylvania, which was meeting in Lancaster. The council, the executive branch of Pennsylvania government, consisted of a representative from Philadelphia and the eleven counties in Pennsylvania at the time. Its president and vice president were the equivalent of a governor and lieutenant governor. The council had ordered Mrs. Ferguson's husband to appear before it on charges of treason, which she felt was unjust because he was a British subject.

Johnstone wanted her to deliver messages to Robert Morris and Joseph Reed.[55] Morris was a Philadelphia merchant who strongly opposed the British Stamp Act of 1765, which placed a tax on newspapers and all financial documents. He was a Pennsylvania delegate to the Second Continental Congress, which contracted with his firm to import arms and ammunition for the Continental Army. Because of his ability to raise money for the army, he would later be called the Financier of the Revolution. His house on 6th and Market streets would be used as British General Howe's residence while the British occupied the city; by American General Benedict Arnold; and by President George Washington from November 1790, to March 1797. Joseph Reed was born in Trenton, New Jersey. During his life he lived there and in Philadelphia. He was a lawyer and politician, and he had served as General Washington's secretary with the rank of colonel. From December 1, 1778, to November 15, 1781, he served as president of the Supreme Executive Council of Pennsylvania.

When the British army evacuated Philadelphia for New York on June 18, the move strengthened American resolve for independence and weakened the position of the peace commissioners.

After the British left the city, Mrs. Ferguson requested a meeting with Reed on June 21. Reed visited her that evening. After discussing her husband's situation, she delivered Johnstone's offer of ten thousand pounds sterling and an office in the colonies as a gift from the king if Reed could effectuate a reconciliation between the two countries. Reed responded, "My influence is but small, but were it as great as Governor Johnstone would insinuate, the King of Great Britain has nothing within his gift that would tempt me." He added that he "was not worth purchasing, but such as he was, the King of Great Britain was not rich enough to do it."[56] In other words, he could not be bought for land, money, or title.

Johnstone had sent letters to Robert Morris and Francis Dana in an attempt to get them to set aside the treaty with France and accept the terms offered by the peace commissioners. Francis Dana was a Boston lawyer and Continental Congressman from Massachusetts serving in 1777 and 1778. He was a secretary to John Adams of Massachusetts, who was appointed a commissioner to negotiate a treaties of peace with Great Britain and a commerce with Holland. On August 11, after citing in the congressional journal the letter to Robert Morris and the verbal offer to Joseph Reed, Congress stated in its journal,

> That the contents of the said paragraphs, and the particulars in the said declaration, in the opinion of Congress, can not but be considered as direct attempts to corrupt and bribe the Congress of the United States of America. [It is] resolved, That as Congress feel, so they ought to demonstrate, the highest and most pointed indignation against such daring and atrocious attempts to corrupt their integrity, Resolved, That it is incompatible with the honor of Congress to hold any manner of correspondence or intercourse with the said George Johnstone, Esq. especially to negotiate with him upon affairs in which the cause of liberty is interested. A motion was made to add, and, whereas, the conduct of the said George Johnstone, Esq. in the aforesaid particulars, unavoidably effects his colleagues in commission, and unfavourably impresses the mind, so that full confidence cannot be placed in them: therefore, Resolved, That Congress will not, in any degree, negotiate with the present British commissioners in America, for restoring peace.

The Earl of Carlisle sent a letter dated August 26, 1778, to the Continental Congress in which he said that France was "a power that has ever shown itself an enemy to all civil and religious liberty," and he accused France of misrepresentation; of deliberately prolonging the war; of making the colonies "the instruments of her ambition; and of misdating treaties." General Marquis de Lafayette, a French aristocrat who joined the Continental Army, took exception to these statements, and on October 5, he challenged the earl, as head of the commission, to a duel, and his aide, Lieutenant Colonel Jean-Joseph Sourbader de Gimat, was to make the arrangements. De Gimat sent the challenge inside a sealed envelope to the British lines and de Gimat requested a response.[57] The earl replied, "The only [answer] that can be expected from me as the King's Commissioner, and which *you ought to have known,* is that I do and ever shall consider myself solely answerable to my country and my king and not to any individual for my public conduct and language. . . . I conceive all national disputes will be best decided by the Meeting of Admiral [John] Byron and Count [Jean Baptiste Charles Henri Hector] d'Estaing."[58]

Johnstone resigned from the commission. He claimed he never attempted to corrupt Reed's integrity. The commissioners sailed back to Britain on November 27, 1778, and the British army now implemented its strategy of taking the war to the American South.[59]

THREE

The British Capture Philadelphia

After their defeats at Trenton and Princeton, New Jersey, during the winter of 1776–1777, the British regrouped at New Brunswick and Perth Amboy, New Jersey. They had lost most of the territory they had captured in New Jersey in 1776. General William Howe had originally planned to take the British army across the Delaware River when it froze and capture the American capital and largest city, Philadelphia—a dream that was dashed by Washington's victories. In the spring of 1777, General Howe still had a dream of taking Philadelphia and making up for the embarrassment of losing at Trenton and Princeton. He wanted to bring the superior firepower of the British navy up the Delaware to assist in his attack on Philadelphia, and he would need the navy to bring supplies to support his occupation of the city. In order to accomplish all this, he needed pilots who knew the river.

Because of Joseph Galloway's intimate knowledge of Philadelphia, Admiral Lord Richard Howe had assigned him the task of obtaining river pilots. Galloway had considerable political power and connections in Pennsylvania. He had been a member of the Pennsylvania Assembly from 1757–1775, and speaker of the House from 1766–1774. He had even been a member of the First Continental Congress.

James Molesworth born in Wolverhampton, Staffordshire, England, had been a clerk to Samuel Rhoads, mayor of Philadelphia from 1774–1775, and Samuel Powel, mayor from 1775–1776. But the position of mayor was vacant beginning in 1776, and Molesworth was out of job. He made his way across

New Jersey to New York City, where Galloway introduced him to Admiral Howe. Molesworth knew Philadelphia, and he knew what people were believed to be loyal to the king. Howe recruited him to go to Philadelphia, secure some Delaware River pilots for the British navy—and specifically one who knew his way through the chevaux-de-frise in the Delaware River—and bring them back to New York City. At one time, Molesworth would claim to have been given a lieutenant's commission, with the help of Captain Thomas Hunlocke of the West Jersey Volunteers. Hunlocke had been the sheriff of Burlington County and lived on Main Street in Mount Holly, New Jersey, before going to the British. Later, however, Molesworth would claim never to have received the commission.

Molesworth left New York and traveled by way of Bullion's Tavern in Basking Ridge, Millstone, and New Brunswick, where he spoke to Brigadier General Cortland Skinner, commander of the British loyalist New Jersey Volunteers (which Skinner had raised), and answered his questions about the Continental Army. Skinner was born and resided in Perth Amboy and was the last attorney general under royal government in New Jersey. He was adept at intelligence gathering in New Jersey for the British.

After a two-day stay in New Brunswick, Molesworth continued on to Philadelphia. There he stayed at a widow Yarnall's residence on Chestnut Street. He made contact with Mrs. Abigail McCoy (sometimes known as McKay), who for the last two years had lived on Union (now Delancey) Street between Front and South Fourth streets.[1] On March 24, Molesworth asked Mrs. McCoy to help him find pilots for the British. He also spoke to Mrs. Sarah O'Brien (sometimes spelled O'Bryan or Brien) about the need for pilots because many pilots boarded with her. She was an acquaintance of his for at least two years, and he had been to her house in the past on several occasions. Later, however, she would claim she only knew him for six months.[2] He told the two women he was a British naval officer.[3]

Molesworth also contacted William Shepard and Joseph Thomas to assist in procuring pilots. Shepard, with his wife, Sarah, two daughters, and one son, lived on Seventh Street in Philadelphia, where he had a farm with stables.[4] Thomas lived on Front Street.

One of the likeliest places to find river pilots who needed money in Philadelphia was the Hatton Arms, where the Sea Captains Club met.[5] The Hatton Arms was the house of the widow Hatton on Third Street. The Sea Captains Club was an organization that helped poor and distressed masters of ships, their widows, and children.[6]

Shepard secured the services of John Keyton, a pilot, and sent him back to New York.[7] Mrs. McCoy went to the house of John Brien, a tailor, on Front Street just above Lombard Street.[8] She asked Andrew Higgons, a pilot, to come to her house at sundown. He did, but she was not there. During the night, Mrs. McCoy sent her female slave with a message that he should come in the morning. That morning she asked him to be one of the pilots for the king's ships. She also asked him to find a pilot who knew his way through the chevaux-de-frise.[9]

About 8 p.m. on March 24, Molesworth went to the home of John Eldridge, a pilot, and told him he wanted to talk to him the next day. Eldridge's landlady, Mrs. O'Brien, had received instructions for Eldridge to go to Mrs. McCoy's house. She took him to Mrs. McCoy, who asked if he would go to New York to bring British ships up the Delaware River. He said no but agreed to meet Molesworth, so Mrs. O'Brien took him to Molesworth's lodging. After some discussion, he said he would consider the project.[10]

Afterward, Eldridge and Higgons contacted each other and discussed the offer made by Mrs. McCoy and Molesworth. They decided to turn Molesworth over to the authorities in Philadelphia.[11]

Eldridge and Higgons contacted John Snyder, a chevaux-de-frise pilot who had arrived from Chester the night before last, and took him to Mrs. McCoy's house. She was in bed so they left. Eldridge and Snyder then went to Turner's Tavern on Market Street Wharf and discussed what had transpired. Higgons then joined them, and they went to Snyder's house, where they was agreed to write out what was happening. At 3 p.m. they went to Mrs. McCoy's. After discussing the idea of going to New York with her, they decided to meet with Molesworth in the evening.[12] Molesworth told them they were being recruited for the warship *Eagle*, and that "arrangements had been made among the disaffected in the city and among the garrison, on the arrival of the fleet, to have the guns at the fort secretly spiked, and the various bridges at the ferries around the town, cut away." He wanted them to be ready to leave Philadelphia that night, and he would provide the horses. Snyder claimed he needed cash to leave with his mother. They discussed amounts, and Molesworth provided him with fifty pounds, which he had received from Shepard.[13]

As Molesworth was preparing to leave Philadelphia, Shepard gave a book to Molesworth's partner, Luke Caton, who went by the alias Warren. It contained invisible writing that needed heat to make it visible. The book was to be delivered to Joseph Galloway. When it was developed, part of Shepard's message was that Caton could be trusted.[14]

Eldridge, Higgons, and Snyder convinced Molesworth that they would spend the night at the Rising Sun Tavern in Germantown.[15] They traveled out of town to see a Captain Thomas Casdorp and told him of their plan to have Molesworth arrested. Casdorp took them into the Boatswain and Call Tavern and read over letters they had written of what had transpired and discussed what they wanted to do. Casdorp suggested they get the city guard, or local police, to make the arrest. The city guard went with them to Molesworth's lodgings and arrested him about 10 p.m. The two women were arrested and placed in the city jail.[16] Shepard, believing he would be discovered, fled to New York City in April.[17]

Because Molesworth's activities were of a military nature, he was subject to a military court-martial. A general court-martial with General Horatio Gates presiding was held in Philadelphia on March 29, 1777, and Molesworth was convicted as a spy for endeavoring "to inveigle three pilots into [British] service, to pilot the ships of war to the attack of this city."[18]

On March 31, John Adams told his wife, Abigail, that Molesworth's "confidant was a woman, who is said to be kept by a Jew."[19]

That same day, Congress confirmed the order of Major General Horatio Gates for the execution of Molesworth's sentence.[20] The president of the Congress, John Hancock, notified General Gates of Congress's decision that Molesworth was to be executed.[21] He was hanged at noon on March 31, 1777, in the presence of an immense crowd of spectators.[22] He was buried in Southeast (now called Washington) Square. When the British occupied the city, his remains were exhumed and reburied in a city cemetery.[23]

The Pennsylvania War Office had decided that Mrs. McCoy and Mrs. O'Brien should be handled in a civilian manner and turned them over to the Supreme Executive Council of Pennsylvania on April 2, 1777.[24] The council sent the case to James Young, justice of the peace, who was to examine them "and thereupon do what you may judge to be right and according to law, either by remanding them to prison or taking bail for their appearance."[25] Young, with the help of attorneys John Moor and Daniel Clymer, examined the women. Mrs. McCoy said that Mrs. O'Brien's idea for getting the pilots to New York was to have them obtain an oyster boat. They would then travel to the area off Cape May, New Jersey, and Cape Henlopen, Delaware, at the mouth of the Delaware River and allow themselves to be captured and taken to New York City. During her examinations on March 28 and on May 13, she admitted discussing with pilot Nathan Church his going to New York as a pilot, and he seemed to agree. She told the same story of the transactions as before.[26] Mrs. O'Brien denied being involved in the plot.[27] Young reported that Mrs. McCoy's confession was complete and that her actions fell within the scope of treason. In the case of Mrs. O'Brien, he concluded that there was insufficient evidence against her but that she was dangerous. He sent both women to the Pennsylvania State Prison.[28]

Joel Arpin was one of the people suspected of being involved with Molesworth. Arpin was a Philadelphia hatter who had been arrested in November 1775, and he had complained to the courts in January 1776 that he had not been informed of the charges against him. He said he was locked up in a cell with no bed and had to sleep on the bare floor. He was released when Israel Pemberton Jr., known as the King of the Quakers, posted a bond.[29]

Henry Stevenson, a surgeon born in Ireland, stated in a letter to General Clinton in 1780 that before he fled Baltimore in August 1777 because of his loyalist activities, he had sent three pilots to the British fleet. One of these pilots was on Admiral Howe's ship when it came up the Chesapeake Bay in the assault on Philadelphia in 1777. He had sent two pilots to Admiral Howe a week before

General George Washington, left, commander of the Continental Army and General William Howe, right, commander-in-chief of the British Army in North America, 1775-1778. (*Library of Congress*)

Molesworth was hanged in Philadelphia for procuring pilots. He claimed Brigadier General Sir William Erskine and Lieutenant Colonel Nisbet Balfour, who managed the intelligence operation in Philadelphia for General Howe, knew of his clandestine activities.[30]

On March 31, John Hancock, the president of Congress, advised General Gates:

> The internal foes of American freedom have been lately making attempts to accomplish our destruction in this place [Philadelphia]. Since the execution of Molesworth, a gang of conspirators has been detected: and seven or eight were yesterday and today committed to gaol [jail] for carrying on a traitorous correspondence with our enemies, or conniving at it. How far their guilt will be made to appear, I am not able to determine. But vigilance and vigor in the administration of our affairs, will, I trust, defeat their deep laid schemes, and enable us finally to triumph over the dark and wicked machinations of our secret foes, and the designs of our open, tho not less cruel and implacable, enemies.[31]

Mrs. McCoy, during her examination, identified Nathan Church as another pilot who had discussed the project with Molesworth.[32] Molesworth identified Hasting Stackhouse as one of his contacts.[33] Thomas Collins, who was a clerk for General Thomas Mifflin, was one of those discovered to be involved in the spy activities as the Molesworth case developed. William Shepard's activities were also revealed. Another person whose actions aroused suspicion was a Colonel John Henry Smith in the area of Bound Brook and New Brunswick, New Jersey. He carried passes from both General Washington and General Howe. Molesworth said he had met him at Bullion's Tavern in Basking Ridge, New Jersey.[34] Colonel Smith of the New Jersey militia, and Collins, formerly a clerk in the Royal Customs House in Philadelphia, were both arrested in New Jersey and sent to Philadelphia, where they were placed in the state prison. Washington informed his aide-de-camp Joseph Reed and Major John Cox of the Pennsylvania Associated Militia that he believed Smith was "the man who was employed by you to act for us, in that capacity" as a spy. "I must beg you will interpose in the affair without delay, and if you find him to be the person I suspect he is, take measures to have him released."[35] It turned out Smith's real name was Joseph Arrowsmith.[36] Reed quickly secured his release and sent him to Washington on June 4, 1777.[37]

Washington wanted Smith's release to appear to be "an accidental escape from confinement" so he might continue his work as a spy. Washington wanted Smith to make his way back to the British as a fugitive. "Great care must be taken, so to conduct the scheme, as to make the escape appear natural and real; there must be neither too much facility, nor too much refinement, for doing too little, or over acting the part, would, alike beget a suspicion of the true state of the case."[39]

Detecting spies was made harder because of individuals who were determined to be independent at all costs. The *Bridgeton* (NJ) *Plain Dealer* reported there were "great numbers of ignorant thoughtless beings who are one day Tories, and the next day Whigs; and the third day nothing at all; who like the pendulum of a clock are perpetually changing sides and strictly speaking [are] as unsteady as the wind."[38] Flexible allegiance makes it difficult to determine who is on your side.

Washington had discovered that two men named "Bowne and Heartshorne [from] near Shrewsbury in Monmouth County [New Jersey] purchase continental money in New York at a great discount, carry this money to Philadelphia and there buy flour &ca. under pretence of shipping it to the foreign islands, but send the vessels to the British in New York City. As those persons are well known in Philadelphia, they may easily be detected."[40]

Washington congratulated the Pennsylvania War Board upon its discoveries of "plans of our internal enemies." The board had collected information from a Joseph Fox, a light-horse farrier. Fox had received a letter from a Mr. Shepard, who suspected a Mr. Hughes, who was a friend of Joseph Galloway's, and Washington thought "that alone is enough to excite suspicion."[41] It is suspected this was William Shepard who was working for Galloway. He was possibly trying to determine the loyalty of Joseph Fox.

The War Board was also looking for proof of guilt against Bowen and Hartshorne. Washington had no documentation against them that he could use. This usually meant the information came from a spy, but to reveal the information would identify the source, and the usefulness of the spy would be lost. Washington decided to tighten the perimeter defenses by issuing "orders to all the officers at the outposts, to suffer no more women to pass in or out, upon any pretence whatever." Washington assured the Pennsylvania War Board that if he discovered anyone suspicious in Philadelphia, he would inform the board. Washington had second thoughts about Hughes being allowed his freedom, so he sent an officer to apprehend Hughes and take him to the war board. In a letter to the board, Washington wrote "if matters should not be fully proved against him, I think it would still be proper, to lay him under injunctions not to return home just at this time, for he is certainly a dangerous person and actively mischievous just now."[42]

John Lee left British-held New Brunswick, New Jersey, using the alias of John Brown. He was collecting intelligence and recruiting for the British. Mrs. Thompson, wife of an American soldier, also left New Brunswick on Wednesday, May 7, 1777, and provided information to the Americans that Brown was recruiting for the British. Alerted to his activities, some American horsemen captured him near the British lines at New Brunswick. A petition to General Howe, offering his services as a guide, was found in his possession. Major John Taylor of the militia of Middlesex County, New Jersey, was the commanding American officer at Cranbury, New Jersey.[43] He contacted Mr. Thompson, who informed Taylor that he knew John Brown in Philadelphia, that his real name was John Lee, and that he had been working as a gunsmith at Bound Brook, New Jersey, during the past summer. Lee previously had lived with William Cliffton, a blacksmith, in the Society Hill area of Philadelphia.[44]

Major Taylor interrogated Brown, who admitted to being John Lee and having recruited five men for the British army. Taylor then sent Lee under guard to William Livingston, governor of New Jersey, who was at Haddonfield, New Jersey.[45] The New Jersey Council of Safety called a Mr. Hall and Thompson as witnesses and examined John Lee on May 12.[46] Lee admitted to the council that he had recruited five men from Northampton County, Pennsylvania, and had taken them to the British at New Brunswick. Lee claimed he was using the recruits as a cover to get into the British camp as an American spy and was on his way to report what he had seen there when he was arrested near the British lines. Lee said his petition was dictated because he could not write. Governor Livingston informed Major General Philip Schuyler in Philadelphia that Lee's story was full of contradictions and that Lee feared being sent to Philadelphia for a court-martial. Livingston wanted a quick military court-martial and wanted to make an example of what happens to recruiters for the British army.[47] Schuyler agreed that Lee was a military prisoner and requested that Livingston send him to the military authorities at Philadelphia.[48] Livingston agreed and sent Lee under guard across the Delaware River to Philadelphia. Livingston was unable to send Mrs. Thompson, as she had returned to the British in New Brunswick.[49]

A court-martial with Colonel Stephen Moylan as president was held May 19 and 20, and Lee was found guilty of being a British spy and of treason. General Schuyler sent the report of the court-martial to Congress that Lee was "guilty of conducting five men to [New] Brunswick; of holding a traitorous correspondence with the enemy, in offering himself as a pilot to General Howe to conduct the British army from [New] Brunswick to Philadelphia; and also promising to discover to the enemy to what place the continental stores, from Philadelphia were removed . . . [and] that he should suffer death."[50] The Board of War consulted with Colonel Moylan, who advised that Lee had provided information on several relatives who were his co-conspirators in Northampton County, Pennsylvania. Due to his ignorance and illiteracy, the court-martial board recommended mercy.[51]

Colonel William Duer of Charlotte County, New York, who was a member of New York's Committee of Safety, wrote to Washington on January 28, 1777, to introduce Nathaniel Sackett of Fishkill, New York, and the plan the two of them proposed for obtaining military intelligence. Sackett personally delivered the letter and the plan.[52] On February 4, Washington appointed Sackett to get "the earliest and best intelligence of the designs of the enemy." Sackett was paid fifty dollars per calendar month and received a warrant for five hundred dollars for the paymaster to pay the spies he was to employ.[53]

In April 1777, Washington instructed General Thomas Mifflin to set up a spy system in Philadelphia, in case General Howe should succeed in occupying the city. Washington told Mifflin, a native of Philadelphia, that the spies "are to remain among them under the mask of friendship. I would have some of those in Bucks County, some in Philadelphia, and others below Philadelphia about Chester, for if any part of their force goes round by water, they will probably land somewhere there abouts. . . . I would therefore have you set about this work immediately, and give the persons you [choose] proper lessons. Some in the Quaker line, who have never taken an active part, would be least liable to suspicion from either party."[54] At the same time Washington also instructed General Israel Putnam to procure spies in New Jersey should the

British come from there toward Philadelphia. He wanted them to be on the lookout for floats for a bridge being brought to Perth Amboy and South Amboy, New Jersey. He knew such bridges were being built in New York and suspected they would be used to cross the Delaware River if the British army came from New Jersey.[55]

Washington had requested that General Adam Stephen, a Scottish-born surgeon from Martinsburg, Virginia, send spies into New York City and New Brunswick to gather intelligence.[56] Lieutenant Colonel George Johnston of Virginia, aide-de-camp to General Washington, sent Stephen a warrant for two hundred dollars for secret intelligence payments. Stephen reported to Washington on April 23 that the spy who had gone to New York and the spy he had sent into New Brunswick reported that a Thomas Long had gone to Philadelphia as a spy two days earlier. Long, nicknamed Bunk Eye because of his prominent eyes, was a schoolmaster near Rahway, New Jersey. Stephen advised that Long was known to associate with Quakers and had somehow "distressed the inhabitants on the passage of the B[ritish] troops through the Jerseys" in the fall of 1776.[57] Upon receipt of the information about Long, Washington wrote to the Continental Congress to be on the alert for him.[58] Washington wrote to Congress that "I do not put entire confidence in [all the information from General Stephen's spy], but the principal reason of sending the intelligence forward is that proper measures may be fallen upon to find out and apprehend Thomas Long."[59]

The British, unable to draw Washington into battle in the Raritan Valley, decided to withdraw from New Jersey and travel by sea to Philadelphia. It would have been unwise to march to Philadelphia across New Jersey with Washington and the American army behind him with the ability to cut off General Howe's supply route from New York. So General Howe evacuated New Jersey by withdrawing his troops to Perth Amboy and then, on June 30, 1777, to Staten Island, New York. Robert Morris on June 24 had written about the good news of Washington's taking possession of New Brunswick and chasing the British back toward Perth Amboy. The news of the withdrawal was received with joy in Philadelphia despite the continuance of a British blockade of the Delaware River. Morris wrote, "I can now assure you of the perfect security of the city."[60] The "perfect security" of Philadelphia would only last through the summer.

Thomas Long was an Englishman who stood five feet six inches tall, was over forty years old, had a fair complexion, and wore white clothes. He apparently escaped detection and completed his spying mission to Philadelphia. The New Jersey militia caught Long on November 1, 1779, while he was hiding in a barn near Rahway.[61] Colonel Moses Jacques of the militia presided over Long's court-martial. Long was found without weapons and was considered to be a spy rather than a soldier. He was convicted as a spy and ordered to be hanged. A man named Ellis Throp was drafted to be the executioner. A William Hadar, a native of Hunterdon County, New Jersey, was with the militia when it caught Long, and he and Henry Williams were in attendance when Long was hanged on Thursday, November 4, at Kinsey's Corner near Rahway.[62] An American newspaper account of the day referred to Long as "a villain noted for his cruelties to many of our prisoners."[63] Loyalist John Smith Hatfield of Elizabeth Town, New Jersey, who worked for the British as a guide and spy, claimed that before Long was hanged, his fingers and toes where chopped off.[64]

Some enterprising individuals decided that Long's hanging should be a warning to loyalists. They dug up his body at night and propped it on its feet with a pail on its head against the door of Tory Englishman Richard Cozen's house. When Cozen's opened his door, Long's body would be standing there. The spot where Long was hanged was near Cozen's garden and sixty-five to eighty-five feet from his window. During the cold night, Long's body froze stiff. When Cozen opened his door in the morning, the body, with the pail on its head, fell into Cozen's house.[65]

On April 27, 1777, General Nathanael Greene wrote that intelligence was received the day before from New Brunswick and New York that the British would take the field by June 1.[66] The spy reported that a portable bridge made of boats at New York was complete and that part of it was said to be at New Brunswick, which was incorrect.[67]

In the spring of 1777, General Howe was trying to draw Washington into open-field combat. Failing to entice Washington out of the security of Morristown, New Jersey, the British army departed from most of New Jersey on June 30, 1777. Howe loaded his army on board ships and departed New York on July 23. They traveled south along the Atlantic coast and were brought up the Chesapeake Bay to the Head of Elk in Maryland. They landed on August 25, 1777. The army would now march to Philadelphia.

In preparation for the army's move against Philadelphia, the British had fake letters, supposedly from Quakers, fall into the hands of General John Sullivan at Hanover, New Jersey, about eight miles east of Morristown. The letters indicated that the Quakers had been collecting intelligence at their Yearly Meeting in Spanktown, near Rahway, New Jersey, and were providing the intelligence to the British. The letters were an attempt to discredit the Quakers and make them appear to be collaborating with the British. On August 25, Sullivan sent the documents to Congress along with a letter of his own. The letters were fakes, because the Quakers never held a Yearly Meeting at Spanktown, and one of the letters, from August 19, reported on Howe's landing in the Chesapeake, which did not happen till the twenty-fifth.[68]

The British had problems with their intelligence operation during their journey to Philadelphia. On September 1, 1777, British General R. Fitzpatrick wrote to the Countess of Ossory, from the Head of Elk, "The maps give us very inaccurate accounts of the country, and our spies (if we have any) give us very little intelligence of our enemy; we heard different stories every moment, but none to be depended upon."[69]

Thomas Badger of Philadelphia was a soap boiler, tallow chandler, and grocer. Prior to the campaign against Philadelphia in 1777, he claimed to have worked as a sutler to the Continental Army providing the British with intelligence. He also claimed to have been a guide for the British army from the Head of Elk to Philadelphia.[70]

During the British army's advance on Philadelphia from the Chesapeake, it won a decisive battle at Brandywine on September 11, 1777. During the battle, the British captured a troop return, or report, of the strength of the Continental Army dated September

10. It noted that General Washington had twelve thousand nine hundred men plus militia and two regiments of light horse fit and ready for battle. British Captain John Montresor wrote in his journal that some of the army's staff believed the report was false, and they were prepared for the deception.[71]

Elkanah Watson was born in Plymouth, Massachusetts, and in September 1773, when he was fifteen years old, he was apprenticed to John Brown of Providence, Rhode Island. In 1777, brothers John and Nicholas Brown sent Watson to their mercantile agents in Charles Town, South Carolina, and Savannah, Georgia. Watson was given fifty thousand dollars to pay the agents, which was hidden in the lining of his coat. At Morristown, he fell into company with two men going to Williamsburg, Virginia. On their approach to Philadelphia, they heard of the British capture of the city two hours earlier, on September 26, 1777, so they crossed north of the city at Cowles' Ferry into Pennsylvania. They were arrested as suspected British spies because of inquiries they made about military events. They were released the next day and allowed to continue on their journey to Charles Town and Savannah.[72]

FOUR

Occupied Philadelphia: The British Move In

George Washington, having realized his mistake when he evacuated New York City in 1776 in not establishing a stay-behind spy network, did not make the same mistake twice. Philadelphia had been the objective of British General William Howe's efforts in late 1776, and in case he should succeed in his quest, Washington, in the spring of 1777, instructed General Thomas Mifflin to set up a spy system in Philadelphia. Washington's instruction specifically included the recruiting of Quakers as spies because they would draw the least suspicion as they refused on religious grounds to serve in a military conflict. Mifflin gave the task of developing and operating a spy system to Major John Clark Jr., Colonel Elias Boudinot, and Captains Charles Craig and Allen McLane. When Howe and the British army marched into Philadelphia at 10 a.m. September 26, 1777, an American spy network was in place waiting for them.[1] Clark's operation was headquartered in Newton Square, Delaware County, Pennsylvania.

When the British army took Philadelphia, British Captain John Montresor observed that about half the city's population had left, as only about twenty thousand people remained. Those were "mostly women and children," he wrote, and all adult males who stayed were suspected of being "connected with the rebels."[2] A British census found that there were 9,423 males and 12,344 females, for a total reported population of 21,767. The census found 5,360 inhabited dwelling houses and 597 uninhabited dwelling houses, which had been deserted by the disaffected, for a total of 5,957 dwelling houses.[3]

While Major Clark was running his spy ring, others were also working different avenues of intelligence. On October 23, 1777, Henry Hesmire was paid $160 for secret services by George Washington.[4] What he did and to whom he reported is unknown.

In December 1777, when the British army was at Philadelphia, and Washington and the American army were at Valley Forge, American Major Benjamin Tallmadge was stationed between the armies with a detachment of cavalry for the purpose of recognizance of the enemy. While on this duty, Tallmadge wrote the following romantic account in his journal:

> Being advised that a country girl had gone into Philadelphia with eggs, instructed to obtain some information respecting the enemy, I moved my detachment to Germantown, where they halted, while with a small party I advanced several miles towards the British lines, and dismounted at a small tavern called the Rising Sun, in full view of their out posts. Very soon I saw a young female coming out from the city, who also came to the same inn. After we had made ourselves known to each other, and while she was communicating some intelligence to me, I was informed that the British light horse were advancing. Stepping to the door, I saw them at full speed chasing in my patrols, one of whom they took. I immediately mounted, when I found the young damsel close by my side, entreating that I would protect her. Having not a moment to reflect, I desired her to mount behind me, and in this way I brought her off more than three miles, up to Germantown, where she dismounted. During the whole ride, although there was considerable firing of pistols, and not a little wheeling and charging, she remained unmoved, and never once complained of fear after she mounted my horse. I was delighted with the transaction, and received many compliments from those who became acquainted with the adventure.[5]

The Darragh family resided in the frame building, known as the Loxley House. It stood at 177 Second Street below Spruce Street at the southeast corner of Little Dock Street. (*Watson, Annals of Philadelphia*)

William and Lydia Darragh were other sources of information coming out of Philadelphia. They lived at 177 South Second Street, opposite the home of American General John Cadwalader, which was at 164 South Second Street. When the British occupied Philadelphia, General Howe used the Cadwalader house as his headquarters and also took over the front parlor of the Darragh residence for use as a meeting room.[6] Family tradition states that the house in which she resided was selected as a meeting place for the British officers by her cousin, Lieutenant William Barrington, of the 7th Regiment of Foot, also known as the Royal Fusileers.[7]

Irish-born Lydia, a Quaker, would overhear what the British high command said in her parlor and tell her husband, William. William, who was a school teacher, would write the information in his special shorthand. Lydia would then sew the messages into cloth-covered buttons on the coat of their fourteen-year-old son, John.[8] He would go from his parents' house in British-occupied Philadelphia to his older brother, twenty-two-year-old Lieutenant Charles Darragh, who was encamped with the American forces in the country outside of Philadelphia during the winter of 1777. Charles Darragh was in the 2nd Pennsylvania Regiment of the Continental Line.[9] Charles would transcribe the messages and send the information forward to the American command.

Years later, Lydia Darragh's daughter, Ann, told Robert Walsh that on the evening of December 2, 1777, a British "officer came and told her [Lydia] to have all her family in bed at an early hour, as they wished to use the room that night free from interruption.

The Rising Sun Tavern was located at the north corner of Germantown Road and Old York Road (at one time called Twelfth Street). (*Library of Congress*)

She promised to do so, and when all was quiet lay down herself, but could not sleep." Lydia got out of bed and went into a closet. (In the eighteenth century, "closet" could mean either a small room for privacy or a large case for curiosities or valuables.) Ann stated that the closet was "separated from the council room by a thin board partition covered with paper."[10]

General Howe briefed his staff on an impending assault by British troops on the American forces at Whitemarsh, Pennsylvania, that would occur in two days, December 4. Lydia, after hearing the plans, went back to bed. When a British officer knocked on her bedroom door, "she did not answer until the third summons," which convinced the officer she had been asleep.

Because of the importance of the information, the next day Lydia went to the no-man's-land that surrounded Philadelphia under the guise of getting flour from the mill in Frankford.[11] She left her sack with the miller to be filled and went to the American outpost at the Rising Sun Tavern, at the junction of Germantown and York roads. There she met Captain Charles Craig of the light horse, or cavalry.[12] She gave Craig the information, which he took to Washington's headquarters. Colonel Boudinot provided the information to Washington but kept the source a secret.[13]

Major Clark reported to Washington from Newtown Square on December 1, 1777, that intelligence had been received stating British troops had been ordered to march at a moment's notice. At 7 p.m. on December 2, Captain Robert Smith reported from Germantown, seven miles northwest of Philadelphia, "Some

Ladies who got out by special favor say as the acc[oun]ts from British officers are to be attended to movement will take place early tomorrow Morning."[14] Captain McLane on December 3 advised that the enemy was moving. Major Clark reported the same at 1 p.m. on December 3: "The enemy are in motion; have a number of flat bottomed boats and carriages and scantling, and are busy pressing horses."[15] At 6 p.m. he sent another letter, saying "one of my spies this moment arrived from the city, which place he left this day at 12 o'clock. He confirms the account transmitted you this day at one o'clock, with respect to the enemy's pressing horses and carriages, but saw no boats."[16]

Colonel Boudinot wrote in his memoirs that he had received secret information from a woman but did not mention her by name. Boudinot said that while the army was at Whitemarsh and he was the commissary general of prisoners, he

> dined at a small post at the Rising Sun [Tavern] about three miles from the city. After dinner a little poor looking insignificant old woman came in and solicited leave to go into the country to buy some flour. While we were asking some questions, she walked up to me and put into my hands a dirty old needlebook, with various small pockets in it. Surprised at this, I told her to return, she should have an answer. On opening the needlebook, I could not find any thing till I got to the last pocket, Where I found a piece of paper rolled up into the form of a pipe [stem]. On unrolling it I found that Gen[era]l Howe was coming out the next morning with 5000 men, 13 pieces of cannon, baggage wagons, and 11 boats on wagon wheels. On comparing this with other information I found it true, and immediately rode Post to head quarters.[17]

Some historians believe that Lydia Darragh was the lady who gave Boudinot the needlebook.

Adjutant General Major Carl Leopold Bauermeister of the Hessian forces wrote on December 16, 1777, that on December 3, 1777, anyone could travel the roads to Frankford, Germantown, and Jenkintown. Loyalists were allowed outside of Philadelphia, and they brought back food. "From these people we receive most of the news about the rebels."[18] American naval Lieutenant Luke Matthewman, who escaped from British confinement in Independence Hall, said that "disguised like a porter, with a bag on my shoulder, [I] passed their lines, and got to Gloster [Gloucester] Point, about two miles below the city."[19] The British defensive lines around Philadelphia were extremely ineffective in preventing an individual from entering or leaving the city.

An American intelligence agent identified as W. D. from Frankford, Pennsylvania, in early December reported the British army had given the soldiers four days of cooked rations, and that they had hitched their horses to the artillery. These were signs of an army preparing to march. The agent had heard that the army would attack when the American troops were in motion, but that it was determined to attack at all costs. W. D. was most likely William Darragh, as the Darragh messages where carried out to the Frankford Mill area, and they were know to be active at this time.[20]

Washington's spy networks provided him with multiple warnings that the enemy was leaving Philadelphia to attack. The British army left Philadelphia on December 4 just before midnight. Washington, expecting an attack, had struck his tents and sent the heavy baggage away from the lines. The two armies, which were of almost equal strength, would engage in a series of skirmishes now known as the Battle of Whitemarsh. On December 8, the British returned to Philadelphia without engaging Washington in a decisive action as was expected. In a report of the activity to Congress, Washington wrote, "in the course of last week from a variety of intelligence I had reason to expect that General Howe was preparing to give us a general action." Washington advised Congress concerning the outcome, "I sincerely wish, that they had made an attack; the issue in all probability, from the disposition of our troops and the strong situation of our camp, would have been fortunate and happy. At the same time I must add that reason, prudence, and every principle of policy, forbad us quitting our post to attack them. Nothing but success would have justified the measure, and this could not be expected from their position."[21]

During the Battle of Whitemarsh, Germantown native Christopher Saur III—most commonly known during the war as

Sower (and also as Sauer in various documents)—guided the British troops to Germantown.[22] He was wounded and captured on December 5, 1777, by soldiers under the command of 1st Lieutenant Nicholas Coleman of the 9th Pennsylvania Regiment. He was held prisoner until January 10, 1778, when he was exchanged for his neighbor George Lush, a gunpowder manufacturer.[23] Sower would go with the British to New York City in 1778 and be involved as a case agent, managing the contact with spies.

With the British army back in Philadelphia and unlikely to attack in force during the winter, Washington and his army proceeded to encamp at Valley Forge on December 19.

The Darragh family espionage activities ceased when the British army evacuated Philadelphia on June 18, 1778. Lieutenant Charles Darragh left military service less than two weeks later, on July 1, 1778.[24]

Lieutenant Colonel Adam Comstock of the 1st Rhode Island Regiment at Red Bank, Gloucester County, New Jersey, reported to Washington on October 27, 1777, that a spy had gone from Red Bank into Philadelphia the previous evening and returned on the twenty-seventh. The spy reported that the British had repaired the lower bridge across the Schuylkill River and were preparing an attack on Fort Mifflin.[25]

Christopher Marshall wrote in his diary that at Lancaster, a report was received on November 10 that in October, two spies were discovered in the fort at Red Bank. One of them said he had been sent to collect intelligence by Samuel Garrigus Sr., Paul Reeves, and Samuel Shoemaker (Shoemaker had been mayor of Philadelphia from 1769 to 1771). The spies were immediately hanged.[26] However, the spies were really sent by Hessian Colonel Count Karl von Donop, who had led two thousand Hessian soldiers that attacked the fort on October 22.[27]

Reverend Nicholas Collin, pastor to several Swedish Lutheran churches in New Jersey and Pennsylvania, wrote in his journal that sometime in the fall of 1777, a Måns Hellms "carelessly went on board an English man-of-war [in the Delaware River], and on being asked about his errand said that he was only curious to see how things were managed there whereupon he was held as a spy, became ill and died shortly after his return home."[28]

The British had taken precautions to protect Philadelphia's eastern flank. By December 1, 1777, a chain had been strung across the Delaware to block fire ships from being floated down the river and into the British ships. The frigate *Delaware* at the New Jersey shore anchored the east end of the chain. The chain ran to a row galley in the center of the Delaware, and another row galley at the Philadelphia shore was the west end. In December, the British fenced off the entire Philadelphia shore so that no one in the city could approach the ships that were docked. The fencing also presented a formidable obstacle for anyone trying to sneak across the Delaware from New Jersey into the city. Additionally, 250 marines made up the night watch at the ships in the river.[29]

General Howe appointed Joseph Galloway superintendent general of police and superintendent of all imports and exports.[30] To control the spy traffic coming into the city from New Jersey under the guise of farmers selling produce, Galloway proclaimed that only two ferries, the old and new ferries near Arch Street, could come within the city.[31]

Galloway was busy collecting intelligence at Philadelphia, which was passed to thirty-five–year-old Ambrose Serle, confidential secretary to Admiral Howe. Serle was providing information to Admiral Howe, General Howe, and Lord Dartmouth.[32] One of Galloway's spies was Andrew Fürstner, a farmer from Lancaster County, located in the south central part of Pennsylvania, and brother-in-law of William Rankin of the York County militia. He and Rankin had been involved in a plot to blow up the American magazine at Carlisle, Pennsylvania, in the summer of 1777. Rankin had recommended Fürstner to Galloway, who had sent him to reconnoiter Valley Forge. Upon his return, he reported to Galloway and Nisbet Balfour, aide-de-camp to General Howe. He was next sent to spy on Brigadier General James Potter's brigade of Pennsylvania militia, then stationed at Newtown.[33] Potter had been busy keeping supplies from reaching the British. Fürstner would also be a courier to a number of British spies.[34]

While General Howe was in Philadelphia from September 1777 to June 1778, he used Nisbet Balfour, Lieutenant John Doyle, and Francis, Lord Rawdon, of the 5th Regiment of Foot, to coordinate his secret service operation.[35] Beginning in January 1776, Rawdon was General Clinton's aide-de-camp; he arrived in Philadelphia on October 18, 1777, with dispatches from Clinton for General Howe and stayed for the length of the occupation of the city.

William Knox, who was undersecretary in the British colonial department from 1770 to 1782, received intelligence from France that General George Washington had left a stay-behind-force in Philadelphia that pretended to be friendly to the king. Knox, in London, wrote to General Howe on December 12, 1777, warning him about several Philadelphia residents—business partners Robert Morris and Thomas Willing, and Samuel Inglis—as well as Christopher Marshall from Virginia.[36]

Robert Proud was a staunch Philadelphia loyalist who had taught Latin at the Friends school and went into seclusion in 1775 as the climate of the city moved toward revolution.

On January 10, 1778, Robert Proud wrote to his brother, John, in England, that the rebels had distressed the inhabitants of the city by preventing provisions from coming in. However, he wrote, "the Royal army appear to be want of nothing." The cost of living in occupied Philadelphia became extremely high and ruined many people.[37] But General Major Bauermeister wrote in his journal on January 20, 1778, that the situation in Philadelphia had changed: "The city market is full of fresh meat, all kinds of fowl, and root vegetables. The residents of the city lack nothing except flour and firewood."[38]

The Reverend Jacob Duché was the rector of Christ Church and Saint Peter's Church in Philadelphia and had been the chaplain of the Continental Congress.[39] When the British occupied Philadelphia, he was arrested and incarcerated. He was released after one day behind bars and changed his allegiance. He now

British map of Philadelphia during their occupation (1777–1778) showing the string of redoubts north of the city between the Delaware and Schuylkill Rivers. (*William L. Clements Library, Clinton Maps 251*)

wanted Washington to give up the rebellion and wrote a letter to the general, but was unable to find a way to get it to him. At this time one of his parishioners, Mrs. Elizabeth Ferguson, received permission from Washington to travel from her country home, Graeme Park, in Horsham, to Germantown to meet her husband, Henry Hugh Ferguson, who was a former collector of the port of Philadelphia. A loyalist civilian, he had taken refuge in British-occupied Philadelphia. Elizabeth Ferguson was the granddaughter of Sir William Keith, a former lieutenant governor of Pennsylvania. Because of her social status and the fact that she had supplied linen to be made into shirts for American prisoners in Philadelphia, Washington granted her request. Her husband talked her into delivering the letter from Duché. On October 15, 1777, she delivered it to Washington at the home of Frederick Wampole, in Towamencin, Pennsylvania.[40] The next day, Washington sent the letter to Congress after he had arrived at Peter Wentz's farmstead in Worcester, Pennsylvania.[41] The Supreme Executive Council found Elizabeth Ferguson guilty of treason, and her property was confiscated and sold at auction.

Soon after the British army occupied Philadelphia, John Brown, a former employee of Morris and Willing Company and a distiller, left the city, claimed to be on private business, and traveled through a large part of Pennsylvania before returning to the city.[42] On November 4, Brown left the city again and crossed the Schuylkill River without an American pass but with a pass from General Howe's aide-de-camp. He passed General Potter's position in the evening and did not stop to procure a pass from him. Brown proceeded to Robert Morris's house on the town square at Manheim, ten miles northwest of Lancaster, Pennsylvania, and waited for him from Thursday till Saturday evening.[43] When he spoke to Morris, Morris sent for William Duer, a member of Congress from New York. Duer then went to Lancaster and then York. With Congress deeming Brown's conduct "grounds of suspicion that he is employed by the enemy for purposes inimical to

Henry William Stiegel, ironmaster and glass maker, built his house, circa 1762, on the town square in Manheim, Pennsylvania. During the British occupation of Philadelphia, the house was occupied by Robert Morris and his family. (*Manheim Historical Society*)

these states," the Board of War of Congress on November 18, 1777, ordered that Brown be arrested and sent to the Pennsylvania authorities.

Brown was arrested, examined by the Pennsylvania Council of Safety on November 21, and kept at the Lancaster County jail for "aiding and assisting the enemies of this Commonwealth, and forming combinations with them for betraying the Unites States unto their hands."[44] Brown claimed to have left Philadelphia on instructions from General Howe, who was acting at the suggestion of Thomas Willing. Howe wanted it made known to Congress that he had the power negotiate with Congress or anyone it would appoint. If Congress would give up its claim of independence, the colonies would be put back in the same state they were in 1763 and given more privileges than they had ever sought at that time. Upon reaching such an agreement, he would remove his army and navy, and no standing army would be kept in the colonies. Brown was found to have no written or public documentation of his mission.[45]

Five days later, George Washington said he was surprised that "Mr. Willing should suffer himself to be imposed on by such flimsy measures. He knows that there is a plain, obvious way for Gen[era]l and Lord Howe to communicate any proposals they wish to make to Congress, without the intervention of a second and third hand. But this would not suit their views. I am sorry that Mr. Brown should have been the bearer of the message."[46] On November 24, the Council of Safety decided that Brown should be held in solitary confinement and that anyone who wished to visit him had to be approved by a member of the council.[47]

The Council of Safety decided to prepare a draft of its findings from the examination of Brown. The report indicated that Brown's tale of a peace offer was ridiculous. Nothing was in writing, so General Howe could deny he ever made such an offer. The council believed the British planned to use the story throughout the state to mislead Americans.[48] Christopher Marshall wrote that on December 1, the council received a letter from Robert Morris requesting the release on parole of "John Brown, and proposing to be his security in any sum that they should require. The same was put to vote, and carried unanimously that he should still be retained a prisoner."[49] Marshall later wrote that Brown was released from prison and sent to Manheim. He was required to stay within five miles of the town and post five hundred pounds for security.[50]

The traffic in spies and prohibited goods into and out of Philadelphia was so great that both Generals Howe and Washington restricted travel into the city. But that did not slow the movement of people, information, and goods.[51]

Howe on November 20, 1777, did allow civilians to leave and return to the city between 8 a.m. and 5 p.m. However, anyone traveling outside of those hours was to be detained. The roads from Philadelphia to Germantown and Frankford, as well as the road to Trenton by way of Jenkintown, were still open for travel to everyone in December 1777.[52] But Howe considered Germantown too close to Philadelphia and a possible base for espionage activities, so he wrote to Washington and requested that future meetings of flags of truce be held at Newtown, Bucks County. [53]

American troops were ordered to stop farmers who were sneaking into the city to sell their goods for hard currency rather than accept the near worthless Continental currency. The troops were to detain anyone leaving the city and send them to Washington's headquarters.

Colonel John Jameson advised Washington on February 2, 1778, that the militia around Philadelphia had abandoned its posts. The mills at Pennypack and Frankford were furnishing great quantities of flour to the British and he was powerless to stop it unless he was with the men on their side of the river both day and night "as they are a set of the greatest villains I ever heard of. Many of them have received bribes to let inhabitants pass, but no proof against any but one Hood and one Reade, both of whom deserted last week. . . . Captain Howard has took about 100 people going to market last week, mostly women."[54] The following were court-martialed for attempting to take provisions into Philadelphia: Philip Culp, David Dunn, Joseph Edwards, John Hambleton, William Morgan, and Henry Norris. G. Ritter of Colonel Thomas Proctor's regiment was caught going into Philadelphia, and James Brown was caught communicating with someone in British-occupied Philadelphia.[55] American Brigadier General John Lacey Jr. sent Jacob Crusel, James McCarty, James McGill, Morgan, Abram Vankirk, John Wiggons, and David Williams to the Supreme Executive Council of Pennsylvania, charged with having sent supplies to the British in Philadelphia.[56]

The New Market was established on South Second Street between Pine and Cedar (South) Streets in 1745. It was called the New Market to distinguish it from the market in High (now Market) Street. Like the High Street market, it was a place where spies who used the cover of smuggling produce into the city would sell their produce and collect local gossip. (*Lisa Nagy*)

An Irish-born surgeon, Dr. Henry Stevenson, was one of the king's commissioners in Maryland. He claimed to have sent by the post riders two pilots to Admiral Howe a week before James Molesworth, a British agent, was hanged in Philadelphia on March 31, 1777. Molesworth was convicted of procuring pilots for the British. In August 1777, Stevenson fled Baltimore, fearing for his life and leaving his wife and five children. He made his way north to Isaac Webster's plantation near Elk Ferry, which crossed the Elk

River at Court House Point and Oldfield Point (also known as Elk Neck), about seven miles southwest of Elkton, Maryland, where he stayed several days. On Thursday evening, August 28, he escaped to the British fleet with the Maryland militia in hot pursuit, but Webster was arrested.[57]

While in Philadelphia, Stevenson procured intelligence working under Brigadier General Erskine and Major Nisbet Balfour, who was promoted in the spring of 1778 to lieutenant colonel of the 23rd Regiment of Foot, also known as the Royal Welch Fusiliers.[58] Stevenson accompanied the British troops when they evacuated Philadelphia for New York City and on April 25, 1782, became a surgeon to the British Legion.

A November 22, 1777, letter from Washington at headquarters at Whitemarsh to Captain McLane acknowledged a letter from McLane that contained proposals of some of the inhabitants near the enemy's lines. Washington's letter said, "I will undoubtedly accept their offers of service on the condition that they give in a list of their names, and engage to be under the absolute command for the time specified of such officer as I shall appoint. This precaution is necessary, for otherwise they may only receive the public money without performing the duty expected of them."[59]

Washington's spy network in Philadelphia was providing him with important information about the British supply situation. It advised him on December 21, 1777, of the British army's intent to plunder in the direction of "Darby, Marple and Springfield townships" during the next week, and of their having assembled approximately two hundred wagons for this enterprise. The spies also advised that there was "a very plentiful market of beef" in Philadelphia, and that the British were not only purchasing hay but that "near 100 Hessians were driving cattle" to the city and could be attacked.[60] When the British did come out to forage, Washington had Colonel Daniel Morgan harass them.[61]

One of Washington's Philadelphia spies was a "Mom" Rinker. According to verbal history, her family was involved at the Buck

Tavern in Germantown.[62] Washington had
visited and stayed at the tavern on September
14 and 15, 1777, and he probably recruited
Rinker for his stay-behind spy network at
that time.[63] She bleached her flax atop a high
rock in the Wissahickon Valley. While performing this chore, she would sit and knit for
hours on end. All the while, she would be
observing troop movements. She would write
down the information and insert it in the center of the skein of knitting yarn. She would
allow the yarn to fall over the edge of the
rocks to the valley below, where it would be
retrieved and then brought to Washington.

John Levering, a
house carpenter, was
a spy for George
Washington, operat-
ing between
Manayunk and
Philadelphia. (*Levering
Family History and
Genealogy*)

Brothers Andrew, Jacob, and John
Levering lived on Green Lane in what is now
the Philadelphia neighborhood of Manayunk
and operated between there and in the city.[64]
Jacob Levering, dressed as a farmer, canoed
down the Schuylkill River to Philadelphia, where he sold produce
door-to-door to acquaintances and brought back military intelligence he acquired from his customers and by observation while in
the city. Upon returning home, he would send one of his younger
brothers—Anthony, John, and possibly Samuel—to American officers with information he collected.

On September 30, 1777, Jacob was on one of his trips and was
arrested by some British light horse soldiers. He was charged with
being his brother John, a known spy. He denied being John. He
had a pass from Washington in his possession that he managed to
eat before he was searched. He was taken to an oak tree on the hill
leading to the middle ferry in Manayunk, where the British were
preparing to hang him. After being told by some neighbors that he
was Jacob and not John, the soldier released him. That evening,
Colonel Stephen Moylan stopped at the Levering house at the
request of General Joseph Reed and was told of Jacob's having
been seized. Moylan reported Jacob's arrest to Washington on
October 1.[65]

The Leverings were part of a group called the Green Boys, who conducted intermittent guerrilla warfare against the enemy. On December 19, 1777, some forty soldiers of Captain Henry "Light-Horse Harry" Lee's Virginia dragoons, on their way to Valley Forge, took shelter for the night in the house and barn at Ridge and Roxborough avenues that belonged to Andrew Wood, a shoemaker. Local legend says that some members of the British 16th Light Dragoons were looking for the Green Boys when, sometime during the night, they found the Virginia soldiers. The soldiers in the house got away, but the British dragoons set fire to the barn and slaughtered the soldiers who tried to escape. Those who stayed in the barn were burned to death. Eighteen Virginia soldiers died and are buried in the Leverington cemetery.[66]

Sometimes even your own people are suspected. An anonymous report was filed on December 11, 1777, against Captain Charles Craig, which was brought to Washington's attention. The report said that a gentleman on horseback had come down the Point Road to within two hundred to three hundred yards of the British guards. Two gentlemen from town came out to meet him. A young woman also met the single gentleman and causally spoke to him. She identified him as Craig. An old woman identified the two men as William Allen and Abel James and told the picket guard on station in the area that the single man was Craig. Allen was a wealthy Philadelphia merchant and loyalist who disapproved of the move toward independence. James was a partner in the Philadelphia shipping firm of James and Drinker and a friend of Benjamin Franklin's. On the report is a transcription of a pass issued by Captain Craig to the servant of a Mrs. Lawrence, which allowed her to enter and leave Philadelphia.[67] On January 15, 1778, to justify his activities, Craig reported that he was trying to catch a Hofman Lowrey and several individuals who were stealing food from the poor and selling it for hard currency.[68] On March 5, Craig submitted his resignation because of the insinuations about his conduct and because another soldier had been promoted over him.[69]

FIVE

The Major John Clark Jr. Spy Ring

As noted earlier, in the spring of 1777, prior to the British occupation of Philadelphia, General Washington instructed General Mifflin to set up a spy system in the city. Washington's instruction included the recruiting of Quakers as spies. Mifflin turned over development and operation of the system to Major John Clark Jr., Colonel Elias Boudinot, and Captains Charles Craig and Allen McLane.

John Clark Jr. was a lawyer from York County, Pennsylvania, which is on the west side of the Susquehanna River opposite Lancaster County. He was born in Lancaster in 1751. On March 15, 1776, he was a first lieutenant in Colonel Samuel Miles's Pennsylvania Rifle Regiment in Captain John Marshall's Company F, which was raised in modern Dauphin County. The regiment was approved by the Pennsylvania legislature on March 5, 1776, and would enlist one thousand men.[1] Clark was later made a captain commanding Company I of the Pennsylvania State Regiment.[2] During the campaign around Trenton in 1776, Clark handled some of the secret service activities. Clark was appointed aide-de-camp to Major General Nathanael Greene on January 14, 1777. Clark managed the spy network in Philadelphia until illness caused him to step down in January 1778. Some of his spies in Philadelphia were Private William Dunwoody and Cadwalader Jones.[3]

Clark had previously advised General Greene that

if a prudent active officer was dispatched among the Quakers near the enemy with orders to engage a few farmers as spies on this condition, that they should be excused from all military service and fines for non attendance or not providing substitutes, it would enable his Excellency to get every information of the enemy's designs etc. and there is not one in ten of those farmers but would be happy to serve America in that situation, permit 'em to carry marketing and give them a few dollars on extraordinary occasions and I'll pawn my life, you succeed.[4]

While the British were advancing on Philadelphia, Clark was at Elizabeth Town, overseeing the operation of several spies: John Meeker and brothers Baker and Captain John Hendricks.[5]

Cadwalader Jones was from Uwchlan Township, Chester County, Pennsylvania.[6] In early August 1776, Jones deserted from Captain John Edwards's Company of the 5th Philadelphia County Militia while it was still in Philadelphia. The unit was to leave for frontline duty at Perth Amboy. A bounty of eight dollars was offered for Jones's capture.[7] Forgiveness for his desertion may have induced him to be one of the Quakers recruited to be an American spy in Philadelphia.

On October 6, 1777, Jones went from Philadelphia to Major Clark at Red Lion (now Lionville), Uwchlan Township. He reported the departure of two thousand Hessians from Philadelphia by the lower ferry the day before on their way toward Chester, Pennsylvania. This was by way of Cedar Street, which today is known as South Street, and then continuing on Grey's Ferry road. He also reported that the British were surprised by the American attack at the Battle of Germantown on October 4, 1777. Jones indicated that he collected his information from Quakers who were in the city at the Yearly Meeting. They informed him of wagonloads of wounded soldiers being brought into the city, and said that a few days earlier, a number of wagons went toward Chester after provisions. He also reported that the Hessians might be planning to set up a post at Derby.

At 5 p.m. on October 6, Clark wrote up Jones's intelligence and sent it with Dunwoody, who was to travel as fast as he could directly to General Washington at Pennypacker's Mills on the Perkiomen Creek, about thirty-five miles northwest of Independence Hall. In his letter, Clark advised Washington that

Jones was "a person of credit" and said he could rely on his information. The letter gave Dunwoody a pass per the orders of General Greene.[8]

Private William Dunwoody, of Chester County, had served in Captain James McClure's company in Colonel William Montgomery's regiment of the Flying Camp. The Flying Camp was a detachment of militiamen, horsemen, and sometimes attached infantry that was a mobile reserve group that operated in the second half of 1776. Dunwoody was taken prisoner at the fall of Fort Washington on York (Manhattan) Island on November 16, 1776. He was part of a large exchange of prisoners on January 3, 1777.[9] Dunwoody then served under Captain Samuel Craig in the 1st Pennsylvania Regiment.[10] On May 2, 1777, he was commissioned a first lieutenant in the 3rd Company of the 6th Battalion of Chester County under Colonel Thomas Taylor.[11]

Five hours after writing up Jones's intelligence and sending it off to General Washington with Dunwoody, Clark was busy updating that earlier report as another of his spies arrived from Philadelphia. Clark did not identify the second spy to Washington, but he described him as a gentleman and an intimate acquaintance. This source had left Philadelphia at 11 a.m. The spy reported that Hessian General Wilhelm von Knyphausen had suffered a wound in the hand. The informant was at Germantown after the battle and saw about fifty enemy soldiers killed. He heard many officers say that the Americans had completely surprised them "notwithstanding a deserter gave notice of your design." Provisions were scarce in Philadelphia and "wagons are constantly going towards Chester" for supplies. "General Howe has ordered the residents of the city to do night watch duty. He believes the British hold about 400 people prisoners."[12]

Major Clark agreed with Washington's assessment of the practicality of using Newtown Square as a base of operations, as he ran his spy ring from the town. Washington had suggested to General John Armstrong of the Pennsylvania militia "that Newtown Square would be a good general place of rendezvous, from which [General James Potter of the Pennsylvania militia] might send out his detachments, as he should judge proper, and to which they might resort, as often as any plan or event should make it requisite. It is not my wish he should be stationary; because by keeping in one place, he would not only be more liable to a surprise and attack; but would have it less in his power to perplex and injure the enemy. These however are only intended as hints, which he can use and improve as his own judgment shall direct. As a few horse will be extremely useful with this detachment, I would have you send such a part of those with you, as you and General Potter shall deem sufficient."13

On October 23, 1777, Washington acknowledged an October 22 intelligence report from Major Clark and told him to continue to provide intelligence. Washington, through Robert H. Harrison, one of his aide-de-camps, gave Major Clark one hundred dollars on October 23, 1777, to pay his spies and to pay Dunwoody. Clark was instructed to keep an account of his disbursements.14

On October 27, Clark, who was at Goshen, Chester County, advised Washington that the British had posted local loyalist guards at every ferry and avenue leading into Philadelphia and that they were examining everyone. This kept his operation from getting intelligence from the city as easily as it had before. His people could "now and then get by," Clark reported. Clark complained about the weather and his failing health. The locals watched him "as a hawk would a chicken," which caused him to change his quarters often to avoid being captured.15

On November 3, 1777, one of his spies arrived from Philadelphia. Clark described this spy to Washington as being "an exceeding intelligent follow." Clark told Washington, "I counterfeited the Quaker for once. I wrote a few lines to Sir William [Howe], informing him the rebels had plundered me, and that I was determined to risqué my all in procuring him intelligence; that the bearer would give him my name." Clark said his spy had given Howe the name of "a noted Quaker who I [Clark] knew had assisted" Howe. Clark's "letter was concealed curiously, and the General [Howe] smiled when he saw the pains taken with it; told the bearer, if he would return and inform him of your [Washington's] movements and state of your army he would be generously rewarded."

General Howe gave the spy a pass to travel about freely. The spy was able to walk the city, where he saw very few troops, only those who kept the guards. He saw thirty-five wagons loaded with

Major John Clark Jr. operated his American spy ring in British-occupied Philadelphia out of headquarters at the William Lewis farmhouse in Newtown Square, Pennsylvania. The house was built circa 1708 with a post-1750 addition. (*Lisa Nagy*)

ammunition at the Pennsylvania State House yard. He questioned the teamsters and was told they were headed to the lower ferry and there was to be an attack at Fort Island. The enemy was stacking hay in great quantities on the commons. Clark asked Washington "to make out a state of the army and your intended movements, according to Sir William's desire, or leave it to me, my spy will carry it and take a further view of their camp."

Clark was also sending information to Washington that he gleaned from refugees. Clark reported to Washington on November 3 that a refugee had assured Clark that the British were building three bridges of boats, with wooden planking laid on top of the boats, at the Schuylkill River. Clark reported on November 8 that the enemy said the bridges would be completed by the following Tuesday. The bridges were at Market Street, Gray's Ferry, and Province Island. It would later be reported that at Middle Ferry, which was the Market Street crossing, when supplies were brought from the western side of the river, they would take up the bridge.[16]

Although Washington was at Whitemarsh, he was still orchestrating deceptions at New York. Major General Philemon Dickinson, commander of the New Jersey militia, had advised Washington that it was believed that General Howe had asked for reinforcements from New York to be sent to him in Philadelphia.[17] On November 1, Dickinson advised Washington that he could get information to loyalist General Cortland Skinner that an attack was intended on New York. He thought this could prevent the reinforcements from being sent to Howe.[18] On the second, Dickinson advised that the British ships were loaded with reinforcements and were at the Watering Place on Staten Island preparing to depart.[19] Washington loved the idea of deceiving the British in New York into believing that an attack was imminent:

Your idea of counteracting the intended reinforcements for Mr. Howe's army, by a demonstration of designs upon New York, I think an exceeding good one, and I am very desirous that you should improve and mature it for immediate execution. A great show of preparatives on your side, boats collected, troops assembled, your expectation of the approach of Generals [Horatio] Gates and [Israel] Putnam intrusted as a secret to persons, who you are sure will divulge and disseminate it in New York; in a word, such measures taken for effectually striking an alarm in that city, as it is altogether unnecessary for me minutely to describe to you, I am in great hopes may effect the valuable purpose which you expect.[20]

At Whitemarsh, Washington set about ensuring that the British bought the rumor. He advised General Israel Putnam, who had served in the French and Indian War and was one of the primary figures at the Battle of Bunker Hill,

In order to distract and alarm the enemy and perhaps keep a greater force at New York than they intended Gen[era]l Dickinson will contrive to convey intelligence that they will look upon as authentic, that he is to make a descent upon Staten Island, you upon Long Island and Gen[era]l Gates directly upon New York. If you throw out hints of this kind before people that you think will send in the intelligence, it will serve to corroborate that given by General Dickinson.[21]

On November 6, Dickinson advised Washington that a heavily laden fleet of thirty-six vessels had left. He had a spy (unnamed) on Staten Island and was awaiting his return. This may have been the spy who was to provide the false information.[22] Dickinson's plan may have been too late to stop the fleet, but General Sir Henry Clinton did visit Staten Island, the British were busy strengthening their defenses on Long Island, and the militia was called out because General Putnam was advancing toward Kingsbridge, which is at the northern end of York (Manhattan) Island.[23] Dickinson's spy on Staten Island probably returned on

the sixth or seventh, as Dickinson reported on the seventh to New
Jersey Governor Livingston that one thousand soldiers remained
on Staten Island.[24]

Because it was in Washington's interests to mislead the enemy
with distorted intelligence, on November 4 he drafted instructions
to Major Clark:

> In your next [letter for the British camp] I'd have you mention that
> Gen[era]l Gates, now having nothing to do to the northward, is
> sending down a very handsome reinforcement of Continental
> troops to this army, whilst he, with the remainder of them and all
> the New England and [New] York militia, is to make an immediate
> descent on New York, the reduction of which is confidently spoke
> of, as it is generally supposed that a large part of Clinton's troops
> are detach[e]d to the assistance of Gen[era]l Howe, and that
> Gen[era]l Philemon Dickinson is at the same time to attack Staten
> Island, for which purpose he is assembling great numbers of the
> Jersey militia, that the received opinion in our camp is that we will
> immediately attack Philadelphia on the arrival of the troops from
> the northward; that I have prevailed upon the legislative body to
> order out two thirds of the militia of this State for that purpose; that
> you heard great talk of the Virginia and Maryland militia coming
> up, and in short that the whole continent seems determined to use
> every exertion to put an end to the war this winter; that we men-
> tion the forts as being perfectly secure, having sent ample reinforce-
> ments to their support.[25]

Washington wrote a second letter to Clark on November 4,
advising that he had received Clark's letter of 8 p.m. the previous
evening and saying he thought Clark had "fallen upon an exceeding good method of gaining intelligence and that too much secrecy cannot be used, both on account of the safety of your friend and
the execution and continuance of your design, which may be of
service to us." Washington included in the letter a false report of
the strength of the Continental Army, with a brief memorandum
of his intended movements, and Clark's spy carried it to General
Howe on his next trip.[26]

Clark, who was at Goshen, Chester County, at 6 p.m. on the
fourth, received Washington's letters and responded that he had
personally gone below Marcus Hook, the southernmost town in

Pennsylvania on the Delaware River, and Chester to view the British ships and that he had trusty people there observing their activities with good spyglasses.[27]

Clark was doing other duty in addition to intelligence gathering. He had left Whiteland, which includes Exton in Chester County and which is about thirty miles from Philadelphia, for the Chester Meeting House near Marcus Hook. There he met Captain Henry "Light-Horse Harry" Lee, a few Virginia dragoons, and sixty foot soldiers, a few of whom were riflemen. Captain Lee said they had been told of some shallops (usually two–masted ships used for rowing or sailing in shallow water) being at Grub's Landing, a few miles below Marcus Hook in Delaware. The vessels had left at 3 a.m. When Clark arrived, all the vessels but a tender to the British warship *Roebuck* had left. Clark and Lee decided to run a little ruse. They captured a Tory resident, whom they sent down to the shore accompanied by a detachment led by one of Lee's lieutenants, a few riflemen, and a few dragoons. The Tory hailed the tender and told some of its crew that his company had some fresh beef for them. Five armed crewmen came ashore in a small boat, and the officer of the dragoons demanded their surrender. They attempted to fire and run, but their weapons did not discharge. The riflemen fired, and three of the crewmen fell dead.[28]

On November 8, Clark was at General Potter's headquarters at Newtown Square.[29] In a letter to Washington, Clark said he was "going to reconnoiter and meet some spies; I hope to give you soon some material intelligence."[30] On the twelfth, Clark was at the home of John Jacob in Whiteland Township. John Jacob had been speaker of the Pennsylvania House of Assembly in 1776. In a letter written there and delivered to Washington by Jacob's eldest son, Benjamin, Clark indicated that he was awaiting the imminent return of his spy from Philadelphia.[31] On the sixteenth, Clark was at the Nathan Lewis house in Newtown Square.[32] He had placed a spy in the British fleet and was expecting a report from him any day. He was concerned that his Philadelphia spy may have been caught. Most likely the spy was late in exiting Philadelphia and making a report. In a letter, Clark told Washington that he wanted to meet with him the next day to inform him of a new scheme to get intelligence but "which I dare not do by letter."[33] That

Major John Clark Jr. used former Continental Congressman Charles Humphreys's home, Pont Reading, as one of his safe houses in operating his spy ring. The center section contains the original house; the kitchen wing on the right and the addition on the left were added in the nineteenth century. (*Old Roads Out of Philadelphia*)

evening he was at Potter's quarters, and he mentioned in a letter to Washington that he had seen two people from Philadelphia, but he did not indicate if they were his spies.[34]

On November 17, Clark was at a Mr. Davis's in Derby Township. He wrote Washington about the troop placement of the 71st Regiment of Foot, also known as Fraser's Highlanders, and some Hessians being on the east side of the Schuylkill River with the main body of the soldiers being in a line down to the Delaware River. He told Washington "two battalions are attempting to be raised called the 1st and 2nd Pennsylvania Royalists, commanded by 'His Excellency Sir W[illia]m Howe.' "[35] He also mentioned that food shortages in the city had driven prices up. People were dying of starvation, and some were enlisting in the British army to avoid it. The British magazine of hay was down to six or eight stacks for the entire army. Prisoners were getting no wood for heat, and residents very little. He reported that large numbers of people were leaving the city. Clark also complained about his failing health.[36]

On the morning of the eighteenth, Clark was in Haverford, Pennsylvania, at the home of former Continental Congressman Charles Humphreys, and he reported to Washington that a gentleman he knew in whom he could entirely confide recommended a young man of character who could be employed as a spy in Philadelphia.[37] Clark had sent him into Philadelphia with orders to mingle with British officers, as he was intimately acquainted with several of them. Clark had "promised to send him a little hard, or old money, to spend in company with them." Clark was going to send the money with the soldiers who were going to take mail to Philadelphia by a flag of truce. The money was for a Mrs. Badden in Philadelphia with whom the spy boarded. The cover story used to get the money past the British guards was that it was from the woman's son, who believed she was in distress. Clark advised Washington that the lady knew the money was for the border but did not know the boy was a spy, and he asked Washington for the hard currency to implement the project. Clark identified the lady as the mother of someone Washington knew, but did not identify her.[38]

At noon on the eighteenth, Clark reported on information on British troop movements obtained from a waiter to one of the officers in Philadelphia.[39] Later that afternoon, Clark was at Lewis's at Newtown Square, having just returned from Chester. He wrote another letter to Washington and informed him that the enemy was encamped at Gallows Hill. Two soldiers had gone into the house of a Mr. Gill, and one of them said they were going to New Jersey. The courier of Clark's letter to Washington had the report from a person who had talked to the two soldiers.[40] On the nineteenth, Clark was at Mrs. Mary Withy's tavern in Chester.[41] He reported to Washington that the enemy was now under the command of Lord Cornwallis. Before the enemy left Chester, they plundered the "inhabitants of everything and ill treated a woman, and committed some other horrid actions."[42]

On November 21, Clark, instead of using a courier to carry the money for Mrs. Badden as originally planned, went to Middle Ferry with a flag of truce. He was met by a Captain Baum, a Hessian officer and a relative of Lieutenant Colonel Friedrich Baum's of the Brunswick Dragoon Regiment, at their advanced sentry. Baum insisted that Clark accompany him to his quarters at the ferry. Clark met Brigade Major Archibald Erskine and gave him a letter and some money for Mrs. Badden, and Erskine assured Clark he would immediately forward them to her.[43] Clark walked to the ferry without any blindfold and observed the bridge, enemy's encampment, and redoubts. When he was leaving, Captain Baum told Clark he was sorry but he had received orders to blindfold him. Clark replied that it was customary and gave Baum his handkerchief to do it. Baum tied the handkerchief rather loosely, and Clark was able to see through it because it was very thin gauze. Clark made mental notes of the defenses. He was taken

HEAD-QUARTERS, 2f 3 Nov 1777
THE Bearer John Fox has the Commander in Chief's Permission to pass the out Posts, without Molestation.
To all Concerned.
NBalfour
Aid du Camp

A preprinted pass completed for John Fox on November 20, 1777, by Nisbet Balfour, aide-de-camp to General Howe. (*Library of Congress*)

blindfolded about one hundred feet, and then the handkerchief was removed. At the ferry he was given a captain's guard, which consisted of thirty men.

On the twenty-second, Clark wrote to Washington and asked if some of the spies who worked for Clark had reported directly to Washington, as Clark had directed. Clark informed Washington that a Mr. Irvine was one of his Philadelphia spies who was to leave the city and report directly to Washington. Clark vouched for Irvine and his intelligence.[44] But Clark informed Washington that John Fox, who was to have reported directly to Washington, had to abort the plan because he was "met by a person who knew him, and told him if he went any further he would bring himself into trouble." Clark sent Washington a pass that a John Fox had obtained in Philadelphia. The name "Fawkes" was often spelled "Fox." Fawkes was a prominent Quaker family in Newtown Square at this time, so John Fox might have been John Fawkes. However, I believe it really was John Fox who was the speaker of the Pennsylvania Assembly for part of the session in 1769 and was the master of Masonic Lodge 3 in Philadelphia in 1771 and 1772. The preprinted pass was completed for Fox on November 20, 1777, by Nisbet Balfour, aide-de-camp to General Howe. The pass would allow the bearer to get through the lines without being molested.[45] Someone did get through, and an intelligence report from Philadelphia dated November 21 stated that supplies were still coming into the city by way of the Schuylkill River. Pork was in plentiful supply, but the army did not have any beef or butter, and the flour was moldy.[46]

John Fox had left Philadelphia sometime after noon. The enemy troops in New Jersey had not returned to Philadelphia. Clark was becoming concerned that his spies had been discovered and were being fed what to report, or that they had turned to the other side, because they all reported basically the same thing, that the enemy soldiers "say that if an attack is made, they must inevitably be defeated, and are fearful it will be attempted. This is all of the talk of the citizens." Clark reported to Washington that one of his spies received intelligence from the enemy that Washington "had tried their lines this morning to find what their strength was." Clark reported that the British had plans to destroy Germantown to prevent troops being quartered in it.[47]

On the evening of the twenty-second, Clark also reported to Washington that he had met that morning with a spy from Philadelphia who had delivered fake dispatches to General Howe and had passed through the army in his travels. The spy reported that the Hessians at Middle Ferry watched the residents carefully and ordered them to disperse when three or more of them congregated.[48]

On the twenty-fourth, Clark reported to Washington that a friend who had left Philadelphia said British officers were alarmed about an unspecified attack. "Orders were given to all the guards to take particular notice of all strangers." Lieutenant Colonel Persifor Frazer of the 4th Pennsylvania Battalion, Colonel John Hannum of the Pennsylvania militia, and other officers who were prisoners of the British, were confined in the Pennsylvania State House.[49] Orders were given not to permit them to walk the State House yard. Clark's friend also said that General Howe had appointed two people to visit the prisoners daily and take care of their needs. Clark also complained to Washington that he had not received Washington's responses to some of his letters.[50]

General Armstrong wrote Washington on November 25 to say he did not have any spies who could provide him intelligence about the enemy's lines in order for him to recommend a plan of attack.[51]

That same day, Washington wrote to Clark to acknowledge receiving his letters of the twenty-second and twenty-fourth. He thanked Clark for procuring intelligence and said he wanted it to continue. Washington enclosed "a list of questions to which I wish the most satisfactory answers that can be obtained. You will direct your emissaries and spies particularly on these heads and will request their pointed attention to them." Washington advised that "no persons employed by you, have been with me. [I] shall be glad to know who John Fox is whose permit you enclosed. Is he the person who carried on the cutlary business in Philadelphia?"[52]

On the twenty-sixth, Clark was at Lewis's house in Newtown Square. He wrote to Washington, acknowledging his letter of the twenty-fifth and saying he would follow the general's instructions. He wrote that a friend had left Philadelphia on the evening of the twenty-fifth, and that before he left he was able to observe the street and wharfs. He told Clark that "the bridge at Middle Ferry has hinges higher this side than the other." He did not know if any hinges were on the other side, or if the bridge was raised at night, but he did not think so. Clark assured Washington, "You may rely on this intelligence, as my friend is a man of sense, and very communicative; in this I am justified by my acquaintance and his attachment to me."[53]

Clark wrote, "Mr. G. F. [Fawkes?] lives in this neighbourhood [of Newtown Square], a man of considerable estate, and never lived in Philadelphia." On December 16, Washington wrote to Clark that he was going to send someone named Fawkes with money for him.[54] Money in the form of coin was always needed to pay spies for the dangers they risked.

Clark wrote to Washington on November 29 and said he had met with a friend who had left Philadelphia on the evening the twenty-seventh and reported that General Howe was billeting troops in the homes of citizens, which the citizens didn't like. Another source who had left Philadelphia the night of the twenty-eighth reported that the British talked of attacking an American position but had not made any preparations in that direction, and the source was unable to predict where it would be. Clark said he was expecting at any moment three spies from the city to arrive at Radnor, fifteen miles northwest of Philadelphia.[55]

Back at Lewis's house at Newtown Square on the evening of December 1, Clark reported that John Jacob had just returned from Philadelphia and said the general opinion was the British army would rest quiet in winter quarters. However, another person who had left the city said that "on Friday evening orders were given to the troops to hold themselves in readiness to march; they have also given out they intend to possess themselves of the heights on this side of the Schuylkill, and make our inhabitants help to stake out a piece of ground to fortify. They either mean to attempt to surprise your army or to prevent your making an attack on them." Another one of Clark's gentlemen friends had gone into Philadelphia, and "by him I expect to find out their secret intention." Clark expected to meet two other people from the city during the day.

Clark had continued to find out more about the bridge at Middle Ferry, which must have been one of Washington's requests in one of the lost letters. He reported on December 1 that the bridge drew in two places and that the hinges were kept loose, which would allow it to be drawn up quickly. No strangers were permitted to cross the bridge after dark. Clark also instructed Washington on how best to arrange to feed disinformation to General Howe. He advised having Colonel Robert H. Harrison, Washington's secretary, write to Clark in confidence in the form of an answer to a question from Clark. That way if the letter fell into British hands, Howe wouldn't think that Clark was the source of the intelligence.[56]

One of Clark's spies, "a delicate, sensible woman," while going into Philadelphia was intercepted by a guard of militia under the command of Colonel Isaac Warner of the 7th Battalion of Philadelphia militia. She had taken with her a pint of chestnuts, which she said she was going to give away to children. The guard stopped her and accused her of planning to sell the chestnuts to the enemy and not give them away. A soldier she knew rode with her in her two-wheeled one-horse carriage as he took her to see Colonel Warner. As they traveled, he used rude language and offered to permit her to go to the enemy with her chestnuts if she would have sex with him. Clark wrote, "Her delicacy would not permit her to tell me, but she told her husband, and 'tis from him I have it."[57]

The female spy's being delayed in going into Philadelphia could not have happened at a more inconvenient time, as the British were making preparations for a move. It shut down one part of the American intelligence-gathering operation. The chestnuts were for an American spy in Philadelphia. The unidentified spy reported the situation in the city. "We are pretty well as yet; have a barrel of good flour and some potatoes. Money is very ill to be got. Numbers of people in town will take no paper money of any currency."[58]

On December 3, Clark reported to Washington that "the enemy are in motion; have a number of flat bottomed boats and carriages and scantling, and are busy pressing horses and wagons. No one was permitted to leave the city except those upon whom they [the British] can depend." Clark had ordered that the spy in Philadelphia, an American soldier under Clark's command, be discharged, and he hoped Washington would approve of his plan and agree with the necessity of not putting it into writing, thereby maintaining his cover. Being discharged from the military would make him a civilian in the occupied city. He would then be able to move about the city, as he would no longer be of concern to the British army. Based on the description of his private supplies, he was probably an officer, as he was not being held in prison with the noncommissioned men.[59]

At 6 p.m. on December 3, one of Clark's spies arrived at Newtown Square from Philadelphia, which he had left at noon. The spy had traveled through most of the city and confirmed the earlier report of the British army's activities, but he saw no boats or carriages. That morning a sergeant, a countryman of the spy's, had assured him that the troops had received orders to hold themselves in readiness and to draw two days' provisions. As the spy was leaving, biscuits were being served to the soldiers. The gossip in the city among the people and the soldiers was that the British army was going to make a move. "Should the enemy move," Clark reported, "it will be sudden and rapid."[60]

Clark, trying to smooth things with his landlord, Nathan Lewis, mentioned Lewis's problem to Washington. "On the 16th of September last, [Colonel] Baron [Henry Leonard Philip Arendt [of the German Regiment] took a mare from my landlord valued at 100, and promised to return her the next day but has never done it. Mr. Lewis begs he may be ordered to do it, as the enemy has taken the remainder of his creatures and he has done me many services for the U.S. I have given his complaint a place in this letter, and beg leave to recommend him as a person worthy of compassion."[61]

Clark also reported to Washington on the third that the militia under Colonel Warner's command "behaved so imprudent in [detaining] my spy yesterday; had not this happened I should have had, early this day, a complete account of the enemy's situation and design." He wanted Washington to order Warner to make immediate restitution for the provisions taken from Clark's spy, a Mr. Trumbull. That would allow Clark to "get some intelligence of the utmost importance, both at present and in future." Trumbull would be able to deliver the provisions and return with intelligence.[62] Washington advised General Potter of the situation. Clark sent Trumbull with a letter that said he had Clark's permission to take the provisions into Philadelphia and waited on Potter for the return of the provisions on December 17, but was unable to get the items. Clark wrote to Washington again on the eighteenth, complaining about the situation. Clark clarified to Washington that Trumbull was sending the provision at Clark's instructions before the enemy attacked Washington at Whitemarsh. Clark

suspected the design, and [was] anxious to get information, the route they intended and their numbers, &c., prevailed on this gentleman to permit an acquaintance to go in with his chair [a one-seat, horse-driven carriage]—money would not tempt him, he said; he had upwards of twenty in family in the country, and several in town, the latter no provisions except flour and potatoes and if I would consent to his sending a little beef and butter he would engage to get me the necessary information, to which I readily consented, and a part was to be given to Mrs. Williams, mother of Major [William] Williams, a prisoner with the enemy in Philadelphia, and thus, because every ignoramus in the militia is not made acquainted with the *secret designs* of the army, he will raise a clamor against an *innocent man*,—but this is not all; a private difference has existed between Colonel Warner and Mr. Trumbull, and the former has been imprudent enough to discover it. I wrote him and informed him, 'twas me that was to blame, (if anyone,) but finding himself disappointed in getting Trumbull under a guard which he sent, and countermanded by me, he never answered by letter, but said he should have me tried by court martial and I have taken no further notice of him; had he been a gentleman he would have excused Trumbull on the reception of my letter, and blamed me.[63]

Clark believed the information the spy would have brought back would have been worth the expense.

On December 16, Washington informed Clark that he had sent an order to Colonel Clement Biddle, commissary general for forage, for one hundred dollars, because he was someone in camp who Washington thought probably had some cash. However, Washington was not certain that Biddle had any money. "If he has Mr. Fawkes will carry it to you. The Paymaster Gen[era]l has not arrived in camp since our late move."[64]

Colonel John Fitzgerald, aide-de-camp to Washington, wrote to Major Clark on December 16 that the provisions he wanted were scarce, and he proposed that he pay Clark a visit.[65] He must have arranged for the items for Clark, because Clark returned the provisions to Trumbull but complained in a December 18 letter to Washington that the militia wanted to keep the provisions for its own use. Clark wrote that there was

no reason the provisions sent by my orders should be detained, my feelings on this occasion are not a little wounded after having given [Trumbull] my word and honor there was no danger to be apprehended from our army; 'tis making me appear in a contemptible light, my word will not be taken hereafter, and let me assure you I have received from this gentleman every intelligence I could wish. Consider his situation; there is no making known his reasons, or he is ruined by one party or the other; he is sensibly injured. I beg leave to recommend him to your Excellency as worthy [of] your compassion, and that the articles may be restored to him. I am sorry those *troublesome gentry* have occasioned me to write you so often on this head.[66]

Washington, in order to give more force to Clark's passes and stop his complaining, included a statement in General Orders on December 18, 1777, that people having any passes from Major John Clark were to be allowed to pass all guards.[67]

Washington wrote to General Potter on December 21 that "a Mr. Trumbull was sending [provisions with a woman] into Philadelphia by [Clark's] permission as a cover to procure intelligence. This provision was seized by Colo[nel] Rankin and has been since detained by him. I desire you will give orders to have it delivered, for unless we now and then make use of such means to get admittance into the city we cannot expect to obtain intelligence."[68]

Clark had sent several spies into Philadelphia to find out the destination of the enemy's march. One of the spies returned at 4 a.m. on December 19 to Lewis's house at Newtown Square. The spy had left the city at 3 p.m. on the eighteenth, at which time there were three hundred horses covered with blankets on the commons. Clark wrote to Washington, "Their light-horse were reconnoitering this morning on Marshall's Road and very inquisitive; I directed my spy to inform them a large body of troops were marching towards Derby, there to take post for the winter, which startled them, he says, exceedingly." When one of his spies was traveling, one of the country people carrying in provisions to the British grabbed his coat and called him a "damn'd Rebel" before the enemy's advanced sentries. The spy put his spurs to his horse to get away. The accuser was captured by some American cavalry. "His name is Edward Hughes, is a papist, and lives in Springfield; I hope an example will be made to deter others."

When Clark had arrived in Pennsylvania in October, he purchased a pony to send messengers express to headquarters, and the horse was now worn down. Washington had instructed him to get a horse from General Potter's quartermaster for Clark to use in meeting his spies, but the quartermaster said he did not have one in good enough condition to give him. Clark wrote to Washington that he had "to ride from 20 to 60 miles a day to meet my friends to prevent suspicion (the people being Quakers.) If you'll please to permit me to purchase a horse, I can do it readily, (and when I have done with him return him to the States) and give an order to the Q. M. G. [Quartermaster General]." He asked Washington to approve of his plan or said he would have to pay for the horse out of his own money, which he could not afford.[69]

A spy from Philadelphia arrived at 8 p.m. Saturday, December 20. He brought "intelligence that near one thousand of the enemy crossed over to Jersey yesterday, with six field-pieces from four to six pounders, with design to let the country people the benefit of

Spies using the cover of smuggling produce into the occupied city would sell the produce at the market stalls, called shambles, adjacent to the High (Market) Street Prison. While at their stalls they would gather intelligence. (*Watson, Annals of Philadelphia*)

the market." They had gone to New Jersey in search of buying supplies for Philadelphia. Clark reported that one hundred Hessians with about thirty wagons went foraging toward Derby and returned loaded with hay and rye straw. His sources told him that the enemy intended "to make another foraging excursion, and haul all the wood they have cut, over the river, and then pull up and destroy the bridge, and remain quiet in winter quarters, for the remainder of the season." Clark reported that his boy, Martin Nicholls, had returned, but Clark did not want to send him to Washington, because his horse was so tired. Lewis lent Clark a horse in order to get the report to Washington. Clark again asked Washington to get Colonel Arendt to return Lewis's horse.[70]

Late the next morning, December 21, a spy arrived from Philadelphia at the same time that the express rider arrived with a letter written earlier that day. The letter gave Clark the authority to buy a horse and bill the government for it. The spy had either received intelligence from, or was, Joshua Humphreys of Philadelphia. Nathaniel Vernon, the former high sheriff of Chester County, in confidence told Humphreys that a detachment was to be sent to Derby, Marple, and Springfield townships during the coming week on a foraging raid.[71] The day before, the spy had seen six large, flat-bottomed boats and about seventy privates who had returned from New Jersey. The boats were loaded with beef, corn, and other food. The spy did not see any more troops returning but understood more were coming back to Philadelphia. About two hundred wagons were moving out, and it was said they were going to Frankford. The enemy was putting some inhabitants out of their homes and quartering troops in them. Many citizens were being forced to live in their kitchens. Some ships had moved down-river, with three or four still at Chester. In a letter to Washington, Clark indicated that he was expecting a spy who would know what was happening with the ships. Clark said he would not allow Trumbull to go into the city, and he indicated he had no plans to use Trumbull in the future.[72]

On December 22, Clark went to Springfield, Pennsylvania, where he met one of his spies on the road. Generals Howe and Erskine were with the troops going to Derby. Clark's spy had been captured by their advance guard on the Springfield road and taken to Howe at Derby. The foraging party started a great number of fires. Clark wrote to Washington, "One of their guards assured my spies they were only on a foraging expedition and intended to pro-ceed toward Chester. No wagons had passed Derby before my spy came away." Clark said he would order his spy to return and get more information.[73]

At twelve o'clock on the twenty-second, Clark wrote from General Potter's quarters, "A large body of the enemy are on their march to Derby, where they must have arrived by this time, the number uncertain but you may rely are formidable; they certainly mean to forage where I mentioned in my letter of yesterday."[74]

Washington had attempted to put a detachment together at Valley Forge to oppose the foraging party but was unable to because of a mutiny over the lack of food.[75] It was a missed oppor-tunity. Clark's spy network delivered the intelligence, but there was no military response.

Another spy, who had just come from General Howe's quarters, reported on the twenty-third that the enemy intended to continue plundering the countryside. Clark went out reconnoitering, and during his absence the enemy's light horse came out to his vedettes. They were in disguise and called to the vedettes, claim-ing to belong to the American army. When they were a few yards away, they fired their carbines and shot one of the vedettes; the other one escaped. They then pursued Clark, but he knew the road and was able to get away just before reaching their picket.[76] On the twenty-fifth, Clark was reporting on the movement of the British foraging party.[77] On the twenty-sixth, a spy left Philadelphia to report that General Knyphausen commanded there with one regiment of English and the rest Hessians, and that they had built a bridge of boats at Gray's Ferry.[78]

A spy from Philadelphia who had left on the evening of December 27 reported that General Howe had returned to Philadelphia and that the bulk of his army had gotten over the Schuylkill River. Clark sent someone to determine if all of the enemy's troops had left Derby. Clark wrote on December 28 to Washington, "If you don't hear from me this evening, you may rely they have returned." Another spy was due to return from the city, he wrote, and "if the enemy are all got into quarters I will write you." He also requested leave to return home to York, Pennsylvania, to see his wife.

While Clark was away on the twenty-seventh, Martin Nicholls, a soldier assigned to him, ran away. If he made it to the British, Nicholls would have been interrogated and could have advised them what Clark was doing. He might have known the names of the American spies and could use that information as a bargaining chip with the British. Clark suspected "he is lurking about camp in hopes of getting over Schuylkill and making his escape to Germantown, and from thence to Philadelphia, where his father lives." Clark asked Washington to put a notice about the soldier in a general order in the hope of recovering him. The notice Clark wanted sent read:

Twenty shillings reward, exclusive of what allowed for taking deserters. Deserted from Major John Clark's quarters at Newtown Square, on the 27th instant, Martin Nicholls, a soldier, about 5 feet 2 inches high, 18 years of age, a barber by trade, wears his hair tied, is of a yellowish complexion, and much pitted with the smallpox; had on and took with him an old felt hat cocked, a blue cloth coat with metal buttons. almost new, a whiteish colored, round waist-coat, buckskin breeches, white yarn stockings, a pair of half worn shoes with yellow buckles, a good blanket coat with-out buttons, two good white linen shirts, an old knapsack with some old shirts, &c. He sometime ago waited on General Minor, and one winter on Col. Biddle. 'Tis probable he may endeavor to go to Philadelphia, as his father lives there. All officers and soldiers are requested to apprehend him, and give notice to [John] Clark, Aid de Camp to Major General Greene.[79]

On December 30, Clark again asked for permission to go home. He also said he was expecting to hear from another spy and would report anything significant.[80] He reported that the British were covering all the crossing points along the Schuylkill River in force, except for the guard at Middle Ferry. Also, the boat bridge at Gray's Ferry had been disassembled. Clark further reported about a group of highwaymen who claimed to be volunteers to the American cause but stopped everyone, even those with passes. They robbed people "without distinction" and blamed it on the army. One of the highwaymen was a Mr. Saunders, who "acts like a Light Dragoon for General Potter." He "has prevented my spies at different times from going" into Philadelphia. "When they produced my passes, he told them I had no right to grant 'em, and spoke so disrespectfully of me that had I caught him I should have made an example of him."[81]

In requesting permission to go on leave, Clark wrote, "I must now remind you of your last words to me. As the armies are both gone into winter quarters, I presume nothing further will be wanting in my department, therefore, beg your permission to visit Mrs. Clark, and prepare some necessaries for myself, which I am in great want of." He also requested a letter of recommendation to the president and Congress.[82]

Clark got his leave, and Washington wrote to Henry Laurens, president of Congress, on January 2, 1778, from Valley Forge:

> I take the liberty of introducing Major John Clark, the Bearer of this, to your notice. He entered the Service at the commencement of the war and has for sometime past acted as Aide de Camp to Major Gen[era]l Greene. He is active, sensible and enterprising and has rendered me very great assistance since the army has been, in Pennsylvania by procuring me constant and certain intelligence of the motions and intentions of the Enemy. It is somewhat uncertain whether the State of the Major's health will admit of his remaining in the military line, if it should, I may perhaps have occasion to recommend him in a more particular manner to the favor of Congress at a future time. At present I can assure you that if you should, while he remains in the neighbourhood of York, have any occasion for his Services, you will find him not only willing, but very capable of executing any of your Commands. I am etc.[83]

When the army first entered Valley Forge, Washington's headquarters was in his marquee near the artillery park. After a week he moved into the two story stone house owned by Isaac Potts. It was from his office in this house from late December 1777 to June 18, 1778 that Washington analyzed intelligence provided by American spies in Philadelphia. (*Lisa Nagy*)

While Clark was home, he wrote to Washington on January 13:

Your kind letter of recommendation, I had the honor to deliver to his Excellency, the President [Henry Laurens], who laid it before Congress in my absence. Since which, they have appointed me an auditor with Mr. Clarkson, to settle and adjust the accounts of the main army. Whether I am equal to the task assigned me or not, I cannot presume to say, but should I accept the appointment, I flatter myself, under your good patronage, I shall be able to acquit myself in the duties of my station with honor. My utmost exertions shall be tried to give general satisfaction, and discharge the trust reposed in me with integrity and impartiality. As I made no application for the appointment, and it being without the line of promotion, I hope it will give no offence to others, whose abilities might have given them reason to have expected it. I have wrote to Major General Greene, informing him of it, and begged permission to resign my commission as an Aide de Camp. . . . I formed a plan by which, I flatter myself, you will hereafter get constant intelligence, if pursued at present.[84]

On January 24, Washington replied, thanking Clark for his letter, saying he hoped Clark would accept the appointment as auditor, and ending his letter, "I am much obliged by your polite tender services."[85]

SIX

Occupied Philadelphia:
The British Move Out

With the arrival of the new year, the British had ceased military operations for the winter. There would be little fighting until spring, which would bring a new season of campaigning. Now was a time for wounds to heal, rest, socializing, and preparing for future operations. Since no offensive operations were planned, intelligence-gathering activities would be reduced, but not suspended. Generals on both sides needed no make sure there were no surprises–that is, that there would not be another surprise like Washington's attack and the American victory at Trenton, New Jersey.

Some of the British spy operations in Philadelphia at this time were the responsibility of Irish-born Francis, Lord Rawdon.[1] His day-to-day operations were handled by Lieutenant Colonel Stephen Kemble of the 60th Regiment of Foot.[2]

Samuel Burling, a New York City merchant, was associated with Joseph Galloway, who had been working as a case agent.[3] During the British occupation of Philadelphia, Burling "was confidentially employed in the procuring of intelligence." He was responsible for appointing people to be stationed at the checkpoints on the British lines. These monitors were to have been acquainted with the people passing the lines. He received the monitors' reports every evening.[4] When the British army evacuated the city, Burling departed with it and was employed as a guide in New Jersey for General Clinton.[5] General Howe used couriers traveling as farmers in wagons to keep contact with the spy network his staff had established from occupied Philadelphia.[6]

On February 16, 1778, Sergeant George Thompson of the 63rd Regiment of Foot also known as the West Suffolk Regiment gave a deposition to John Potts, magistrate of police in Philadelphia, stating that on December 27, 1777, the brig *Symmetry*, which was transporting soldiers fit for duty and invalids, ran aground in the Delaware River. The crew of the *Symmetry* was discovered by the Americans and taken prisoner to Lancaster. Two sergeants, Donald Cameron of the 42nd Regiment of Foot and Matthew McMahon of the 16th Regiment of Light Dragoons, who accompanied a British flag of truce were also captured and jailed, and were to be treated as spies.[7] General Howe wanted the sergeants released because they had been traveling under the protection of a flag of truce. On February 21, he wrote to General Washington about the sergeants, enclosing depositions from a Thomas Franklin, a Thomas Wileman, and a Sergeant George Thompson about the two sergeants.[8] Howe wrote again on March 21 for the release of Cameron and McMahon or an explanation of why they were being held.[9]

In a reply to Howe, Washington stated that the sergeants "were taken at a distance from their party, whither they had straggled, under very exceptionable circumstances, and were confined in Lancaster [jail], on suspicion of their being spies. I have sent directions to have them conveyed to your lines, which nothing but a regard to the promise of my Aid de Camp would induce me to do, the conduct of these men having been so irregular and criminal, as to make them justly amenable to punishment. The particulars of this affair shall be the subject of future [criticism]."[10]

James Parker was born in Port Glasgow, Scotland, in 1729, and emigrated to America in 1750.[11] He became a wealthy merchant in Norfolk, Virginia, in partnership with William Aitchison, his brother-in-law.[12] Early in the war, Parker was involved in gathering intelligence, which he brought to John Murray, 4th Earl of Dunmore, the royal governor of Virginia. Lord Dunmore was living on a British naval vessel in Hampton Roads, Virginia.[13] Dunmore appointed Parker a captain in his troops, and he relocated to Philadelphia during its occupation. He was sent out of the city to make a detailed drawing of the American camp at Valley Forge, which he accomplished.[14] Another British spy, William McKay, was not as successful as Parker. McKay used the cover of selling fresh meat to the starving troops at Valley Forge. He eventually was discovered and hanged as a spy in the presence of the Continental Army on April 15, 1778.[15]

In February 1778, the Americans had a plan to cause confusion in Philadelphia by burning the South Street theater, which was above South Fourth Street, and Smith's tavern (also known as City Tavern and the New Tavern at 138 South Second Street).[16] In the resulting commotion, they would attack the city's line of defenses. On February 23, a soldier who had deserted from Washington's camp and made his way to the British in Philadelphia "was in one of the redoubts within the British lines when he saw a woman going out [whom] he told the officer of the guard he [had seen] only the day before in the rebel camp speaking to General Washington."[17] She was Miss Anne Myers of Philadelphia who provided intelligence at American headquarters on the activities of loyalists.[18] She was detained and taken to a guard room. "A letter being discovered in her hair, she snatched it and burnt it in the fire." Immediately she was taken to headquarters, where General Howe interrogated her. She had a pass in her possession to go through the British defenses. Major Alexander Campbell, who gave the woman the pass, was ordered into confinement, and a court-martial was begun.[19]

Campbell was born in Scotland but served in the French and Indian War as an officer in the provincial army. He had lived in Boston for a number of years and volunteered for the British service. General Clinton, while in Philadelphia, appointed Campbell deputy quartermaster under General Erskine, quartermaster general.[20]

Campbell was arrested on suspicion of correspondence with the enemy.[21] His trial was completed as it was snowing and sleeting on March 10. The only evidence against him came from the woman suspected of being a spy. Campbell had an alibi and presented a

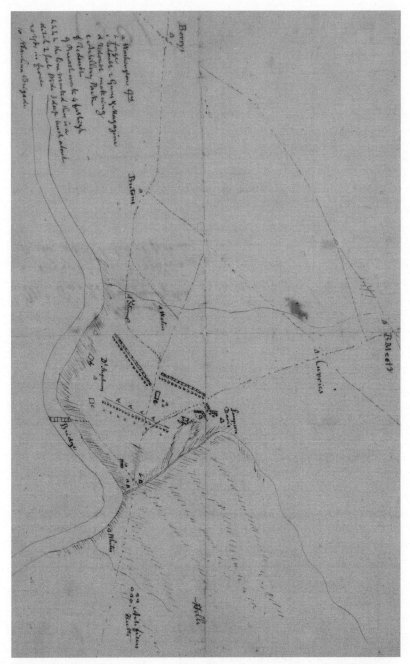

Plan of Washington's position at Valley Forge, Pennsylvania, made by James Parker, a British spy. (*William L. Clements Library, Henry Clinton Maps Map no. 256*)

strong defense. On the eleventh, he was acquitted for lack of evidence against him.[22]

Jacob Bankson was an American spy who reported to Brigadier General William Maxwell of New Jersey.[23] Bankson operated in British-held Philadelphia with such ease that Washington suspected him of being a double agent.

Bankson's father owned property in the 1740s and 1750s at Moyamensing and Passyunk townships in Philadelphia County.[24] The former townships now make up the southeast section of Philadelphia. Jacob was born September 27, 1751, and was one of seven children. He attended the College of Philadelphia from 1764 to 1767, when he received a bachelor of arts degree; he earned a master of arts degree in 1770. He delivered the salutatory oration at the college on November 19, 1767.[25] He later became an attorney.[26] He received an honorary master's degree from the College of New Jersey now known as Princeton University at its commencement exercises in 1771.[27] Bankson married Elizabeth Bedford on February 13, 1772, at the Second Presbyterian Church in Philadelphia.[28] In 1773, he was living at Wilmington when he became a Freemason in Philadelphia; he later became secretary, worshipful master, and an officer in the Grand Lodge.[29]

In March 1778, while the Banksons were living in Princeton, Washington wrote to Governor Livingston:

> I have strong reasons to suspect a Mr. Bankson, late a Captain of Marines in our service, of being in the employ of the enemy as a spy. We have nothing against him that amounts to proof, and to seize him at present would answer no end; but to put it out of our power to detect and punish him. It were to be wished, your Excellency, without discovering our suspicions could fall upon some method to have him well watched, and, if possible, find out something to ascertain the fact. He is lately from Philadelphia and has offered me his services in that way, as he proposes to return in a few days, taking this camp in his way. If in the mean time any circumstance should arise within your knowledge you will be pleased to transmit it to me.[30]

Washington gave Lieutenant Colonel Alexander Hamilton, one of his aides-de-camp, the job of checking up on Jacob Bankson. On April 3, Hamilton wrote to Colonel Stephen Moylan of the Fourth Continental Dragoons that Bankson was suspected of being a spy for General Howe. Bankson had left Valley Forge on March 24,

> on pretense of making a visit to his family, and is now returned with renewed offers of service. It is doubted whether he has not, in the mean time, been at Philadelphia. The General wrote some days since to Governor Livingston, requesting he would take measures to explore Mr. Bankson's conduct and views. He directs you immediately to see the Governor and learn from him, if he has been able to make any discovery, and to take cautious methods to ascertain whether Bankson has been at home, since he left camp, how long, and when he left home, in short any thing that may throw light upon his designs. Let him hear from you as soon as possible about the he subject. Manage the business with caution and address.[31]

On April 11 and May 1, 1778, the Continental Army Warrant Book recorded payments to Bankson of one hundred dollars for secret services.[32]

On May 17, Livingston wrote to Washington, and because he thought Bankson would carry the letter, he wrote it in Dutch.[33] The letter said Bankson "pretends to have a commission from General Washington for secret business as I am told, he goes frequently from this place [Princeton] to the camp, he pretends that he undertakes this journey on business with General Green."[34] Livingston advised that Bankson's brother was apprehensive that Bankson was suspected and "officiously told me that he could produce a pass from your Excellency if I desired to see it. I answered that I knew nothing of his brother, nor had any reason to question his right of passing especially as he was employed by your Excellency. I have since learnt that he has plenty of gold and silver. If he had no business with General Green in his last jaunt, as he told his brother he had, it will increase the suspicion against him."[35]

On May 21, Washington wrote back to Livingston that the courier who brought the letters was one of the army's hired express riders. "So is the man now for whom, I presume, you took him; nevertheless, I am not the less indebted for your attention and cautious notice."[36] On May 23, Livingston advised that there was confusion over which Bankson was under suspicion because there were three brothers named Bankson at Princeton. Livingston had been at a tavern in Princeton with the Bankson who was under suspicion. Livingston, apparently upset with Bankson's behavior, had sent him into another room in the tavern because of his "profane swearing, an accomplishment in which he seemed to excel the whole navy of Britain."[37]

Hamilton eventually found the suspicions about Jacob Bankson's being a double agent to be unfounded.[38] On June 1, Washington advised Livingston that the person of interest was named Jacob Bankson. He further advised that he was now satisfied with Jacob Bankson and that Livingston need not trouble himself further in the matter.[39]

Although Washington's spies used the cover of trading with the enemy to accomplish their mission, he was upset with their volume of merchandise changing hands with the British. He was also concerned about the dangers the army might be exposed to if the flow of information was not shut off. He instructed Brigadier General John Lacey Jr. of the Pennsylvania militia, who was at Warwick Township, central Bucks County, Pennsylvania, twenty-two miles north of Philadelphia, to try his best to slow the communications and goods going into and out of Philadelphia. In order to motivate Lacey's troops, Washington was going to allow "every thing actually taken from persons going into and coming out of the city" to be kept by those who intercepted the goods. Washington also cautioned Lacey "to prevent an abuse of this privilege, since it may otherwise be made a pretext for plundering the innocent inhabitants. One method to prevent this, will be to let no forfeitures [of intercepted goods] take place, but under the eye, and with the concurrence of some commissioned officer." He wanted Lacey to move closer to Philadelphia and to "to ramble through the woods and bye ways, as well as the great roads." He wanted him to search out and find those transporting goods to Philadelphia and "to fire upon those gangs of mercenary wretches."[40]

Washington later wrote that he wanted the state to take over the responsibility of granting permission for people to enter Philadelphia:

> If the state would take them in hand, and deal properly with them, it would be more agreeable to me than to inflict military punishment upon them. The evidences seldom appear against those guilty of small crimes and then they escape. If you think that the state will receive those persons you have taken, I am willing that they should be given up to them, either to be punished as criminals or kept to exchange for those inhabitants lately taken away from their families.[41]

Sometime during the British occupation of Philadelphia, Mary Hutchinson of Philadelphia went behind American lines to Valley Forge to collect intelligence for the British.[42] She may have been the same person as Margaret Ann Hutchinson, a milliner and widow of Philadelphia who was employed as a courier between British officers. She estimated her annual income from the millinery business at seventy-eight pounds.[43]

Also during the British occupation, Martin Blackford of Warrington, York County, Pennsylvania, joined the British army. He wrote in a summary of his military service that while serving in the army, he was sent out of Philadelphia for intelligence.[44]

The British army was paying reward money for turning in American spies. Margaret Locke of Philadelphia, in her claim for losses to the British government, stated that while the British army occupied Philadelphia, she had discovered an American spy in the city, and when offered a reward did not take it.[45]

The British also recruited from disaffected American soldiers. Thomas Shanks had been an ensign in the 10th Pennsylvania Regiment. He was court-martialed in the fall of 1777 for stealing a higher-ranking officer's shoes, found guilty, and discharged from the army. He went into Philadelphia and offered his services to the British. General Clinton teamed him up with a British sergeant, William Sutherland of the Grenadiers. Sutherland was to show Shanks through the British lines. Once through the lines, the sergeant was to return to Philadelphia, and Shanks was to continue onto Valley Forge to spy on the Americans. After getting Shanks through the British lines and on his way, Sutherland changed his plans. He would not return to Philadelphia but desert to the Americans at Valley Forge. He had a bargaining chip—Shanks—to play to his financial benefit. Sutherland arrived at Valley Forge first and informed the American command of Shanks's spy mission. When Shanks arrived, he was arrested.[46]

On June 2, 1778, at Valley Forge, Shanks was convicted as a spy at a Board of General Officers. He was sentenced to be hanged on June 3 "at guard mounting at some convenient place near the Grand Parade."[47] Shanks was hanged on June 4 on the grand parade.[48] His body hung from 10 a.m. till retreat, at which time it was cut down and given to the surgeons for their use.[49] Elijah Fisher a Massachusetts soldier at Valley Forge, recorded in his journal that on June 4, 1778, "there was a spye hung on the grand parade from the enemy he formerly belonged to our army and was an ensign in the Second P[ennsylvani]a Reg[imen]t. His name was Thomas Church."[50] Fisher must have been describing the hanging of Thomas Shanks.

The Americans were also busy with their espionage activities. Alexander Clough had been the adjutant of the 1st New Jersey Regiment in 1775. On January 8, 1777, Clough was commissioned a major of the 3rd Continental Dragoons.[51] At Valley Forge, he was assigned to receive and forward spy and intelligence reports from Captain Allen McLane's spy network.[52] Clough, in answer to a letter of January 21 from Colonel Alexander Hamilton, told Washington of McLane's stopping people who were coming from south of Germantown and then releasing them "as if they were not answerable to any one for their conduct."[53] Clough assumed that some of these persons must be involved in smuggling and should be searched and charged. Upon Washington's instructions, Lieutenant Colonel John Laurens informed Clough that "Captain McLane frequently employs spies to bring him intelligence, it would be improper for him to subject persons whose safety depends on secrecy to the examination of any but the officer in whom they have a confidence, and who has engaged them to act."[54] Although we do not know who provided information to McLane, being accused of spying or involvement in suspicious activies was a common charge among the populace. Washington had noticed that Pennsylvanians were often placed in the provost, or military jail, on charges of disloyalty or spying "which upon examination before a court martial appear groundless and those persons consequently subjected to needless imprisonment." Washington wanted a high-ranking administrative officer to refer cases with little evidence that did not involve going into or coming out of Philadelphia to the judge advocate, who was in charge of the administration of military justice. Washington believed that this way, cases with little evidence would be dismissed, and the jails would not become clogged, decreasing the drain on army resources, such as food for prisoners and men to serve as guards. These men would then be available for combat duty.[55]

Nonetheless, actual British and French spies and disloyal behavior continued to be discovered in 1778. On February 24, 1778, Joseph Worrell, an inhabitant of Pennsylvania, was brought before a court-martial presided over by Colonel Philip van Cortland of the 2nd New York Regiment. Worrell was charged with giving intelligence to the British and acting as guide and pilot to the enemy. He was acquitted of giving intelligence but found guilty of acting as a guide, and was sentenced to death. Washington approved the sentence and ordered Joseph Worrell to be executed March 3.[56] On March 2, Washington ordered the execution postponed.[57] Worrell was hanged on March 7.[58]

A French spy who had left Philadelphia was captured on March 9. The spy was being guarded by a detachment of soldiers under Captain James Lang of the 10th Pennsylvania Regiment and was to be interrogated by Paul Fooks, the French- and Spanish-language professor at the College of Philadelphia.[59] No other information has been found regarding this spy.

On May 6, 1778, a loyalist spy was discovered observing the celebration at Valley Forge of the recent French alliance with the United States.[60] A member of Washington's staff decided it would be more beneficial to take no action against the spy and allow the spy to return to Philadelphia and report on the excellent drilling by, and condition of, the American army.[61]

Washington, in the spirit of the day "being more desirous to reclaim than punish offenders and willing to show mercy to those who have been misled by designing Traytors and that as many as can may participate [in] the pleasures of the truly joyful day," pardoned William McMarth, a matross who assisted the gunners in loading, firing, and sponging the guns in Captain James Lee's company of Colonel John Lamb's 2nd Battalion of Continental Artillery; and John Morrel, a soldier in Colonel Henry Jackson's Additional Continental Regiment, both of whom faced death sentences, and he ordered their immediate release, "hoping that gratitude to his clemency will induce them in future to behave like good soldiers."[62]

The alliance with France gave the Americans something they did not have—a naval presence—and the game changed. Britain's prized possessions, the sugar islands in the Caribbean, were now at risk. The other British possessions around the globe also required attention. The small American privateers had been a nuisance but never a serious threat to the British navy's ships of the line. Now the British had to contend with French warships. All the sugar islands now needed to be defended, thereby reducing the men and ships available to deal with the American colonies. Everyone knew new directives were forthcoming from England that would change how the war would be fought. With fewer ships and troops available, the British needed to consolidate their forces in one place. It was decided that New York would be the best location, necessitating an evacuation of Philadelphia. Because of an insufficient number of ships, some people had to make the trip by land across New Jersey.

By mid-May 1778, Washington's intelligence network was reporting that indeed the British were planning to evacuate Philadelphia. These sources included deserters, respectable townspeople, prostitutes, and his spies.[63] Lieutenant Colonel Laurens mentioned, "the greatest part of this intelligence was given by a Mr. Combs, father of the clergyman. The old gentleman is come

Christ Church was built from 1727 to 1744. It was the largest church building in eighteenth-century British North America. The steeple was added in 1754 making it the tallest building in North America until 1810. Saint Peter's Church was built from 1758 to 1761 for parishioners of Christ Church who lived in the Pine Street area. (*Lisa Nagy*)

out to make his peace and take the oath. He will be sent back to town with consolation for repentant sinners."[64] "Mr. Combs" was actually Thomas Coombe; the clergyman was his son, Thomas Coombe, D.D., of the united churches of Christ Church and St. Peter's Church in Philadelphia.[65]

On May 20, McDonald Campbell of Warren County, New Jersey, enlisted for nine months as a fifer in the 4th New Jersey Regiment under Captain Jonathan Foreman.[66] During his time at Valley Forge, he was sent out "in the disguise of a cobbler amongst the Tories." His cover story was that he was sent "to obtain bread for the subsistence of the Army."[67]

Because the British were preparing to evacuate, every kind of carriage, from wagons to wheelbarrows, was moving belongings and military supplies between the houses and the waterfront for several days at this time. A report that soldiers were even pulling light carts, such as a goat cart, indicated the urgency, as the evacuation would happen quickly. On May 17, Governor Livingston of New Jersey told Washington that intelligence from New York City said houses there were being prepared to receive refugees from Philadelphia.[68] Washington on May 17 wrote to General Greene that it was more and more probable that the enemy was preparing to evacuate Philadelphia and that he had reasons to believe its destination was New York.[69] Washington even was receiving word from Philip General Schuyler at Albany, New York, who took a deposition from an American spy identified as "J.T." who had gotten on board a British warship in Lake Champlain. He reported that the army was to come up the Hudson River from Philadelphia.[70]

On May 25, Washington gave instructions to General William Maxwell to proceed with two regiments of his brigade to Mount Holly, New Jersey, going by way of Coryell's Ferry.[71] Once there, he was to "take the greatest care to procure exact intelligence of what is passing in Philadelphia" and report to Washington "information of the discoveries you make, and the earliest advice of any movement that may happen."[72] On May 31, Maxwell sent a letter to Major General Philemon Dickinson, who was at Trenton, that he was at Mount Holly. In the letter, Maxwell reported the intelligence he had acquired and asked that it be forwarded to Washington. A spy sent to Philadelphia had returned and reported that a large detachment on foot and horse had been sent from Philadelphia to New Jersey to reconnoiter Maxwell's taking position at Mount Holly. The British had moved sixty wagons and pack horses from Philadelphia to New Jersey. Wives and belongings were being loaded onto vessels and passing below the chevaux-de-frise. The universal opinion in Philadelphia was that the British would march across New Jersey. It was reported that they "have held several councils concerning their movements." A second spy, an unidentified woman, came from Philadelphia later in the evening and reported that the British troops on the New Jersey side "had struck their tents and had set all that cord wood on fire."[73] On June 1, Dickinson sent Washington Maxwell's letter and added some secondhand information he had obtained.[74]

On June 1, Maxwell sent Washington information collected from deserters and a letter from Colonel Israel Shreve of the 2nd New Jersey Regiment.[75] Shreve was four miles closer to Philadelphia, at Fostertown, and reported on the observation of ships at Philadelphia as seen from Gloucester, New Jersey.[76] The report Shreve received said there were seventy ships at Philadelphia, sixty between Gloucester and the chevaux-de-frise, and that twenty had passed the chevaux-de-frise the previous day, bringing the total number of ships to 150.[77]

Colonel Stephen Moylan of the 4th Continental Dragoons at Trenton reported to Washington that on May 10, he had sent a woman to Philadelphia to determine British intentions.[78] She returned May 13, and reported that General Clinton had taken command of the British forces, and General Howe was preparing to go home. Moylan reported "there was great talk of the troops embarking, the transports were taking in wood and water, indeed their burning the shipping looks very [much] like a move." But the woman was unable to determine if the British were planning an offensive maneuver or were evacuating the city.[79]

Washington was so convinced the British were evacuating that on June 1, he sent instructions to Major Clough on how to proceed to enter Philadelphia when it was determined the British had left.[80] (There is a story that Washington received a report on June 16, 1778, from a man whose mother was a washerwoman in Philadelphia that the British peace commissioners had ordered their linen delivered at once, "finished or unfinished."[81])

On June 17, 1778, Joseph Galloway wrote a five-page letter on the reasons against abandoning Philadelphia and Pennsylvania. He wrote "there is no place in America where the persons attached to government are so numerous—where there are so many good intelligencers, guides and faithful refugees and which its middle and inland situation renders so conv[en]ient to them to resort to."[82]

The British evacuated Philadelphia on June 18. Some took a twelve-day journey down the Delaware River to New York, traveling around New Jersey. The rest marched across New Jersey to New York.[83]

With the departure of the British, most of the American espionage efforts were relocated to New York. But the British still maintained a spy network in Philadelphia because of the return of the Continental Congress. Silas Deane, a former Continental congressman and an American commissioner to France sent by Congress, claimed that the British left behind agents whose job was to foment discord among residents and push people into a "state of licentiousness."[84] But there was no such plot. British espionage efforts were aimed at discovering the activities of Congress and the Continental Army.

In 1776, Philadelphia farmer Frederick Verner was an American express rider traveling to Cumberland, Lancaster, and York counties in Pennsylvania.[85] When the British occupied Philadelphia, he changed sides. When the Americans returned to Philadelphia, they charged him with acting as a spy and guide to the British army. On July 29, 1778, he was tried at a court-martial and convicted of being a spy for the British army. In February 1778, he had been used as an interpreter in a British court-martial.[86]

On August 15, 1778, Congress read a letter from American Major General Benedict Arnold, who had ordered the court-martial, that accompanied a report on Verner's court-martial and sentence. Arnold thought there was insufficient evidence that Verner was a spy; therefore, he "suspended the sentence until the pleasure of Congress is known."[87] Congress, not wanting to burden itself with the case, ordered that it be turned over to the Supreme Executive Council of Pennsylvania for study and that the council be requested to report back with its opinion on the matter.[88]

The council received the case and referred it to Thomas McKean, chief justice of Pennsylvania, for an opinion. In that opinion, dated August 22, 1778, McKean said that Verner should be tried for treason under Pennsylvania law, that witnesses should be bound over to give evidence at the trial, and that Arnold should send for McLane "or any other person now in the army in the state of New York, who can give evidence against the prisoner, for the purpose aforesaid." The council agreed and informed Congress of its opinion.[89] Congress received it on August 28, 1778.[90]

Verner was placed in the new Philadelphia jail on the southwest corner of Walnut and Sixth streets.[91] On December 7, he sent a petition to Congress, which was read the same day and referred to the Board of War.[92] Pennsylvania Governor Joseph Reed had doubts about the legality of the trial and the evidence upon which

Walnut Street prison was built in 1774 at the southwest corner of Walnut and Sixth streets. During the British occupation it was used as the provost or military prison. (*Watson, Annals of Philadelphia*)

the original conviction was based. In March 1779, Reed reported to John Jay, president of Congress, that the British had offered to exchange Robert Taylor, an American being held in New York, for Verner. The British had caught Taylor trying to take goods out of occupied Philadelphia for the American army.[93] Reed asked Congress to instruct the jailor to deliver Verner to the sheriff of Philadelphia so the exchange could be made.[94] Reed had informed the Supreme Executive Council of his actions, and on March 13, the council sent Congress a letter supporting Reed's request.[95] On March 15, Congress issued an order to turn over Verner,[96] which the council received the next day.[97] A letter dated April 12, 1779, from Brigade Major Aaron Ogden of General Maxwell's brigade included a receipt for Verner, who was sent to New York City in exchange for Taylor.[98]

Tried with Verner was George Spangler, charged with being a spy for the British. He was convicted, and on August 14, 1778, he was hanged at the Philadelphia Commons, also known as Center Square, which was beyond the developed area of the city. Spangler's wife, Mary, wrote to New York Governor James Robertson on May 11, 1780, saying she and her three children were penniless. Samuel Shoemaker, a former mayor of Philadelphia, certified that the statement was true. Governor James Robertson had Thomas Murray, his aide-de-camp, approve rations to be provided to them.[99] The Supreme Executive Council on July 7, 1780, granted Mary Spangler permission to immediately leave Pennsylvania for New York with her children, her bedding, one chest, and a small box.[100]

John Roberts was a Quaker miller from lower Merion Township in present-day Montgomery County, Pennsylvania. Roberts was hanged as a traitor in November 1778.[101] He had been charged with providing intelligence to General Howe on his approach to Philadelphia. Howe received the information at Swedes Ford on the Schuylkill River about seventeen miles from Philadelphia. Also convicted and executed was Abraham Carlisle, a Quaker lumber merchant near Vine Street in Philadelphia.[102] After had Howe captured Philadelphia, he ordered Carlisle to examine anyone who entered or left the city, looking for American spies.

The British had sent three peace commissioners to Congress: Frederick Howard, fifth Earl of Carlisle; William Eden, later Lord Auckland; and George Johnstone, who had been governor of West Florida from 1763 to 1767. In June 1778, Johnstone tried to employ Elizabeth Ferguson as an intermediary with Joseph Reed, Pennsylvania delegate to the Continental Congress and later president of the Supreme Executive Council.[103] Mrs. Ferguson in October had been talked into delivering Reverend Jacob Duché's letter to General George Washington, encouraging him to give up the fight.

Mrs. Ferguson had seen Governor George Johnstone three times at the house of Charles Stedman, a friend of hers. She believed that Johnstone was a friend to America and wanted to see the bloodshed stopped. At the time, her husband, Henry Hugh Ferguson, was being summoned to the Supreme Executive Council, then meeting at Lancaster, to answer to a charge of treason. She was going to respond for him that he was born British and had left a year before the Declaration of Independence was signed and should not be charged with treason. Governor Johnstone had heard her mention this situation and her planned travel to Lancaster. They were in Stedman's tearoom between 10 and 11 a.m. on June 16 when Johnstone gave her a manuscript book to read. She had completed a quarter of it before he retrieved it. He talked her into being an intermediary in his negotiations with Joseph Reed. By means of a confidential courier, Mrs. Ferguson wrote to Reed requesting a private meeting. The British evacuated Philadelphia on June 18, and the meeting with Reed occurred three days later, on the twenty-first, when he received the letter. She related Johnstone's comments, including an offer to Reed of 10,000 pounds and any colonial office for his influence in helping to form a reunion of the two countries. Reed laid the overture before Congress. Governor Johnstone had also sent letters on the same subject to Robert Morris of Pennsylvania and Francis Dana of Massachusetts.[104]

Many courts-martial were held at Valley Forge for people caught trying to take supplies into British-occupied Philadelphia, or leaving the city and attempting to return. A good cover used by spies to move between the lines was as a smuggler. If you were caught, the penalty for being a smuggler was less severe than the penalty for being a spy: death. For example, at a general court-martial held April 4, with Colonel Joseph Vose of the 1st Massachusetts Regiment presiding, Pennsylvania residents John Bloom and Philip Culp were tried for attempting to carry flour into Philadelphia, found guilty, and sentenced to receive fifty lashes and be employed in some public work while the British army remained in Pennsylvania, unless they chose to enlist in the army or navy during the war. At the same court–martial, John Evans, also a Pennsylvania resident, was tried for attempting to send provisions into Philadelphia, found guilty, and sentenced to be employed in some work for the benefit of the public in Carlisle while the enemy remained in Pennsylvania.[105]

People were also caught going in the other direction. William Morgan of Pennsylvania was tried at a general court-martial on March 24, with Colonel Matthias Ogden of the 1st New Jersey Regiment presiding, for leaving Philadelphia, stealing a horse, and attempting to take him back to the city. He was sentenced to be kept at hard labor during the war not less than thirty miles from the enemy's camp. If he was caught trying to escape, he was to be executed. General Washington approved the sentence on April 3.[106]

The Grand Parade at Valley Forge was the site of the execution of spies by hanging. (*Lisa Nagy*)

Matthias Tyson, a Mennonite from Bedminster Township in Bucks County, was arrested while smuggling butter and eggs to Philadelphia. Colonel John Piper of the 1st Battalion of Pennsylvania militia had him tied to a tree, let soldiers pelt him with his own eggs, and then sent him home with a warning.[107]

In May 1778, Captain McLane was instructed to stop everyone entering or leaving Philadelphia, question them, record every piece of intelligence and the hour he obtained it, and send the information every morning to Washington. Anyone who disobeyed general orders was to be kept under guard until a court-martial was held and the offender punished or sent to headquarters.[108]

Joseph Murell of Pennsylvania was tried in 1778 for giving intelligence to and acting as a guide for the British. He was convicted of being a guide and sentenced to death. His execution was postponed, and it is suspected he may have escaped.[109]

After the British left Philadelphia in June 1778, a number of lawsuits were brought against people for having entered the city during the occupation with provisions for the British army. Charged in Justice Peter Evans's court in Philadelphia County were Christian Benner and John Benner of Franconia Township (Philadelphia, now Montgomery County) who were members of the Indian Creek Reformed Church; John Hackman; Isaac Penner; Martin King; Jacob and John Sowder; and John Wright (who went with the British to New York).[110]

SEVEN

Chasing a Fox

Edward Fox was born in Dublin, Ireland, in 1752. He fled Ireland because of his involvement in an insurrection against the British government, and arrived in America with letters of introduction and some money. He studied law with Samuel Chase of Maryland and was admitted to the bar, but he practiced only briefly.

By May 18, 1778, Fox was a clerk in the Continental Treasury.[1] He was one of a number of people recommended by the Board of the Treasury to sign Continental currency.[2] He was also nominated by John Penn, a Continental congressman from North Carolina, to be a commissioner of accounts.[3] In 1779, Fox was captured by the British and sent to detention at Jamaica, Queens County, Long Island, New York.

Fox wanted to gain his freedom by arranging his exchange and return to Philadelphia. He proposed to send to the British intelligence that he would gather from his friend and business partner, Samuel Chase, a former (and future) member of the Continental Congress.[4] This offer to spy for the British got him a meeting with Major John André, aide-de-camp to General Clinton. At the conclusion of the meeting, André did not think Fox could provide any essential military information through this method.

On September 11, 1779, Fox, who had once held a minor position in Maryland under Royal Governor Robert Eden, wrote to Dr. Henry Stevenson, whom he probably knew from his time in Maryland. Stevenson was a Maryland refugee living in New York City. He had practiced medicine in Maryland since about 1760. In 1769, he turned his stone house into an inoculation hospital and was very popular. He also made his loyalist feelings known. In August 1777, fearing for his life, Stevenson fled his home, Parnassus Hill, in Baltimore, leaving his wife and five children. He made his way to Elkton, Maryland, and out to the British fleet in Chesapeake Bay. He accompanied the British army to Philadelphia. While Stevenson was in occupied Philadelphia, he procured material intelligence for the British army and had some connections.[5] He accompanied the British army on in its withdrawal to New York.

In his letter to Stevenson, Fox mentioned his meeting with André and the fact that André did not think Fox's plan would produce important results. Fox tried to convince Stevenson of the significance of the information he could obtain at Congress and from other offices. However, he wrote, "this is not to be had without money; without gold." Fox said he needed Stevenson to go with him to get someone from Boston to go to Philadelphia to help him accomplish his plan. Fox needed a cover story of why he needed to go to Boston. He created the cover story that he had "made disadvantageous purchases there," which he said people sometimes do when they get involved in this kind of clandestine operation. He added:

The expense would be considerable, and ought not to be even in the first instance out of my pocket; and if I was never so willing my connections would not always enable me to make the necessary advances upon great occasions. I cannot but view the procuring the gentleman from Boston as a very great occasion and one that would make an immediate supply of ready money absolutely requisite.

Fox was trying very hard to con the British out of money. Fox continued, writing that

persons engaged in speculative trade, as I am, are as often without ready money as with it; but if I was disposed to offer Continental money, you know it would not have that weight in this kind of negotiation that even a small sum in gold would have; and you I think will be of opinion with me, when I say that the object is worth trying to be obtained even at the risque of a few hundreds; or say a few thousands [of pounds].[6]

James Rivington, publisher of the *Royal Gazette*, a loyalist newspaper in New York City, had been and probably still was printing counterfeit Continental currency. So Fox had to explain why Rivington's counterfeit notes would be of little or no value to him, even though they were available just for the price of the paper. Counterfeit Continental currency would depreciate as fast as real Continental currency. Fox wanted to make sure that his money retained its value, which is why he wanted hard currency.

As one reads Fox's letter, one can see the sting getting bigger and bigger. He starts out requiring small amounts of money but then escalates what he needs. To justify needing that much money, he claimed he could turn Samuel Chase to the British side, but said it would take time and be costly.

Chase had lost his seat in November 1778 because of reports of his being a speculator. Congress on August 24 had resolved to buy twenty thousand barrels of flour in Maryland and Pennsylvania to ease the shortage in New England due to the arrival of the French fleet of Jean Baptiste Charles Henri Hector Comte d'Estaing and the requirements for the French army. Chase had advised his business partners, John Dorsey and Company, to buy wheat and flour in August and September 1778. In 1781, Chase claimed that he did not use information obtained from Congress but used what was available to the general public. Commissary General Jeremiah Wadsworth had found when he arrived in Baltimore that the mills were busy processing flour for private companies. Wadsworth complained that the resolution of August 24 should have been kept secret but was known in Baltimore before his arrival. The main buyer was John Dorsey and Company. Although no direct proof of Chase's breaching Congress's trust or his intention to enrich himself was ever produced, many considered him guilty based on his associates and the circumstantial evidence.

Fox claimed in his letter to Stevenson that in Philadelphia he had papers from former Royal Governor Eden of Maryland that would remove any suspicion about him. Eden was back in London, so the claim would take months to verify if anyone tried to contact Eden. Fox asked Stevenson, who was planning to go to England, to mention him in a good light to Eden, and he offered to do anything he could to help Stevenson's family, which was not accompanying him on the trip. Fox did not want anyone else to see the letter, because they might recognize his ploy, so he asked Stevenson, "Pray destroy this as soon as you have perused it."[7]

André, writing from British headquarters in New York City on September 15, 1779, told Stevenson he was sorry Fox did not find him to be confident about the information Fox was offering, but added that they had other sources of intelligence. He explained that he had no reason to trust Fox because he did not know him and only had Fox's claim that he was trustworthy. André said Fox had to show that he had the ability and desire to accomplish the task of collecting and providing the intelligence, and he added that he wanted Fox to provide useful information before he paid him anything. André said he concentrated on military intelligence because it was the most useful to the army. He proposed that Fox be allowed to leave New York City it order to quickly prove that he was going to do as he had proposed. André told Stevenson, "[A] man shall moreover be sent to Philadelphia or wherever he [Fox] pleases to receive his dispatches." André also offered to detain Fox as a suspected person and put him on bail. As a detainee rather than a prisoner, Fox could "sollicit the correspondence of C[hase] by means we will procure him and if he deems any other persons willing and capable of serving us."[8]

The British believed they could turn Chase to their side because of his financial problems. He always lived well, but his political activities and the lack of business for his legal practice was causing him a financial strain. He had been selling property to raise cash and was involved in a speculative operation to buy flour. In 1777, he and William Whetcroft, who made cast-iron parts for muskets, became partners in a salt works that was not a financial success, despite the shortage of salt. In 1778, he entered a partnership with John and Thomas Dorsey of Baltimore for foreign trade and privateering. He also formed a company with Luke Wheeler, called Dorsey, Wheeler and Company. These businesses were draining his money.

Fox eventually realized he was not going to get big money and might not even be allowed to leave the British lines, so he changed his story. On the morning of September 16, Fox wrote to Stevenson and said he had been misunderstood. He said he had confidence in British justice and generosity, and would transmit useful intelligence before getting "any liberal pecuniary advances. I have no desire to receive such; my views would [be] extended to a permanent provision, in some measure equal to my services." Fox, whose nose must have looked like Pinocchio's, went on to say it would take "pecuniary tho' not liberal advances." In this entire negotiation, he never stopped trying to get hard currency. He said that a spy needed to be planted in the office of Charles Thompson, secretary of Congress, in Philadelphia. He again mentioned bringing someone from Boston. He also told Stevenson to check if the person from Boston could appear publicly or must remain incognito. He discussed André's two offers of going on parole or being held as a suspected person and claimed that either was acceptable, but then he pushed to be sent to Philadelphia. Being in Philadelphia would get him away from the watchful eye of the British military. Fox then asked Stevenson to set up a meeting with André for that evening. He told Stevenson he wanted to deal with this quickly, "as I shall otherwise be reduced to a very disagreeable situation; Mr. A[ndré] having put me off too often to put any dependence in him."9

On September 17, Fox accepted thirty-one pounds and ten shillings as payment for future intelligence he would provide. He left New York City the next day for Philadelphia. He left an alphabetic code for his correspondence with British headquarters. Fox, when in Philadelphia, was to send Stevenson the message "the compliments of Clapham." Upon Stevenson's receipt of Fox's message, André was to send a message to Philadelphia. "The messenger [from André] is to make a cross in chalk on the pit door of the play house at night and in the next day is to find an hour and address mark[e]d over it when to call for a parcel." Should Fox and the messenger need to meet, then "Monmouth" would be the first word of a recognition sign, and "Penobscot" the response.10

On September 25, 1779, George Washington wrote a report to Congress that summarized some intelligence he had received. One of the items was a report dated September 22 from Elizabeth Town that stated, "On the 20th a Mr. Edward Fox of Philadelphia an exchanged prisoner, came out of New York. He says the embarkation [of the British army from New York] was by accounts to consist of seven thousand men, and that a number of Hessian and English regiments had embarked before he came away, their destination said to be Virginia."[11]

In May 1780, William Churchill Houston, a Continental congressman from New Jersey, nominated Fox to be commissioner of the chamber of accounts.[12] In 1782 and 1783, Fox was Congress's superintendent of finance, responsible for settling the accounts of the Continental Army's hospital department.[13]

No evidence has been found that indicates Fox ever gave the British any information.[14] And the October 18, 1781, edition of the *Pennsylvania Packet or General Advertiser* newspaper contained an ad on page 4 that could have been a message from Fox to British army headquarters dissolving their agreement. The ad, with the names Alexander Nelson and Edward Fox at the bottom, read, "The partnership being dissolved by mutual consent, such persons as have any demands against the same are requested to apply for payment; and those who are indebted thereto will please to settle their accounts with Edward Fox, at their late store above Walnut Street in Water Street. Sept[ember] 22, 1781."[15] Alexander Nelson was a resident of Philadelphia and co-owner with Philip Roche of the privateer *Adventure*.[16]

EIGHT

Commuter Spies:
New York and Philadelphia

Ann Bates was a schoolteacher in Philadelphia who supplement-
ed her income by keeping bees and selling the honey in a small
store she ran. She began her career in espionage under General
Clinton starting in 1778. She disguised herself as a peddler and
passed through the American soldiers and camp followers, observing the numbers of weapons and men in each camp she visited.
Her husband, Joseph Bates, was a British soldier and gunsmith.
She learned how to distinguish the different weapons and was able
to report on them and the numbers of cannons, men, and supplies.
When her inventory of goods was depleted, she would return to
the British lines. There she would report her findings to her contact, Major Duncan Drummond, an aide to Clinton.[1] Bates sometimes used the name Barnes.

During one of her excursions among American troops in New
York, she was arrested, searched, and imprisoned for a day and
night before being released. She reported to Drummond, and on
July 29, 1778, Bates was sent out again to spy on the American
troops. She was told to find a disloyal American soldier named
Chambers. However, Chambers had been killed in battle about
three weeks earlier. Bates wandered about the American camp for
three or four days, counting 199 pieces of cannon and 23,000
troops. She tried to gather information on the troops' movement to
Rhode Island and erroneously reported to Clinton on August 6
that they had not yet gone there. As soon as she returned to New

York, she was sent out again to gather more intelligence. Bates went to Washington's headquarters in White Plains, New York, and overheard one of Washington's aides say that boats were being prepared for landing on Long Island and that part of Washington's troops had already left for Rhode Island. Bates was back in New York City to warn Clinton of the American troop movements on August 19, 1778, and her information influenced Clinton's decision to send more men to defend Rhode Island, forcing the American and French armies to withdraw from Newport on August 31. Most of her exploits were in New Jersey and New York.[2]

Samuel Shoemaker, a Philadelphia attorney and merchant, and his wife, Rebecca, lived on the north side of Arch Street between Front and Second streets in Philadelphia. They were married on November 10, 1767.[3] Shoemaker, a Quaker, was politically connected, having been treasurer of Philadelphia from 1767 to 1776, and mayor in 1769 and 1770. He was a magistrate during the British occupation of Philadelphia. During the British evacuation, he left Philadelphia for New York City on a British vessel. While in New York, he lived on Wall Street and kept up a surreptitious correspondence with Samuel Wallis until Shoemaker's connection with Wallis was passed off to Colonel Beverly Robinson in the spring of 1781.[4] Wallis was a shipper and speculator who lived at both Philadelphia and Muncy, Pennsylvania. He began his secret service work for the British in January 1776. Shoemaker corresponded with his wife, who had stayed in Philadelphia.[5]

In May 1779, Rebecca Shoemaker tried to get a pass to go to New York but was denied.[6] On March 7, 1780, her journal was seized and turned over to the Supreme Executive Council of Pennsylvania. In a meeting in Philadelphia that day, the council determined that the journal proved that she had "by letters of recommendation and otherwise, assisted prisoners and others, enemies to government to pass clandestinely to New York."[7]

On May 16, 1780, the council approved her petition to travel from Philadelphia to New York City on the condition that she not return without the council's approval.[8] She passed through Elizabeth Town on June 20, 1780, on her way into New York City. At Elizabeth Town she picked up mail from Captain George Beckwith for then-Captain John André, adjutant general on the staff of General Clinton, and transported it to New York City. Once in New York, she carried on a social correspondence with her daughter, Anna Rawle, who was in Philadelphia. The letters were carried by friends, returning paroled soldiers, and ships traveling to Philadelphia.[9] After one year in New York City, she wanted to return to Philadelphia, but the Supreme Executive Council did not give its approval.[10]

George Henry Playter was born in Surrey, England, about 1736, and emigrated to New Jersey about 1758. He married Elizabeth Welding around 1765 in Pennsylvania and became a Quaker. In 1776, he was a cabinetmaker living at Crosswicks Creek at the Bridge Ferry in Nottingham Township, New Jersey.[11] Captain Thomas Trewren of the 16th Regiment of Light Dragoons, also known as the Queen's Own Light Dragoons, sent him to fix a bridge that traversed Crosswicks Creek and had been damaged the day before by the Americans. From Nottingham Township, Playter infiltrated the American lines and seized important information and documents for the British. When the British occupied Philadelphia in 1777, he went into the city in October. With the recommendation of Joseph Galloway, he was employed by General Howe to procure intelligence. He was sent on missions out of the city by either Galloway or Howe's aide-de-camp.[12] General Cortland Skinner said in 1789 that Playter had performed secret service activities from November 1777, working out of Staten Island.[13] When General Clinton became commander in chief of the British army in 1778, Galloway and Colonel Balfour recommended that Playter continue to perform secret service duties.[14] When the British army relocated to New York City, Playter carried cipher letters to loyalists outside the lines and brought back naval intelligence that was turned over to the admiral commanding at New York.[15]

In 1780, Playter had been working for the British commander in chief for four years. Playter and Christopher Sower proposed to General Clinton that Sower would set up a communication code and recruit a Peter Miller of Philadelphia to transmit every transaction of Congress. The plan was that Playter would travel from his house in Bucks County, Pennsylvania, to Philadelphia weekly. He would contact Miller and collect his letters and papers. Playter would then travel across New Jersey to South Amboy, where John Rattoon, a tavern owner there, would receive the letters and papers. According to the plan, Rattoon would "hang out a certain sign, or give some other sign to the row galley lying off" Staten Island. The row galley would come in the night to pick up the items and arrange for their transport to New York City.[16]

Playter used the code names Dr. Welding, Dr. Wilding, DW, and GP in his correspondence with Sower and British headquarters. Using the code name Dr. Welding, he sent an intelligence report to Sower on November 5, 1780, saying he had received information from a member of Congress on a wide variety of subjects.[17] Playter used the cover of Dr. Welding another time, in an unsigned report of December 11, 1780, that was annotated on the back, "Intelligence [from] Dr Welding."[18]

In January 1781, the largest mutiny ever experienced by the United States Army occurred when approximately two thousand five hundred soldiers of the Pennsylvania Line of the Continental Army forcibly left camp. A number of soldiers and officers were wounded or killed during the event.

British headquarters tried to send spies to entice the mutineers to come to the British in New York. It was a high risk assignment for a spy. If the spy contacted a loyal American, the spy would assuredly be hanged, which is what happened to two British spies. Playter did not want to have anything to do with this assignment.[19] He complained about having to be visible in a tavern for two nights, which might make people suspicious.[20]

During the mutiny, he attempted to sneak from Staten Island over to South Amboy, which led the British to suspect he was a double agent. Playter never explained his reason for attempting to leave, but he may have been pressured into doing something he did not want to do, or he may have been working as an agent for both sides. General Clinton ordered that a guard be put on Playter.[21]

On January 11, Playter agreed to take a letter from Major Oliver De Lancey, who was running the British secret services from New York, to American Brigadier General William Thompson, who lived near Carlisle, Pennsylvania. Thompson had spent five years as a prisoner of war and was bitter over the delay in his being exchanged.[22] After completing his assignment, Playter returned to New York in March and reported that Thompson was friendly to their overtures.[23]

A letter from W (Dr. Welding, or George Playter) on September 21, 1781, indicated he wanted to resume his situation with British headquarters but knew the British did not have confidence in him because of his attempt to secretly leave Staten Island.[24] Playter did provide intelligence from Philadelphia on the American and French troops' passage across New Jersey on their way to Yorktown.[25] He later arrived in New York City from Philadelphia and reported on October 26 that General Cornwallis had surrendered at Yorktown on the seventeenth, and that the French fleet of thirty-six ships of the line with three thousand troops had left Chesapeake Bay on October 18.[26] At the time Playter reached New York, British General Clinton was on the warship *London* off the Virginia capes attempting to confirm the rumors that Cornwallis had surrendered. General Wilhelm von Knyphausen who Clinton left in charge of the British forces in and around New York in his absence immediately sent Playter's report to General Clinton.[27]

In 1783, General Sir Guy Carleton wrote to Governor John Parr of Nova Scotia and described Playter as "a man much employed in the King's service, by which conduct he has forfeited his property and expects to be driven from his country."[28] Carleton was trying to get preferential treatment for Playter, who was going to Nova Scotia. John Graves Simcoe, lieutenant governor of Upper Canada, in 1796 stated that Playter was a loyalist and had joined the King's Standard.[29] Playter left Pennsylvania in 1785 for the east coast of New Brunswick, and by 1796, he was in Kingston. He was given half pay as a lieutenant and two thousand acres on the Don River in York, now part of Toronto.[30]

Despite George Playter's reluctance to carry General Clinton's message to entice the Pennsylvania Line mutineers at Princeton to come to the British side, Clinton was able to find several spies who were willing to take on the dangerous mission. John Mason, a loyalist who was in a British jail in New York, volunteered in order to gain his freedom. He was to carry Clinton's proposal in a lead-covered envelope. He was guided across New Jersey by James Ogden, a young newlywed who apparently needed the money. When Mason and Ogden arrived in Princeton on January 5, 1781, they went straight to the college, where John Williams, who was in command of the mutineers, was located. Upon their arrival at Nassau Hall, Mason asked the sentry for the commanding officer and was sent up to Williams's room on the second floor.[31]

Mason told Williams that he had come from Elizabeth Town and had an express for him. During Williams's interrogation of Mason, he asked if the British were coming and was told no. When asked who had sent him, Mason replied that Clinton had, and he handed over the proposal still in its lead covering. After opening and reading the unsigned letter, Williams asked who had sent it. When he was told that it came from Clinton, Williams had Mason and Ogden placed under arrest. Williams, with the two agents in tow, went to the Committee of Sergeants who quickly agreed that they should turn over Mason and Ogden to General Anthony Wayne. Although Wayne was the commander against whom they had mutinied over lack of pay and desire to be discharged from service, the Pennsylvania Line soldiers had no intention of joining the British. Wayne persuaded the sergeants to send Mason and Ogden to Joseph Reed, president of the Supreme Executive Council of Pennsylvania, who had traveled from Philadelphia to Trenton to keep abreast of the mutiny.

With Mason and Ogden now imprisoned, Major General Lord Sterling, the highest ranking Continental officer at Trenton, called for a court of inquiry to meet at 4 p.m. on January 10 at Summerseat, a private residence across the river in Pennsylvania, to determine if Mason and Ogden were spies. The court of inquiry was finally able to meet at 8 p.m.

There is no record of the testimony at their trial. The court of inquiry ruled that they were "decidedly of opinion that the said John Mason and James Ogden came clearly within the description of spies and that according to the rules and customs of nations at war they ought to be hung by the neck until they are dead." Sterling confirmed the verdict and the sentencing by the court of inquiry. He fixed the time for the hanging at 9 a.m. the next day

Summerseat is a Georgian manor house built in 1764 for Adam Hoops in the town of Colvin's Ferry (Morrisville), Pennsylvania. When Hoops died, his son-in-law Thomas Barclay bought it from Hoops' estate. Summerseat served as George Washington's Headquarters from December 8 to 13, 1776. On January 10, 1781, it was the site for the trial of British spies John Mason and James Ogden. It would later be owned by George Clymer and Robert Morris, both signers of the Declaration of Independence and the Constitution. (*Library of Congress*)

"at the cross-roads from the upper ferry from Trenton to Philadelphia at the four lanes' ends," with Wayne's aide-de-camp, Major Benjamin Fishbourne, in charge.[32]

Early on the morning of January 11, the Philadelphia Light Horse broke camp at Trenton and crossed to the opposite side of the Delaware River at Colvin's Ferry.[33] Mason and Ogden, their hands bound, were brought out of confinement. They stood as their sentences of death by hanging were read to them.

The light horse then took the men to the intersection near Patrick Colvin's ferry, where Colvin's black slave was commandeered to be the hangman.[34] The entire business was concluded by noon, and the light horse, having received orders to return to Philadelphia, departed quickly, leaving the two spies hanging from the tree.[35] They were still swaying in the wind on the sixteenth.[36]

Daniel Coxe was an attorney from Trenton and a large landowner in western New Jersey. During the British occupation of Philadelphia, he was appointed magistrate of police. He accompanied the army when it retreated to New York City in June 1778. While in New York he collected intelligence from Philadelphia and Trenton. When he attempted to leave for England in 1780, General Clinton requested that he stay and help the British war effort.[37] Coxe wrote on March 28, 1780, from New York to John André in Charles Town, South Carolina, that he had just received information from Philadelphia that the value of the continental dollar had fallen from sixty paper dollars for one silver coin to seventy-five for one when news of the siege of Charles Town was received. Coxe told André that after the fall of Charles Town, a military move by the British up Chesapeake Bay would cause Maryland and Virginia to be unable to provide troops and support for the American cause. He suggested that the current year's campaign end with the possession of Philadelphia for the winter season.[38]

Another British spy in Pennsylvania was Samuel Wallis, a Quaker born about 1730 in Harford County, Maryland.[39] He went to the west branch area of the Susquehanna River as a surveyor in 1768, and worked the Juniata River area up to Frankstown. He was also a shipping merchant in Philadelphia prior to the revolution. He had a seven-thousand-acre plantation and began building his stone house early in 1769. The house was built on high ground on an arm of the river near the mouth of Carpenter's Run. A few hundred yards north of the house, Fort Muncy was later erected and became a rallying point for the settlers.[40]

On September 24, 1780, Wallis, who was a wealthy merchant and land speculator, reported from Philadelphia to Coxe on Congress's activity. He most likely obtained most of his information from his business associates in Philadelphia. On October 19, he wrote from the tiny hamlet of Squan, New Jersey, that since September 24, "nothing material has transpired.[41] The affair of Gen[eral] [Benedict] Arnold has been the wonder and surprise of the people for a few days, but like everything of the trivial, it begins to grow old."[42]

On November 8, Wallis wrote to Coxe from Philadelphia while the messenger waited, so he advised Coxe that his report would be

brief. (Abiah Parke was the British contact in Squan and was probably the coastal contact for Wallis and Coxe's communications.)
Wallis reported that the fleet was getting ready to leave
Philadelphia, as he had reported a few days earlier, and move
down to Chester, Pennsylvania. He told about movements and
conditions to the south, and he advised that "I shall carefully
attend to every material matter &c and convey them to you in the
best way I possibly can, but those conveyances are attended with
a thousand difficulties and risks to the messenger and to myself,
which you cannot be a stranger to."43

General Clinton thought so highly of the information Wallis
submitted through Coxe from January 25 to February 9, 1781, that
he sent it to Lord George Germain, first lord of trade and secretary
of state for America, and said it was from "a Gentleman in
Philadelphia (whose information may be relied upon) to Mr. Coxe
the acting Secretary to the Commissioners."44 Clinton periodically
sent reports to Germain on the British military situation in
America.

After Samuel Shoemaker evacuated Philadelphia, he and Wallis
kept up correspondence until 1781. On March 24, 1781, Wallis,
using the code name "A Gentlemen from Philadelphia," wrote to
Captain Beckwith, an assistant to Major De Lancey, and apolo-
gized that he was so late in answering Beckwith's letter of January
31. Wallis mentioned that

I had frequently wrote long trusty Friend Shoe____r [Samuel
Shoemaker], but receiving no answer from him nor any kind of
advice of the receipt of any such letters, I was led to conceive, that
there was either a want of confidence in me, or that their contents,
were of very little consequence to you; under these considerations I
was much hurt and had concluded to remain silent in [the] future;
but on being urged by my friend Mr. [Daniel] Cox[e] I opened a correspondence with him: perhaps Mr S___r [Samuel Shoemaker] may
have not received my letter's or that his to me may have miscarried.

Wallis added that Colonel Robinson would be corresponding
with him, and said he did not know Robinson but "I take it for
granted, that you would not introduce me to any one on so serious
a subject, in whose hands you were not sure I was perfectly safe."

Wallis provided information to George Beckwith on the actions of Congress and the conditions of the army in general.[45]

On April 18, 1781, Wallis reported to Beckwith on the falling value of the new issue of Continental currency and on the movements of the army and the two fleets. He reported to Beckwith on April 21 that Captain John Paul Jones was being sent to France with dispatches for the American commissioners there. Jones had commanded the *Ranger* and then the *Bonhomme Richard* and had brought the war to the British and Irish coasts. The British viewed him as a pirate. Wallis sent another letter to Beckwith on April 23, saying:

> I was greatly dispirited on Friday last on not getting my dispatches forwarded by our confidential messenger. He was obliged to conduct Colonel R[ankin] to New York. . . . Our spirits are all up again; nineteen sail of vessels have arrived in this port within the last three or four days, with merchandise from the West Indies—many of them from Havanah, which brought in real specie upwards of 160,000 Dollars in exchange for flour.

Wallis wrote on April 25 that the rumor in Philadelphia was that George Washington believed four thousand British and Hessian troops would be sent to the Delaware River area, and the soldiers were told to be ready to embark on ships for the journey.[46]

In a letter to Wallis on May 15, Beckwith offers some insight into what he thought of Wallis's information-gathering—unless he was just flattering him when he wrote, "I am persuaded, that you survey public affairs, with a cool observant eye, neither suffering yourself to be swayed by prejudice, biased by the sanguine hopes of our friends, or led by the false enthusiasm of our enemies: extremes equally dangerous, and at times avoided with some degree of difficulty." He then asked Wallis to find out how Congress was perceived by the French court and where General Greene was in Virginia.[47] General Clinton wanted the navy to use a fifty-gun ship and two frigates to blockade the entrance to the Delaware River and Philadelphia. He indicated in a letter written June 20 to Admiral Mariot Arbuthnot, who was in command of the North American British fleet, that his request to do so was based on information he had received from behind enemy lines—information from Samuel Wallis.[48]

Wallis wrote to Coxe on June 27 concerning the American financial situation, saying that the British had left the port of Philadelphia so wide open that seven-eighths of the American agricultural trade had been delivered to the West Indian markets for nearly a half million dollars. The French and Spanish appeared to be removing their trade barriers and would start buying American provisions for their armies and their fleets. Congress was ready to remove all trade barriers except those with the "Common Enemy," Great Britain. This influx of French and Spanish money was exactly what the Americans needed to help finance the war effort. Wallis wrote about seeing the source of these agricultural commodities: "There never was so great an appearance of crops since the settlement of North America as is at present all over the middle colonies. I have been very lately thro' [a] great part of the [Delmarva] Peninsula, as well as over a great deal of Pennsylvania and [New] Jersey and in the whole course of my ride, I did not see a single field that was not uncommonly fine." He recommended that the British navy cruise the Delaware River and bay to interrupt the shipments.[49]

Coxe wrote to Major De Lancey on July 2 and included an extract of a letter he received July 1 from Wallis concerning the British army assisting Admiral Thomas Graves, who succeeded Arbuthnot as commander of the North American British fleet, in stopping the Delaware River trade.[50] On July 6, John Stapleton, assistant adjutant general at British headquarters in New York City, noted on a copy of Wallis's report that Wallis's information was copied and sent to Commodore Edmund Affleck on the warship *Bedford*, who in turn would forward it to Graves.[51]

Asher Levy, who was born in New York in 1756, served as a cadet, or officer's apprentice, under Lieutenant John Flahaven in the 1st Regiment of the New Jersey Line of Continental Troops at Valley Forge from December 1777 to May 1778.[52] He was an ensign in the same unit from September 12, 1778, until he resigned on June 4, 1779. He was suspected of being a Tory. Lieutenant Colonel William De Hart of the 2nd New Jersey Regiment wrote to the Supreme Executive Council of Pennsylvania in February 1780 and advised that Levy was in Philadelphia and "there was great reason to believe he was a spy."[53] He was arrested and confined in the jail in Burlington, New Jersey. He escaped on March 25, 1780, and was recaptured. He escaped again on August 9, 1780. This time he went to New York to join his family, who were Tories. After the war, Levy and his wife, Margaret Mary Thomson, moved to Philadelphia, where he died in 1785.

One of George Washington's resident spies in New York City was John Vanderhoven, who used the code names "Littel D" and "VDH." He sent information to Captain John Hendricks, a resident of Elizabeth Town who was controlling Colonel Elias Dayton's spies while Dayton was sick, "that a person who is called George [Andrew] Fürstner of Lancaster, and who is brother in law to Rankin formerly of York County, comes frequently out as a spy by way of Shark River thro' [New] Jersey and from thence to Lancaster. He left New York the 27th."[54] Fürstner was "to meet some officer of distinction" in either New Jersey or Pennsylvania. Major De Lancey accompanied Fürstner to the schooner *Fly*, which took him to New Jersey. Before Fürstner left New York City, he stopped in to get a flask of cherry brandy from John Vanderhoven. The two were introduced to each other by Lieutenant James Moody, a British spy, whom Vanderhoven said he was on very good terms with:

I often give him an invitation to come and dine with me and sup and so forth. Mr. Fürstner one night after we was well warmed with wine, and I began to tell what very great exploits I had done in going through the meadows for intelligence. [He] opened him self to me and informed me that he was sent out the time he got the brandy to meet an officer in the Continental army one of Arnold's associates, and that the boatmen put him on shore near Middletown, and that he had a horse provided for him and that he rid all that night and the best part of the next forenoon before he met with him that he spent all the afternoon and evening with him. So far as this he told me that it was an officer, who was on his way from headquarters to Philadelphia. . . . I am working on Mr. [Andrew] Furstner [Fürstner] and Lieutenant [James] Moody every night and I believe that I shall find out all their secrets in a time as Moody has informed me that one of the Governor's own counsel sent him word every day, while he was out after him and I intend to find out his name in a day or two, and his guide.[55]

Captain B. Edgar Joel claimed he deserted from the British in New York to Washington's camp at Springfield, New Jersey, in June 1780, because he was disgusted with service in the British army.[56] Washington wrote to the Board of War that Joel "pretends to have left the British Army in disgust. I cannot determine whether this is true or false; but I cannot but view him with an eye of suspicion. I think it necessary at least, in the present conjuncture of things, that he should be safely kept and I wish the Board to have him so confined as to prevent him any opportunity of escaping."[57] Because Washington suspected Joel had come as a spy, he had Joel transferred to Philadelphia, where he was kept at the Philadelphia Barracks. On July 21, Joel wrote to Washington in an attempt to get out of confinement. He said the War Board would not act without instructions from Washington.[58]

On August 8, Joel wrote to Washington again and said he had served six years in the British army. He asked Washington for a brevet rank, which he believed would protect him in case he was captured by the British. He wanted the opportunity to serve under a Major Lee in the next campaign.[59] Washington answered his pleas on August 14:

Whatever favourable opinion I might entertain of your military abilities and knowledge in your profession or however I might be disposed to foster and cherish genius and merit wherever they are discovered; circumstanced as you are; I should not think myself warranted to give you an employment in the army under my command. Altho I do not conceive it expedient, from a variety of considerations which must occur to every one, for you to engage in the service of the United States; yet I have given directions to the Board of War for your immediate liberation from the restraint of which you complain.[60]

In September the Board of War summoned Joel to appear before them. Joel wrote to New Jersey Governor William Livingston, requesting a horse so he could make the journey. Livingston sent Joel to the Board of War and requested that they "dispose of [him] in some interior part of the country where he cannot with equal probability of success carry into execution any pernicious designs." Livingston believed that because Joel could be in contact with the British in New York, it was too risky for him to stay in New Jersey.[61]

Before the Board of War, Joel claimed to be the son of the Duke of Richmond.[62] He also claimed that Major General Robert Howe was in the pay of the British. The Board of War did not believe this but reported it to Washington.[63] Washington responded:

> It will be the policy of the enemy to distract us as much as possible by sowing jealousies, and if we swallow the bait, no character will be safe, there will be nothing but mutual distrust. In the present case, from every thing I have heard of your informant, I should suspect him of the worst intentions; and notwithstanding what we are told about the motives which obliged him to leave the enemy, I still think it probable he came out as a spy and that the assigned causes are either altogether fictitious, or being real were made the inducement with him for undertaking the errand to avoid punishment, as well as obtain a reward.[64]

President of Pennsylvania Joseph Reed on November 13 advised Governor Livingston that Joel had started to provide information on people from New Jersey and Pennsylvania corresponding with the British in New York. Joel was going to court in Trenton to answer a lawsuit there. Reed suggested that Livingston have someone follow up with Joel to see if additional people communicating with the British could be discovered.[65] Livingston wrote on the fifteenth that Joel had made himself unwelcome in New Jersey due to his "insufferable insolence" to the authority of the state and had made connections with persons of suspected disloyalty when he was there.[66]

Based on information provided by Joel, eight people were rounded up in Philadelphia, suspected of communicating with the British by way of Shrewsbury, Monmouth County, New Jersey.

The suspects were interrogated, which led to the discovery of invoices concerning large amounts of goods having been brought from New York to the American areas. It was disclosed that a lumber ring operating out of Egg Harbor, New Jersey, was sending lumber to the enemy in New York. Also, ships left Philadelphia bound for a friendly port but went to the British in New York. Goods purchased with the proceeds were shipped to Shrewsbury, which had a high loyalist population. The goods would then be smuggled to Philadelphia. William Black, John Shaw, and James Steelman were the captains of some of the vessels involved. Also discovered was information about the exchange of gold and silver for American paper money at a rate that would depreciate the American money. The conspirators also transported loyalists, escaped prisoners, and spies secretly to New York City.

Joel's information led to the arrest of Joseph Stansbury, a Philadelphia merchant who had secretly been a conspirator in the Benedict Arnold treason. The lumber ring was exposed from Stansbury's papers. In one of the letters, Stansbury used the alias J. Sterling. Stansbury's business receipts also described his store, located opposite Christ Church on Second Street, as selling china, glass, and earthenware. In 1776, he sold George Washington two cut vinegar cruets and four heavy salt cellars.[67]

Joseph Reed sent Governor Livingston nineteen documents concerning approximately fifteen people in New Jersey involved in the nefarious activities. He warned that R. J. Smith of Moorestown was deeply involved in Stansbury's dealings. Reed said they were still trying to locate the papers of Joseph Ball, Richard Price, and J. Salter, which would disclose the identities of more participants.[68]

Also arrested were Joshua Bunting of Chesterfield, New Jersey, who operated a tavern that was one of the stations along the way to New York; John Cummins, a Philadelphia merchant; Patrick Garvy (sometimes spelled Garvey), an assistant apothecary, or pharmacist, in the Continental Army who was a part owner of a boat that plied the waters transporting people between Squan, New Jersey, and New York; Samuel Clark, who lived near Princeton; and Joseph Grieswold, who was a business partner of Samuel Clark's.[69] Some were questioned and released. Those from

New Jersey were transferred there for a resolution of their cases. Joseph Stansbury was exiled to the British in New York.

There were several other spies operating between New York and Philadelphia that I have identified but whose stories are incomplete. John Turner of Spotsylvania, Virginia, had fled to New York City in 1778. He was put in charge of a group to intercept dispatches from Congress to George Washington. Once they intercepted the mail, Turner took the items from Brandywine, Pennsylvania, across the Delaware River to New Jersey. He made his way to Little Egg Harbor. He traveled by sea along the New Jersey coast toward New York until he was taken prisoner by two American whale boats. In his after-war claim for losses to the British government, he claimed he had been hanged three times by the Americans trying to extort a confession. He escaped, and in 1781, James Moody sent him back into Pennsylvania with Moody's brother, John, to intercept the mail, hoping to find American military correspondence.[70]

In 1782, Jonathan Paul of Bucks County, Pennsylvania, was convicted of being a spy and sentenced to death. He was being held prisoner in General Lafayette's camp, and on the night before his scheduled execution, he escaped. In 1783, he settled in Pennfield, New Brunswick, Canada.[71]

Samuel R. Fisher, a Quaker from Philadelphia, was tried in 1779 for sending information to the British at New York. He was not convicted of treason but of concealing an act of treason and sent to jail.[72] The Supreme Executive Council of Pennsylvania received a report from two doctors saying Fisher was dangerously ill and his life might in danger. They recommended that he be moved someplace where he might be better accommodated. The council approved his being allowed out of prison if a bond was provided before any justice of the peace of Philadelphia. Fisher was instructed that he was to return to prison on the demand of the sheriff.[73]

John Pafford of Hampstead Hill, Charles Town, South Carolina, was a bricklayer. He lived in Charles Town for about eight years before the start of the war and owned a brick works at Goose Creek. He fled to New York City in 1776 for his safety. At Charles Town, his wife and family with two slaves were persuaded to go on a rebel galley rather than a British galley, which took them to Philadelphia. Pafford followed them to Philadelphia, where he was arrested and imprisoned for two years as a spy until he was exchanged.[74] In 1781, he wrote to British Brigadier General Samuel Birch, commandant of New York, asking for a fixed allowance of food until he could secure passage to Charles Town. Birch passed the request to Governor James Robertson on July 28, and rations were approved in August.[75]

NINE

Spies along the Susquehanna River: Lancaster, Muncy, and York

When the British occupied New York and Philadelphia, loyalists along the lower Susquehanna River in Lancaster and York counties reached out to the royal forces, hoping they could restore the former order. The leaders of this central Pennsylvania loyalist contingent were Dr. Henry Norris and Colonel William Rankin.

Norris, son of Henry Norris, was born around 1740 in Elizabeth Town, New Jersey.[1] He moved to York County, Pennsylvania, where he practiced medicine prior to the Revolutionary War. He fled in 1775, but he returned to York County the following year. The Reverend Daniel Batwell, an Anglican minister at York, York Springs, and Carlisle, Pennsylvania, called Norris "madly loyal."[2] In December 1776, Norris was arrested and imprisoned for three weeks. In 1777, he traveled to New York City, and during his return he was arrested in Philadelphia. He was sent to the jail at Morristown, New Jersey. When he was released, he returned to York County.

Norris decided to move to Chester County, Pennsylvania.[3] In 1778, he was returning from British-occupied Philadelphia when he was arrested and confined at Valley Forge. On March 18, with Colonel Heman Swift of the 7th Connecticut Regiment presiding, Norris was convicted by a court-martial of supplying the enemy with provisions. He was fined fifty pounds, which was to be used for the care of the sick at camp. Norris was also sentenced to one month's hard labor, which almost killed him. At night he was to be kept in the provost, or military, jail.[4]

Norris joined the Associated Loyalists of York County as a captain under the command of Rankin, who was a landowner, a justice of the Court of Common Pleas, and a colonel in the York County militia. Andrew Fürstner was Rankin's brother-in-law and a courier to New York City. In August 1777, Fürstner was compelled to leave his farm in Allen Township, Cumberland County, Pennsylvania. He joined the British army at Newark and served in New York and Virginia.[5] In his claim for losses to the British government, Fürstner said that on his first visit to New York, he was authorized to represent Rankin, Captain Martin Weaver of the Northumberland County militia, and an unidentified colonel in the Lancaster militia.[6] On a number of trips carrying intelligence between Rankin and Christopher Sower, Fürstner was accompanied by John Roberts, a Quaker miller from lower Merion Township in present-day Montgomery County, Pennsylvania. Roberts was hanged as a traitor in November 1778.[7]

Sower resided on Germantown Avenue in Germantown.[8] When the British occupied the city, Sower, a Quaker, printed an English newspaper for them. He left Pennsylvania when the British army evacuated in June 1778. He was considered a collaborator, and his property was confiscated and sold. Once in New York, he became Fürstner's contact. Sower sent "A. F." (Andrew Fürstner) out in the fall of 1778 to York County to contact Rankin and Weaver about enlisting loyalists, and he returned in December. Rankin and Weaver promised to enlist troops who would rise up when called upon by the British army. They also inquired about orchestrating a general uprising of loyalist.[9] Lieutenant Colonel Erskine gave Sower an answer from General Clinton in response to the inquiry from Rankin and Weaver. Sower wrote that General Clinton, the commander in chief, instructed Rankin and Weaver to continue in their respective positions in York County, and he would hold them harmless even if they had to take on the cover of loyal patriots.

Erskine gave Sower a spoken watchword to be passed on to Rankin and Weaver so they could identify messengers from British headquarters, but there is no record of what it was. Fürstner was also supplied with some kind of sign or mark on a six dollar Continental bill so he could identify true couriers from the British.

Fürstner was sent from New York to Rankin and Weaver but did not return to New York City for three months.[10] Fürstner was later sent to gather intelligence on the Pennsylvania Line Mutiny. He left New York on January 15, 1781, returning on the twenty-fifth with a detailed report of his travels through New Jersey to British headquarters.[11]

In autumn of 1777, Rankin and Batwell had plotted to destroy the American military supplies at Carlisle and Lancaster. They also plotted to capture the Continental Congress while it was in session at York. George Stephenson of Carlisle identified William Willis of Newbury Township and James Rankin of Manchester Township—both in York County—and Sheriff John Ferree of Strasburg Township in Lancaster County as the leaders of the plot. Daniel Shelly, of Shelly's Island in the Susquehanna River, implicated Batwell and the Reverend Thomas Barton, the Anglican minister at Lancaster, in the plot. He also provided evidence against Norris, who lived near the Warrington Quaker meeting house in York County, and Alexander McDonald, who lived near Carlisle.[12]

William Rankin began organizing a loyalist militia in 1778. He was in contact with British headquarters, as John André, at this time aide-de-camp to General Clinton, wrote to Rankin sometime after June 20, 1779, that Alexander McDonald had come to New York. MacDonald had arrived with the watchword provided to Rankin indicating that Rankin had sent him, which MacDonald must have assumed would protect him. Because McDonald was a deserter from the British army, he was arrested. Deserting was a habit of McDonald's. After leaving the British army and making his way to the frontier, he enlisted in the 7th Pennsylvania Regiment. On June 4, 1777, he was brought before a court-martial, charged with "Intending and threatening to desert." He was found guilty and sentenced to fifteen lashes.[13] On June 18 and 19, he was brought before another general court-martial, charged with attempting to desert a second time, with a Colonel Stevens as president. Again he was found guilty. This time he was sentenced to receive one hundred lashes on his bare back and to be placed on a Continental frigate to serve during the war.[14]

Two other men, named Cooper and Gray, also came in the British lines.[15] In August 1779, Fürstner told Sower that they should be treated as spies.[16] Sower, who was also Rankin's contact in New York, warned André that Samuel Wallis's friend in Philadelphia, Joseph Stansbury, "insinuates to be employed on secret services for government." Unknown to Sower, Stansbury had been involved in the Benedict Arnold conspiracy as a coder and decoder of Arnold's correspondence. Because Rankin had given his watchword to McDonald, Rankin was given a new watchword and told to use it as they had initially directed as a check on a false messenger to him.[17] Rankin went by the pseudonym Mr. Alexander in some of the correspondence sent to British headquarters.

John Vanderhoven, one of Washington's spies in New York City, informed the general of Fürstner's activities. Fürstner "comes frequently out as a spy by way of Shark River thro' Jersey and from thence to Lancaster." Vanderhoven also informed Washington that John Staria, also known as "the Irish Dutchman, because he speaks both languages, . . . goes constantly between New York and Lancaster, accompanied by a lusty old Man called John Smith, who serves as a guide to him."[18] John Staria is believed to be the person known as "Roving John." In January 1781, Roving John had planned to smuggle two deserters from the Continental Army named Peter Dill and Francis Steel from Pennsylvania into Maryland. The plan did not work, and Dill and Steel were captured.[19]

When the Revolutionary War started, William Rankin was on the York County committee that met on July 28 and 29, 1775, with militia officers and divided the county into districts and battalions.[20] Rankin had formed a plan to destroy the American arsenal at Lancaster and requested Clinton's approval to seize the weapons rather than destroy them. According to Christopher Sower, the people who would accomplish this task were to proceed to New York, where they would be handsomely rewarded.[21] "Some of [Alexander] McDonald's party had inadvertently betrayed the secret and thereby alarmed the rebels."[22] When Washington became aware of Rankin's plot in March 1781, he had Rankin arrested and imprisoned at York. Rankin escaped and made his way to New York City.[23]

Captain Beckwith, in writing to Major De Lancey on July 1, advised, "My F___d is just come from Phil[adelphi]a and I have rec[eive]d letters as late as [June 27 and] four days ago I am decyphering them. I give you this notice to prevent any bad consequences which might arise from the meeting of my little Doctor [Henry Norris of York County, Pennsylvania] and the Captain now suspected by us." Beckwith added, "I have not seen the doctor who left the packet for me and is to call again in an hour."[24]

Wallis wrote in code in an undated letter to Beckwith that Beckwith's letter of May 30 did not get to him till June 23. He urged the closing of the ports on the Delaware River. He mentioned that his Lancaster friend, Dr. Norris, a leader of a central Pennsylvania loyalist contingent, had been ill the last two months. Wallis indicated that the bearer of his encoded letter would bring the British payments for his secret services to him.[25] Beckwith had paid Wallis fifty-two pounds and ten shillings.[26] Wallis wrote to Beckwith on July 24 that Washington had stopped using the regular post to carry his messages to Congress and was now utilizing an express system that used different routes and operated as secretly as possible.[27]

Norris wrote to De Lancey on June 17 about the living conditions of seven hundred to nine hundred British prisoners at the Lancaster Barracks. He also advised that there was a large supply of gun powder at Lancaster, and one thousand barrels of flour at Philadelphia. Someone at British headquarters who was familiar with Dr. Norris added an identification of Norris on the letter. The added note said Norris had carried letters and other items from Colonel Rankin and that he was trustworthy "concerning any attempt toward the prisoners".[28] On August 10, Norris secretly arrived in New York City. Beckwith wrote that Norris "seems very zealous and clear, in his plan which I think most deserving of notice." Beckwith told De Lancey that he would explain the plan later that evening.[29] Norris made another trip to New York from Philadelphia on December 9.[30]

Norris planned to use force to free the large contingent of British prisoners at Lancaster. General Clinton considered Rankin's proposal of a general uprising important but did not make plans to execute his plans until 1781. Rankin and Sower (who traveled under the fictitious name of Captain Longstreet) were sent to General William Phillips in Virginia, who was to give his appraisal of Rankin's plot.[31] But Phillips died without providing any analysis. General Benedict Arnold, who was in Virginia, was heading back to New York and was to provide his analysis in person. Lord Cornwallis was to supply the troops, but his surrender at Yorktown caused the plan to be canceled.

Norris left Philadelphia on December 9, 1781, for the safety of the British army in New York.[32] After the war, he went to London and was given a British military pension of ninety pounds per year. Rankin also took refuge in New York. In November 1783, he left New York and went to England. When he filed for a half-pay pension from the British government, Clinton recommended him "in the strongest manner as an active zealous man who encountered many dangers for the good of the King's service and as one highly deserving the attention of government." Rankin was granted a pension of 120 pounds per year and over 2,300 pounds for his losses.[33]

In central Pennsylvania the Mennonites and the Dunkers, two Pennsylvania German Christian sects, were loyal to the crown. The Dunkers were also known as German Baptist Brethren. The leaders of the two groups were from Lancaster County: Michael Kauffmann Sr. and Jr., and Melchior Brenneman were Mennonites. Philip Shoemaker was a Dunker. The two societies sent Christian Musselmann to the British commander in chief seeking reconciliation with the crown and pledging their goods and chattels to the effort. However, Musselmann was captured by the rebels, who destroyed the documents. In a letter written September 1, 1780, Christopher Sower told De Lancey that the two sects were loyal and had helped British and Hessian soldiers who were being held captive in their area. He wanted to get the younger members to be active participants in the war. He indicated that there were two thousand to three thousand Mennonite families and that the Dunkers numbered about three thousand adults. The older men of both sects were conscientious objectors, but the young Mennonites "are not so much contracted. They have ever since the beginning of this rebellion excommunicated every person that took up arms against the King, or otherwise voluntary assisted the rebels." Sower volunteered to "Safely & privately convey any Message unto them without any particular expense to government."[34]

Former Mennonite preacher Henry Funk, a miller from Upper Milford Township in Northampton County, Pennsylvania, was arrested by John Laub and Philip Walter on August 8, 1777, on suspicion of being a British spy. He was traveling on errands when Walter stopped him as he passed Walter's house. Walter arrested him because he had not taken the oath of allegiance to Pennsylvania. He was brought before Justice Frederick Limbach. He was asked to take the oath and refused. Limbach gave him a day to think it over. When asked the next day if he would take the oath, Funk cited Saint Paul in Romans 13 of the New Testament: "Let every soul be subject to higher powers: for there is no power but from God: and those that are, are ordained of God." Limbach asked Laub and Walter if they were convinced that Funk was a spy, and they said they were. They said he was acting very suspiciously, traveling forward and backward covering the same ground. Limbach had Funk jailed as a spy.[35]

Don Juan de Miralles was a wealthy Cuban merchant who was a Spanish secret agent. His control agent was the Spanish governor of Havana, with whom he corresponded. He landed in Charles Town, South Carolina, in April 1778, claiming he had problems with his ship. He went overland to York, where the Continental Congress was meeting, and arrived on June 9, 1778. He reported on the activities of Congress.

Miralles, Don Francisco Rendon (Miralles's secretary), and the Chevalier de la Luzerne, French minister to the United States, in company with General Washington, arrived at the encampment of the Continental Army at Morristown, New Jersey, from

Philadelphia in April 1780. Miralles took sick and on April 24 was confined to Washington's headquarters in Mrs. Theodesia Ford's house, where he died of pneumonia at 3 p.m. on April 28. Father Seraphin Bandol, chaplain of the French minister, conducted a Catholic funeral, and Miralles was buried with military honors the next day in the Presbyterian graveyard in Morristown.[36]

In 1779, General John Sullivan was being sent with an army into the Indian lands of upstate New York in retaliation for loyalist and Iroquois raids on American patriot settlements. Colonel John Cox, a Philadelphia merchant, introduced Colonel William Patterson of the Lancaster County militia to Washington and claimed him "as a person capable of giving the best information of the Indian Country between the Susquehanna and Niagara of any man that could be met with; and as one, who had it more in his power than any other to obtain such intelligence of the situation, number and temper of the Indians in those regions as I wanted to enable me to form the expedition against them."[37] Washington told General Lafayette, "in this light, and as the brother in law of General James Potter who is known to be a zealous friend to America I viewed and employed Patterson for the above purpose. Concealing as much as the nature of the case would admit my real design. If I have been deceived in the man, Colonel Cox is the author of the deception and is highly culpable, because he represented him to me as a person he was well acquainted with."

Washington called Sullivan's expedition a "rod of correction" against the Six Nations–the confederation of the Cayuga, Mohawk, Oneida, Onondaga, Seneca, and Tuscarora Indians in upstate New York west of the Hudson River. Before the expedition could begin, Washington wanted more intelligence of the area.[38] On March 1, 1779, he assigned Patterson to determine "the situation of the towns belonging to the six nations and their dependent tribes. The strength of each town their disposition and designs with respect to war or peace; the relative distances of all remarkable places as well as between each of them and the navigable waters of the Susquehanna, Allegany and Seneca Rivers."[39]

In order to accomplish his mission, Patterson recruited a Getshom Hicks and provided him with a suit of Indian clothes.[40] Patterson was unable to get anyone else to go on the mission with Hicks. Washington sent instructions to Colonel Zebulon Butler at Wyoming, Pennsylvania; Major Barnet Eichelberger, of the Pennsylvania militia, at Sunbury; and to the commanding officer at Fort Willis.[41] They were to allow the bearer of Patterson's pass to come and go through the lines without interruption and without being searched, supply him five days of provisions if he asked for it, and help him in any other way required. The pass read: "This will serve as passport for Getshom Hicks who may appear in Indian Dress, and the Officer commanding will receive him. W. Patterson. 25th March, 1779."[42] Captain George Bush of the 11th Pennsylvania Regiment helped get Hicks through the frontier country north of Fort Wallace (later Fort Muncy) at Muncy, Pennsylvania.[43]

Hicks had been to Shamong, where he fell in with a group of twenty-five white men under the command of a British sergeant and about thirty Indian warriors of the Mingo, Muncy, and Tuscarora tribes. Hicks spoke to the sergeant, who said their officer had gone to Lake Ontario to get reinforcements. The sergeant also said "the six nations and their dependents were all preparing for war." Hicks noticed that they were low on provisions. The Indian chief of the town provided Hicks with a safe method to communicate with him. Other Indians were not happy with Hicks's presence, and he left.

On April 11, Washington wrote to Patterson and told him to stop his intelligence-gathering until Patterson contacted General Edward Hand, who would soon be in his area. Washington complained about the expense involved in the Hicks case and said he thought the results were not worth it.[44] Patterson consulted with Hand, and they agreed to discontinue the effort. Patterson wanted to know what to do with the money he was holding for intelligence work.[45] He wrote to General Greene, who was quartermaster general at the time, saying he wished to settle the account but wanted to buy the Indian clothes.[46] Washington instructed Patterson to turn in the balance of the intelligence money to the paymaster general or his nearest deputy.[47] In May, Cox and Patterson completed a list of questions for Washington on their knowledge of the Six Nations.[48]

The British had their spies with respect to Sullivan's expedition to upstate New York. Samuel Wallis had residences in Muncy and Philadelphia. Before the Revolutionary War, he lived some years at Muncy only during the summer.[49] He was elected a captain in the 6th Company of the Northumberland County militia.[50] He usually operated as a British spy from Philadelphia, where he was a shipper and speculator. He lived in Philadelphia during its occupation by the British. While operating from his stone house in Muncy, on the west branch of the Susquehanna River, in June or early July 1779, he proposed, through Joseph Stansbury in Philadelphia to John André in New York, to provide an exact account of Sullivan's army approximately every week. Wallis had a friend who would volunteer to serve with Sullivan's army and report back to Wallis, who in turn would report to British headquarters through Joseph Stansbury in Philadelphia.[51] This was a long, circuitous route, and the information would be out of date by the time it reached New York, making it too late to develop any plans against an army on the march. No such reports have been found among the British headquarters papers.

Wallis had another plan. He would provide Sullivan with an inaccurate map of the New York Indian country but would provide an accurate version to General Clinton. André, writing under the name Joseph Andrews to Stansbury, requested that he thank Wallis for his "exactness and assiduity" and give Wallis Clinton and André's "compliments and thanks." André also instructed Stansbury to tell Wallis that when a specific word was provided to him, he was to send intelligence of Sullivan's expedition to British Colonel Joseph Brant and raise up loyalists to assist Brant in his military actions against Sullivan's army.[52] Wallis would later become a courier for Benedict Arnold in his secret communications with British headquarters. In July 1780, he carried two hundred and ten pounds from Captain Beckwith to Benedict Arnold.[53] Sometime in 1782, Wallis ceased his espionage activities.

Other spies were also operating along Pennsylvania's northeastern frontier with New York. Edward Hicks, listed as being from Susquehanna, and New York native Robert Land were the subjects of a court-martial held March 17–19, 1779, at Minisink, New York, by order of General Hand, Lieutenant Colonel Eleazer Lindsley of Spencer's Continental Regiment as president.[54]

Land was charged with being a spy and taking intelligence to the enemy.[55] Witness James Vanokee testified that early in the war, Land was suspected of being a Tory and brought before the Northampton County (Pennsylvania) Committee. After Land swore allegiance to the United States, he was allowed to go free. Arthur Vantoil testified that on March 11, he saw Land with a musket and fixed bayonet eating supper at the home of a Courtwright.

A Lieutenant Decker testified that on the fourteenth, he and a detachment where going toward Coshithton in pursuit of a group of Tories who were traveling from New York to Fort Niagara, which stands on a bluff at the intersection of Lake Ontario and the Niagara River in northwestern New York. About 3 p.m., he captured Hicks and Land. Land admitted he was going to the enemy at Fort Niagara. A Captain Tyler, who once lived in Coshithton, testified that Land was a resident of Pennsylvania.[56]

The *Pennsylvania Gazette* of April 21 reported the story of the capture of Hicks and Land, saying,

> Four armed men were discovered passing privately through the mountains in the eastern part of Sussex County [New Jersey]. The inhabitants pursued them and having excellent dogs for tracking followed by different routes upwards of 30 miles, when they were discovered. Two of them made their escape, the other two were lodged in the provost of the Continental troops at Minisink. They proved to be spies sent from New York with dispatches to those infamous butchers Butler and Brant. One of the prisoners is named Robert Sand [Land], formerly a Magistrate. No doubt but the court martial which is now trying them will honor them with a share of Continental hemp.[57]

Captain Tyler testified at the court-martial that a few days earlier, he heard Land's wife say that "when he was searched for letters

in 1777 that he outwitted those who searched him by having a letter concealed in his ink stand that was sent from General Howe to
the Commanding Officer at Niagara." Tyler admonished her that
"she was as bad as her husband and in his opinion she had letters
from New York concealed, she declared that as God was her judge
she had not, that her husband had hid them for fear they would be
found with him as he expected every minute to be taken prisoner."[58]

Land testified that a Hugh Jones, a John Lord, and an Indian
had come to his house one evening in April 1777, and that Jones
told him he was going to join British Lieutenant Colonel John
Butler and Captain Joseph Brant. Before the American Revolution,
Butler had lived near Fonda, New York, and was the second
wealthiest person in the frontier area of upstate New York. He
raised a loyalist corps known as Butler's Rangers. Joseph Brant
was also known as Thayendanegea. He was a Mohawk Indian
leader who had traveled to London in 1775 where he became a
Mason. He was a captain in the British army over both Indians
and white loyalists. Late in 1779, he would be promoted to colonel.
Jones's plan was to get Indians to destroy the frontier settlements.
He went with them to try to prevent their destroying the country,
and on his way he met Brant, who told him he had no orders to
destroy the frontier settlements. Land then returned home to
Coshithton, where he remained till February 21. When he heard
the Indians were coming to destroy Coshithton, he went to New
York to try and put a stop to it.[59]

Land told the court that after being in New York a few days, he
"was informed that the inhabitants [of Coshithton] would kill him
if he returned." He decided to stay in New York, and in February
1778, he entered into the king's service as a carpenter. He did this
for just over a year, until the last day of February 1779. Land then
left New York to see his family, which was about twenty miles west
of Coshithton. He decided to move them to the safety of Fort
Niagara. Land testified that he refused a request of General
Clinton's to carry a letter to the British commanding officer at
Niagara.

The court unanimously found Land guilty of being a spy and
carrying intelligence to the enemy, and he was sentenced to
death.[60]

Hicks was also charged with being a spy and carrying intelligence to the enemy. Lieutenant Caleb Bennett testified "that about two years ago he heard the prisoner say that he would as willingly kill a man that fought against the British Troops as kill a dog."[61] A Captain Spalding testified that at the start of the war he knew Hicks, and that Hicks was going to enlist in the service of the United States but was persuaded not to by his father.

Hicks testified that in April 1777, "he left his father's house and went to Niagara in company with about sixty Tories where he continued about two months, then entered into the bateaux service to carry provisions from Niagara to Oswego." The bateaux service was responsible for transporting boats and items in them. He did this for six weeks. Hicks said he "heard that General Washington had issued a proclamation offering pardon to all those who had joined the Indians if they would return to their homes." He left immediately but arrived too late to take advantage of the pardon. He was captured by some American militia and incarcerated at Hartford, Connecticut, as a prisoner of war until September 1778, when he was exchanged and transferred to New York. Hicks's name appeared on the payroll in Captain William Caldwell's company in Butler's Rangers for the period December 24, 1777, to October 24, 1778.[62]

While in New York City in 1778, Hicks enlisted in the British army and was placed in the commissary department. He deserted on February 28, 1779. He was on his way to Niagara when he was captured near Coshithton on March 14. The court unanimously found him guilty of being a spy and sentenced him to be kept in close confinement during the war.[63] Hicks managed to escape. He may have been a double agent, or just pretended to be one to escape from jail, in which he may have had some help.[64]

On April 9, 1779, Washington wrote to Colonel Oliver Spencer of the Additional Continental Regiment that Hicks had escaped. Washington wrote that he wanted Land sent to Easton, Pennsylvania, where he would be turned over to the state. Washington said Land was not subject to military jurisdiction. Spencer was to provide the state whatever documents he possessed concerning Land, including a copy of the court-martial proceedings, which Washington enclosed.[65] But at the supreme court of

Northampton County, a judge did not find Land's name in the Supreme Executive Council's proclamation of traitors, so he allowed Land to post a bond.[66] While on bail awaiting a new trial, Land escaped.

On May 12, 1780, Ralph Morden, a Quaker, was arrested while helping Land, his friend and neighbor, flee to the British in Canada.[67] Colonel William Bond of the New Jersey militia had received information that a party of Tories had planned to meet near the Delaware Water Gap that day and be taken by Land to meet with some Indians. Bond placed a few volunteers in ambush. They shot two Tories, one of whom was Morden, and took them prisoner. Land, according to a report, "was seen to fall when fired upon and dropt his knapsack, beaver hat and cane. Tis supposed he was mortally wounded as there was plenty of blood discovered next morning. A diligent search [was] made but to no purpose. Tis thought he was either killed or conveyed away privily by the Tories as a number of them reside near this place where the action happened."[68] Land, although wounded, did escape.

Morden went on trial on October 30, 1780, at Easton, Pennsylvania, charged with being a British spy.[69] The presiding judges were Thomas McKean, George Bryan, and William A. Atlee. There were seven witnesses for the prosecution and only one for the defense. Morden had pleaded innocent, saying his only acts had been acts of mercy and kindness. He further claimed he was only helping out a friend.

Morden's captors said that when he was taken prisoner, he had in his knapsack what appeared to be a general letter of protection from the British army or a pass. However, his name did not appear anywhere on the letter. Still, the possession of a pass from the enemy was enough for Morden to be convicted of high treason. He was hanged on Gallows Hill at Easton on November 25, 1780.[70]

A trail from New York to Fort Niagara met the Susquehanna River about twenty miles north of present-day Wilkes-Barre, Pennsylvania. John Secord, who was known to harbor suspicious people, lived about ten miles north of where the trail met the

Susquehanna River. Because of Secord's suspicious associates, he was suspected of being a spy and giving them intelligence. After several British prisoners (a Captain Hume, Lieutenants Richardson, Hubbage, and Burroughs, and their servants) escaped from Lebanon, Connecticut, their guide followed the trail and met the river. Secord was suspected of providing them with provisions and aiding their flight to Niagara, so the local committee had him arrested.[71]

Secord sent a petition to Congress for redress of his arrest on suspicion, and the case was referred to a committee consisting of John Jay, John Penn, and Edward Rutledge.[72] The committee's report was read to Congress on April 11, and on April 15, Congress ordered that a copy of Secord's petition be sent to the governor of Connecticut.[73] The governor was to investigate Secord's claims and, if they were found to be true, it was recommended that he "cause restitution to be made to the petitioner." Secord was ordered released. He spied on the Whigs in the vicinity of Wyoming, Pennsylvania.[74]

TEN

The Traitor and the Merchant

After the British evacuated Philadelphia on June 18, 1778, American Major General Benedict Arnold arrived there, a wounded hero.[1] As a colonel, he had led his troops on a perilous journey through the Maine wilderness to attack Quebec. His debilitating injury from the Battle of Saratoga in 1777 prevented him from returning to a field command.

To some members of Congress led by Joseph Reed, Arnold was guilty of mismanagement of the $66,671 that was advanced to him for his 1775 expedition to Canada. More than $55,000 was not properly documented. Arnold claimed to have given the money to officers and other people for public use. Congress was withholding reimbursement to Arnold for his expenses until the situation was resolved. Arnold watched as the money Congress owed him shrank to 10 percent of its value as the Continental dollar depreciated.

Arnold was passed over for a promotion because of congressional politics. Congress decided to limit each state to a maximum of two major generals. Since Connecticut already had two, Arnold could not be promoted. He was forced to watch people with lesser ability and weaker credentials be promoted ahead of him. On February 19, 1777, Congress promoted five brigadier generals to major generals—Benjamin Lincoln, Thomas Mifflin, Arthur St. Clair, Adam Stephen, and William Alexander—while passing over Arnold.[2] Washington was surprised that Arnold's name was not on the list. He informed Arnold of the promotions and said he was "at a loss whether you have had a preceding appointment, as the news papers announce, or whether you have been omitted through some mistake."[3] Washington was informed by General Greene of the events that led to Congress's actions. He then informed Arnold, "General Greene, who has lately been at Philadelphia, took occasion to inquire upon what principle the Congress proceeded in their late promotion of general officers. He was informed, that the members from each state seemed to insist upon having a proportion of general officers, adequate to the number of men which they furnish, and that as Connecticut had already two major generals, it was their full share. I confess this is a strange mode of reasoning, but it may serve to show you, that the promotion which was due to your seniority was not overlooked for want of merit in you."[4] Arnold felt he was betrayed by the politicians. On January 20, 1778, he received from Congress a predated commission as major general, which restored him to his original seniority in the Continental Army.

On May 28, 1778, Arnold was appointed military commander of Philadelphia,[5] a role he would assume after the British left on June 18. The next day, Washington instructed Arnold, "You will take every prudent step in your power to preserve tranquility and order in the city and give security to individuals of every class and description; restraining, as far as possible, till the restoration of civil government, every species of persecution, insult, or abuse, either from the soldiery to the inhabitants or among each other." Arnold was to adopt whatever measures he thought "most effectual, and at the same time least offensive, for answering the views of Congress."[6]

Congress feared looting or the "removal, transfer, or sale of any goods, wares, or merchandise in possession of the inhabitants" until it and the state of Pennsylvania could "determine whether any or what part thereof may belong to the King of Great Britain or to any of his subjects," and it asked the military to ensure that merchandise did not disappear.[7] All military goods and supplies left by the British were confiscated. Arnold complied with Congress's request and ordered the city's shops closed until further notice to prevent items needed by the quartermaster and commissary for the army from going astray. After a week had passed and shops were still shuttered, citizens and merchants became angry with the delay. No business was being conducted for the merchandise in the shops.

With the outstanding audit of his handling of funds in 1775 fresh in their minds, the members of Congress did not vote Arnold a budget for the administration of the city for four months.[8] But Arnold, who was short of money, was not about to let a golden opportunity pass. On June 23, 1778, four days after his arrival and before the shops could reopen, he entered into a secret written agreement with James Mease, clothier general, and his deputy clothier general, William West. Arnold arranged that goods purchased by the clothier general, or persons appointed by him, for the public use that were not wanted for the intended purpose could be sold at the price originally paid. This would be an extremely lucrative deal for the three men. Mease and West could buy large quantities of merchandise at bargain prices using government money, then sell anything the army didn't need for whatever price they could get. Mease and West had to pay back the government only what the government originally paid for the merchandise. Because merchandise and food was scarce, there was a significant profit to be had and shared. Arnold had requested that a brigade of government wagons remove merchandise that belonged to Arnold, Mease, and West that was at Egg Harbor, New Jersey, which he said was in imminent danger of falling into enemy hands, and bring it to Philadelphia.

The secret agreement was exposed, and the Supreme Executive Council of Pennsylvania compiled a list of charges against Arnold. It sent copies of the charges to Congress on February 9, 1779, and had them published the next day in the *Pennsylvania Gazette*. Arnold accused the council of purposely waiting until he left Pennsylvania and was on his way to Poughkeepsie, New York, before issuing its charges so he could not quickly respond to them. The council claimed that Arnold had left so it could not deliver the charges until he had taken flight. Later in February, Arnold met with Washington at Middlebrook, New Jersey. Washington advised Arnold to demand a court-martial to clear his name rather than allowing Congress to send the matter to committee, where Arnold would not be able to defend himself.

On February 15, 1779, Congress "resolved, therefore that the Commander in Chief be directed to cause the said Major General Arnold to be tried by a Court Martial for the several misdemeanors with which he so stands charged, in order that he may be brought to punishment if guilty; or if innocent, may have an opportunity of vindicating his honor."[9]

The Pennsylvania legislature wanted to take back control of the state from Arnold and the military. Congress voted on February 16 to postpone action on Pennsylvania's motion to suspend Arnold from command as military governor of Philadelphia. The congressional committee dealing with the charges against Arnold did not report its findings until March 17, because Pennsylvania was slow in producing the evidence. The report indicated that four of the five charges were grounds for a court-martial.[10] Arnold demanded that a court-martial be speedily convened, and he wanted an immediate decision. With a court-martial on the horizon, Arnold would not be able to effectively continue as military commander of Philadelphia, so on March 17, he resigned the position. His letter to Congress stated he resigned for the recovery of his health and wounds, and for the settlement of his public as well as private affairs.[11]

Arnold had made a house at Sixth and Market streets his residence and headquarters within about a week of his arrival. In April 1779, thirty-seven-year Arnold married eighteen-year-old Margaret "Peggy" Shippen. She was the daughter of Edward Shippen, a wealthy, politically conservative Philadelphian.[12] It was Arnold's second marriage. In 1767 he had married Margaret Mansfield of New Haven, Connecticut. She died at age thirty-one on June 19, 1775, in New Haven.

On April 20, Washington set the starting date for the court-martial as May 1, 1779.[13] There were delays, and cross-charges between Arnold and Joseph Reed, president of the Supreme Executive Council of Pennsylvania, as to the cause of the delays. On April 27, Washington had to postpone the trial until June or July.

On May 5, Arnold wrote a crazed, hysterical letter to Washington. In the letter, Arnold mentioned his ungrateful countrymen and the ingratitude of Congress, and said he had nowhere to turn. He felt that despite "having made every sacrifice of fortune and blood, and become a cripple in the service of my country," he had been stabbed in the back:

If your Excellency thinks me criminal, for heaven's sake let me be immediately tried and, if found guilty, executed. I want no favor; I ask only Justice. If this is denied me by your Excellency, I have nowhere to seek it but from the candid public, before whom I shall be under the necessity of laying the whole matter. Let me beg of you, Sir, to consider that a set of artful, unprincipled men in office may misrepresent the most innocent actions and, by raising the public clamor against your Excellency, place you in the same situation I am in. Having made every sacrifice of fortune and blood, and become a cripple in the service of my country, I little expected to meet the ungrateful returns I have received from my countrymen; but as Congress have stamped ingratitude as a current coin, I must take it. I wish your Excellency, for your long and eminent services, may not be paid with the same coin. I have nothing left but the little reputation I have gained in the army. Delay in the present case is worse than death.[14]

This image of Benedict Arnold was published in 1776 by Thomas Hart, London. Arnold was both a hero and a traitor during the American Revolution. (*William L. Clements Library*)

Arnold's feelings of betrayal, ingratitude on the part of his compatriots, and helplessness are clear, and he seems unlikely to be loyal to a cause and a Congress that in his mind betrayed him.

After the war, General Clinton wrote in a memorandum that Arnold "supported the Rebellion as long as he thought the Americans right; but when he thought them wrong particularly by connecting themselves with France he told them so, opened a correspondence with me offering his services in a manner I would accept them. He gave me most important information. . . . [H]is conduct does not seem to have been influenced by any interested motives."[15] Clinton also wrote that "Arnold offered [to] either join or give information or be otherwise serviceable in any way we wished."[16] And on October 4, 1780, Clinton wrote to his sisters that Arnold made the first move and offered his services "without any overtures from me."[17]

On August 6, 1783, Joseph Stansbury wrote that Arnold sent for him around June 1779, a year after the British had evacuated Philadelphia. Arnold was aware of those individuals who had been appointed to positions of importance and trust when the British army occupied the city. Stansbury had been appointed to oversee the city watch (patrolling guards) and as one of the managers of a lottery. When Arnold was setting up housekeeping in Philadelphia, Stansbury sold him expensive dining room furniture. Stansbury wrote that Arnold told him of his wishes to open a line of communications to the commander in chief of the British forces. Stansbury secretly went to New York City with Arnold's offer of his services to General Clinton.[18]

Stansbury, probably with the assistance of the Reverend Jonathan Odell, a fellow author and friend, met on May 10, 1779, with John André, adjutant general on the staff of General Clinton, British commander in chief. In Philadelphia, General Howe had appointed Odell superintendent of the printing presses, and John André was living in Benjamin Franklin's house. André and Odell would have known each other in Philadelphia. Loyalists Odell and Stansbury wrote satiric poetry for the British that was read on special occasions and also published in *Gentlemen's Magazine* in London and the *Pennsylvania Ledger* and *Pennsylvania Evening Post*.

It was a mere five days after Arnold's hysterical letter to Washington, and it would have taken a couple of days for Stansbury to clandestinely journey from Philadelphia across New Jersey to New York City.

Arnold's message that Stansbury carried to British headquarters was totally unexpected. André, in a letter to General Clinton, referred to "such sudden proposals." Later that day, André wrote a response to Stansbury in which he promised Arnold that he would be handsomely rewarded if he could accomplish a major coup, and that he would even be rewarded according to his efforts if he made a good faith effort but failed:

On our part we met Monk's [Arnold's] overtures with full reliance on his honorable intentions and disclose to him, with the strongest assurance of our sincerity, that no thought is entertained of abandoning the point we have in view.[19] That on the contrary, powerful means are expected for accomplishing our end. We likewise assure him that in the very first instance of receiving the tidings or good offices we expect from him, our liberality will be evinced; that in case any partial but important blow should be struck or aimed, upon the strength of just and pointed information and co-operation, rewards equal at least to what such service can be estimated at will be given. But should the abilities and zeal of that able and enterprising gentleman amount to the seizing an obnoxious band of men, to the delivery into our power or enabling us to attack to advantage and by judicious assistance completely to defeat a numerous body, then would the generosity of the nation exceed even his most sanguine hopes; and in the expectation of this he may rely on that honor he now trusts in his present advances. Should his manifest efforts be foiled and after every zealous attempt flight be at length necessary, the cause for which he suffers will hold itself bound to indemnify him for his losses and receive him with the honors his conduct deserves.[20]

Arnold maintained a correspondence from Philadelphia to British headquarters in New York City by having Stansbury in Philadelphia and Odell in New York City processing the coding and decoding of the correspondence.

John Rattoon, a South Amboy tavern owner, was a British mole who used the code name Mercury.[21] He provided intelligence, secreted messages across the lines, and arranged for guides to take spies to their destination. He was the person responsible for the movement of letters across New Jersey. Captain George Beckwith told of his handling communications with Rattoon in the Raritan Bay area of New Jersey when Beckwith was running the intelligence operation in New York City. The messages had come through "the armed vessel stationed off the Raritan [Bay]."[22] This would be the British ship that was usually stationed at Princess Bay, Staten Island.[23] Beckwith wrote that the commander of the vessel had been instructed to use his seaman instead of the troops when they had to land on the Jersey shore to pick up letters. He was to forward all the letters to the redoubts on Staten Island, and they were to be sent immediately to British headquarters in New York City. The letters he received were to be placed inside an outer envelope and marked to the care of Beckwith, and they were to be given to someone the commander trusted highly.[24] These precautions were taken to protect the identity of Rattoon, an extremely reliable and valuable agent.

In one incident, Rattoon gave a copy of a message to a Mrs. Gordon, who was accompanying a Mrs. Chamier to Philadelphia.[25] Occasionally, Rattoon would venture a trip to New York City to personally deliver a letter to Odell, as he did in June 1779.[26]

Odell and Stansbury used a code keyed to a volume of Blackstone's *Commentaries*. Three numbers were used to identify each word of the cipher: the first number was the page, the second number was the line on the page, and the third number was the word in the line. For example, 45.9.8 would have referred to page forty-five, line nine, word eight. The numbers would appear on a page in one of two ways. They were written following each other in lines running left to right, as if the numbers were words in text, or they were inserted in lines of text when a specific word was to be hidden.

André planned to bury messages for Benedict Arnold in letters written to Peggy Arnold and her friends. A draft of a letter from André to Margaret Chew, believed to be dated in May 1779, was marked with the letter "A," which indicated it contained a hidden part that needed acid or a reagent to make it visible.[27] They also used *Bailey's Dictionary*, 21st edition. Stansbury wrote in May of 1779 that he renumbered the pages of the dictionary for Arnold, beginning with "A," and paged each side, resulting in 927 pages. One number would be added to each page, line, and word. Thus, "Zoroaster will be 928.2.2 and not 927.1.1. Tide is 838.3.2 and not 837.2.1."

Arnold was off to the American camp at Middlebrook, New Jersey, where his court-martial convened on June 1, 1779, and from there he sent in his correspondence direct to New York. In order to disguise his correspondence with New York, Arnold addressed the letters to captured American Colonel Edward Antill, but to the care of John André. Arnold was going to use the signature "AG," or a name beginning with "A."[28] André would have the mail to Antill intercepted. Antill, of the 2nd Canadian Regiment (also known as Hazen's Regiment), participated in General John

Sullivan's raid on Staten Island on August 22, 1777, which did not go well. The Americans lost 13 killed and 172 captured, including Antill.[29]

Because of some misunderstandings at a public meeting in Philadelphia, as Stansbury explained to Odell in a May 26 letter, he took refuge in Moorestown, New Jersey.[30] Despite the relocation, he was still Arnold's go-between and signed a letter May 26, 1779, using the name Paliwoledash. Stansbury also signed letters as Jonathan Stevens. There is no indication how messages got from Arnold in Philadelphia to Stansbury in Moorestown.[31]

Sometimes, things went astray. On May 31, 1779, Odell had to advise André that a letter written on May 21 in invisible ink had gone terribly wrong. Based on a "private mark agreed between" him and Stansbury, the letter indicated that "it contained an invisible page" that required heat to make it visible. When Odell held it near a fire, he "found that the paper, having by some accident got damp on the way, had spread the solution in such a manner as to make the writing all one indistinguishable blot, out of which not the half of any one line can be made legible."[32] Odell wanted Stansbury to stop using the invisible ink and put the letter in the form of a business deal to hide the true intent, stating "our little matters of trade and commerce; for thus our correspondence, though secret, will be harmless, and we shall have no cause to repent our choices." He also told Stansbury to "stick to your Oxford Interpreter," that is, his Blackstone's *Commentaries*.[33]

Odell pointed out that the letters between himself and Stansbury were passing each other in traveling across New Jersey. This situation was causing confusion. He wanted a quicker way of getting through the bureaucracy at British headquarters to get his translations to André. He apparently wanted to deal directly with André. He tried to get the cooperation of Captain John Smith, General Clinton's secretary who would have been processing all mail coming to British headquarters, but got nowhere. Odell then told André that he had apparently given André's personal cipher to Stansbury to use.[34] André's personal cipher involved, "Reversing the alphabet, using the last as the first letter, in the first line, in the second line, using the last but one as the first, continuing to drop a letter each line in that manner to O inclusive, then beginning again as at first."[35]

André wrote a letter in mid-June offering him money, but the offer was not good enough. Clinton was offering a set amount per soldier that Arnold would deliver to the British.[36] However, the total amount of money discussed would require Arnold to deliver more men than he could. Arnold wanted guarantees for his effort even if they did not result in success for the British.

On July 11, Arnold reported that General John Sullivan and five thousand men were sixty miles north of Wyoming, Pennsylvania, and that Detroit was believed to be their destination. Arnold also reported that General Benjamin Lincoln had three thousand regulars and five hundred militia in South Carolina and was "not likely to collect an army of consequence."[37]

Arnold also used the code name Mr. Moore. He even found time to send in a shopping list of items for his wife, whom he called Mrs. Moore. Odell advised André that Arnold and Stansbury were using the 23rd edition of *Bailey's Dictionary*, which was a different edition from the one Odell originally sent to André. Odell believed that André originally had a 23rd edition and told him to use it.[38] But a copy of the 23rd edition could not be found in New York, so Stansbury sent one by way of Rattoon to Odell, with a bill for sixty dollars for it. Odell cautioned André to use the edition that André took with him after visiting with Odell.[39] The shipment of goods for Peggy Arnold was sent, and a second parcel was prepared and ready to be sent on December 24, 1779.[40]

André wrote two letters at the end of July that he sent to Odell for encoding. The first letter concerned Wallis's efforts to gather intelligence on General Sullivan's expedition into New York state, but Sullivan was too far away for the British in New York to respond. The other letter went to Arnold concerning the negotiation of terms for his efforts.

Stansbury wrote a letter believed to have been sent on December 3, 1779, that was a mixture of plain text, code, cipher, English, and French. He reported that the army was going into winter quarters but had only four days' supply of flour: "[Philadelphia] has not enough flour to subsist her inhabitants." He also reported that there was a militia call for two thousand five hundred men to turn out in North Carolina, but no more than one thousand were expected to answer the summons. He also warned the British that "some insect of your place hath written the President of Congress that the October packet was arrived, the contents not transpired, but that your officers looked very blue."[41]

As the armies went into winter quarters, the correspondence stopped. It was a time for armies to heal and prepare for the spring campaign to begin. The American army was camped at Morristown. It would suffer through the lack of food and proper clothing. Private Joseph Plumb Martin described winter encampment as "the time again between grass and hay, that is, the winter campaign of starving."[42] Starvation would be their hut mate for the next several months. This

John André was the adjutant-general of the British Army in America when he conducted the correspondence with Benedict Arnold. He was captured by Americans as he tried to return to New York City in disguise. He was executed as a spy. (*William L. Clements Library*)

would be called the "hard winter," as it was the coldest in the eighteenth century.

The British army officers prepared for the winter season of balls and plays in New York City. Everyone in the city complained about the shortage of fuel—that is, the firewood needed to keep them warm through the long, cold winter—and of price gouging by woodcutters.

Come spring of 1780, activity in both camps became electric. It was time to get ready for soldiering and to ensure that everything was ready to move on short notice.

Stansbury was sent to New York City to re-establish the chain of correspondence. When he arrived in New York, he found that General Clinton was in South Carolina conducting a siege against Charles Town (now Charleston), and that General Wilhelm von Knyphausen was in charge of the British forces in and around New York. Before departing for South Carolina, Clinton had left instructions with Odell that all letters he received from Mr. Moore (Arnold), when deciphered, were to be sent to Beckwith, Knyphausen's aide, at the Morris house on York (Manhattan) Island north of New York City.[43]

About May 1780, Stansbury went to New York to restart the negotiations. Knyphausen, now in charge, responded to Mr. Moore (Arnold) that he did not believe he could speak on such an important matter for General Clinton but would cultivate their communication. He procured two identical rings, which would later serve as identification, and two pocket dictionaries. The dictionary (which one is unknown) was for Stansbury to use for his coded correspondence, and Stansbury was to deliver one of the rings to Arnold.

British headquarters documents from 1780 that summarize the previous year's correspondence show Arnold and his family were to receive five thousand pounds for the loss of his private fortune and five thousand pounds owed him by Congress.[44]

On June 7, Arnold wrote a letter to Beckwith that was keyed to the small pocket dictionary. The letter was addressed "G. B. Ring executor to the late John Anderson [John André], Esquire to the care of James Osborn [Jonathan Odell]." In it Arnold asked for a meeting with someone who had the other ring. If Arnold met a person in his travels from Philadelphia to New Haven, Connecticut, and then to Morristown, New Jersey, "who has the token agreed upon, you may expect every intelligence in my power which will probably be of consequence." He also directly asked for a meeting with an officer.[45] Accompanying Arnold's letter was one from Stansbury, which was also keyed to the small dictionary. It contained a coded copy of a proclamation to the Canadians.[46] The document used a small dictionary and a cipher that was a one-letter shift, where *a* equaled *b*, *b* equaled *c*, and so on. The original was prepared by General Lafayette and sent on June 4 by Washington, who was at Morristown, to Benedict Arnold in Philadelphia with instructions to get a printer to make a proof copy with a possible final run of five hundred copies.[47]

The correspondence between Arnold, Stansbury, and Beckwith continued, but only extracts of the letters are available. In one of the extracts, Arnold indicated that he was to have command of

West Point and that there were only one thousand five hundred soldiers there. Arnold also provided a description of the state of the defenses. And in a letter from Stansbury dated July 7, 1780, Arnold asked for a direct answer to his request for an interview with Major General William Phillips. The letter was keyed to the small pocket dictionary and decoded by Odell.[48]

Arnold also sometimes disguised his handwriting for secret correspondence. His letter of July 11, 1780, was written that way, and it was addressed, "J. Moore to John Anderson [John André] merchant to the care of James Osborn [Jonathan Odell] and to be left at Mr. [Jonathan] Odell's," in an attempt to make it harder to unscramble should it be intercepted.[49] A letter of August 30 from Gustavus (another alias for Arnold) to André also used a disguised handwriting and was addressed in a similar roundabout way.[50]

Arnold sent another letter in code that was keyed to the small pocket dictionary. Odell decoded it. Wallis delivered the letter.[51] Arnold mentioned his spy reports providing intelligence and that he would soon be in command of West Point. He reported that with the arrival of French troops, Washington planned to attack New York "as the first object." He reiterated he "wish[ed] an interview with some intelligent officer in whom mutual confidence can be placed."[52]

On July 15, Arnold responded to an undated letter from André and upped the ante. He now wanted ten thousand pounds sterling in case of loss and one hundred pounds per year for life. He also wanted twenty thousand pounds if he could turn over West Point and its garrison to General Clinton. "I think will be a cheap purchase for an object of such importance," he wrote. "At the same time I request a thousand pounds to be paid my agent—I expect a full and explicit answer."[53]

On July 24, Odell wrote a letter using his code name of James Osborne to Mr. Stevens, who was Stansbury, to be relayed to Arnold that General Clinton would reward him for his efforts, but that "indemnification (as a preliminary) is what Sir H[enry]: thinks highly unreasonable."[54] Clinton was willing to pay Arnold for his action but was not going to guarantee him a large endowment before he exerted any effort. Clinton also agreed to a meeting at West Point by a flag of truce. A flag of truce would provide protection from seizure for anyone traveling with the flag. "Mr. Anderson [John André] is willing himself to effect the meeting either in the way proposed or in whatever manner may at the time appear most eligible."[55]

Beckwith traveled from the Morris house to meet with Wallis in New York City and give him the two hundred and ten pounds that Arnold requested be paid to his agent. Beckwith told André that he hoped to get reimbursed for the expense.[56] Odell advised André that he believed that Arnold sent Wallis "chiefly with a view of ascertaining whether [Stansbury] or your humble servant had faithfully conducted the correspondence."[57]

Arnold sent two letters, dated July 30 and August 5, addressed to his wife but written with the intention of them going to his contacts in New York City. Should his correspondence to his wife be discovered, he would be accused of being careless in divulging to her the plan to attack New York, Washington's movements, and supply problems. He would not be thought of as what he was at this point: a British spy.

Finding dependable couriers could be a challenge. A letter in Odell's handwriting replying to an August 14 letter from Stansbury to Odell said "Mr. Moore [Arnold] commands at West Point, but things are so poorly arranged that your last important dispatches are yet in her hands [Margaret Arnold], no unquestionable carrier being yet to be met with." The August 14 letter took nine days to clandestinely travel from Philadelphia to New York City and was delivered by John Rattoon.[58] Arnold was now at West Point, and his letters were being sent to Philadelphia and then across New Jersey to New York City, with the process reversed for letters from New York to him. On August 27, Beckwith advised André that he believed that Arnold had taken over command of West Point.[59]

Arnold wrote a letter that Stansbury, using the name Thomas Charlton, encoded and sent on August 25. It reached Odell on September 3. The letter said that Washington was planning to attack New York, but that for the past three days there was no meat for his men because the commissaries sold it to the French, who paid more.[60]

Later in September, Arnold wrote a short, encoded note to

British headquarters. It provided the British with enough information to ambush Washington and capture him. The translation was done by Odell and carried the date September 15. The note told of Washington's travel via "King's Ferry on Sunday evening next on his way to Hartford, where he is to meet the French Admiral and General. And will lodge at Peak's Kill [Peekskill, New York]." It is unknown if the British tried to ambush Washington. If they did, they waited in vain, because Washington did not follow the agenda in the note.[61]

On September 20, André boarded the *Vulture*, a British sloop of war in the Hudson River off Teller's Point on Croton Bay, which is forty miles north of New York City. Arnold arranged for his passage through the American lines. André was to wait for an American ship to pick him up and take him to Colonel Elisha Sheldon's headquarters of the 2nd Continental Light Dragoons. On the night of the twenty-first, André was picked up by Joshua Hett Smith and taken to meet with Arnold. Smith had been a member of the New York Provincial Congress. He tried to ingratiate himself to Arnold in order to obtain favors, such as passes for people to go to New York. As instructed by General Clinton, André wore his British uniform in order that he not be taken for a spy. If things went wrong and André was arrested, he could only be treated as a prisoner of war.

André and Arnold met on the shore near Haverstraw, New York, and went to Smith's house behind the American lines. Arnold gave André the plans of West Point containing the placement of troops and other military intelligence. Their conference was completed in the morning. However, the *Vulture* was fired upon by the Americans and forced to move, stranding André behind American lines. Arnold wrote a pass with the name John Anderson for André to use in his attempt to get back to New York by a land route.

André decided it was best for him to change out of his uniform and travel in disguise. On September 23, Smith, who was guiding André, departed and left him near Pine's bridge, over the Croton River. André and Smith thought André had "clear sailing" to the British lines. Around 9 a.m. he was stopped by some militiamen in neutral territory near Tarrytown. André reported, "I was taken by three volunteers who, not satisfied with my pass, rifled me and, finding papers, made me a prisoner."[62] When news of André's capture reached Arnold, he fled to the protection of the British. Arnold received a general's commission in the British army. He spent the rest of 1780 raising a new regiment called the American Legion. He was sent to Virginia to raid Richmond and take a position at Portsmouth. When General Cornwallis brought his army into Virginia, Arnold was called back to New York. In September 1781, he led a raid on New London, Connecticut. In December he sailed for England.

A board of inquiry was held with General Greene as president. The board determined that André changed clothes within the American lines and "under a feigned name and disguised habit passed our works at Stoney and Verplank's Point[s] the evening of the twenty second of September instant and was taken the morning of the twenty third of September instant at Tarry Town in a disguised habit being then on his way to New York and when taken he had in his possession several papers which contained intelligence for the enemy." The board also determined that "Major André Adjutant General of the British Army ought to be considered as a spy, from the enemy, and that agreeable to the law and usage of nations, it is their opinion he ought to suffer death."[63]

Washington approved the board's sentence and directed on October 1 that it should be carried out "in the usual way this afternoon at five o'clock precisely."[64] André had asked to be shot, which would indicate he was considered to be a gentleman, and no gentleman could be a spy. But because the board of inquiry decided he was a spy, he was only entitled to be hanged, so he was.

A letter in a disguised handwriting dated September 30 and believed to be from Alexander Hamilton to General Clinton had offered to exchange André for Arnold. Clinton added a note to the letter that it was received after André's death.

ELEVEN

Pittsburgh: Pennsylvania's Frontier

The British encouraged the frontier Indians to be their friends, and many of them were under the influence of British Lieutenant Governor Henry Hamilton at Fort Detroit.[1] Because of the threat from this situation, Congress, in response to there being British Indian commissioners, appointed its own commissioners for the northern, middle, and southern colonies. They were to coordinate relations with the Indians, winning their friendship and convincing them of Congress's good intentions. George Morgan was made Indian commissioner for the Middle Department of the United Colonies on April 10, 1776. Since the mid-1760s, Morgan had been a partner in the trading firm of Baynton, Wharton, and Morgan, and he had spent much time on the western frontier trading with the Indians prior to his appointment. The Indians referred to him as the "truthful white man." The Delaware Indians, whose language he spoke, gave him the Indian name Tamanend (the Affable One).[2]

Morgan left Philadelphia for Fort Pitt at Pittsburgh in April 1776.[3] In May he sent Paul Long to Fort Niagara as a spy. Long was questioned by British Colonel John Butler at Fort Niagara and released.[4] Morgan, in a letter written on June 10 at Moravian Town (Walehaketopack) and marked "secret," instructed a Mr. J. Vraiment on what intelligence he had gathered at Detroit and other British posts.[5] Moravian Town was on the eastern bank of the Muskingum two and a half miles south of Coshocton. It was also known as Lichtenau and existed from April 1776 to March 30, 1780.

Morgan went on an intelligence-gathering mission at Fort Detroit, and he returned to Fort Pitt on December 12, 1776. He provided a detailed report on the conditions at Detroit during his visit on October 18. His report told of naval vessels and the armament they carried. He also reported on the numbers and positions of cannons, the officers and men stationed there, and the makeup of the militia. He reported that the British were employing Indian runners to carry intelligence, and that they were constantly alarmed by rumors of Americans coming to attack Fort Detroit. Morgan reported on the lack of support the British would receive from their French settlers if attacked. The French settlers had refused to turn out during an alarm, which caused a British ship to fire on their houses. Some French were taken prisoners, and others fled to a settlement on the Wabash River. Morgan also reported on the lack of maintenance on Fort Detroit, for when the fort fired a single round in celebration of Captain George Foster's victory in May 1776 at the Cedars, the blockhouse fell down. Morgan reported that it had been repaired.[6]

Morgan also said he was often been able to get over the fifteen-foot-high cedar pickets of the fort by using the five-foot-high fascines and the pounded earthen embankment at night without being discovered by the sentries. His report identified the weakest part of the fort as being nearest the town and the King's Garden. He also advised that about three hundred yards from the back of the King's Garden was a high ground from which the fort and its batteries could be commanded.[7]

David Zeisberger also was an American spy.[8] He was born in Moravia in 1721, and immigrated to British North America in the late 1730s. He joined the Church of the Unity of the Brethren, commonly known as the Moravian Church, and became a missionary to Native American groups in Pennsylvania and New York. During the 1760s, Zeisberger lived with the Delaware Indians in Pennsylvania. As the colonial population grew and the need for more land arose, the Delaware Indians moved west to Ohio in 1772, and Zeisberger followed.

Zeisberger and John Gottlieb Ernestus Heckewelder, a Moravian missionary, founded a settlement at Schoenbrunn near modern-day New Philadelphia, Ohio, which is seventy-one miles south of Cleveland on the Tuscarawas River.[9] When that community prospered, they quickly founded other communities, including Gnadenhutten and Lichtenau. At the beginning of the American Revolution, the Christian Delawares feared the non-Christian Delawares, and they abandoned Schoenbrunn in 1776. Heckewelder would later admit in writing his participation as an American spy.[10] Heckewelder and Zeisberger's reports were sent to the commander at Fort Pitt.

British officials arrested Heckewelder and Zeisberger in 1781 for treason, as they believed they were spying for the Americans. They were taken to Detroit for trial but were released due to insufficient evidence.

The Indians were not innocent bystanders in the Revolutionary War. General Clinton wrote on a letter, "It may likewise be observed that the Indians are naturally our friends as these inhabitants of the frontiers must be for it is ever in our power to let [the frontier settlers] loose on [the Indians to take their land]."[11] On April 5, 1780, Arent Schuyler De Peyster, commander of Fort Detroit, wrote, "The Michilamahinac Indians and from thence to the Sioux Country are stanch for the King and propose attacking the Illinois soon."[12] De Peyster reported that the Indians had defeated Colonel David Rogers and his men—fifty-five rebel soldiers—while the Americans were returning from New Orleans on their way to Fort Pitt.[13] He reported that "the great Huron Chief Sasterassee is returned from Niagara and brings belts with him from the five Nations, to be sent to the Southern Indians, requesting them not to make peace with the Virginians 'till required to do so by the Great King of Great Britain."[14]

Matthew Elliott of Pittsburgh was the business partner of Alexander Blaine of Carlisle, Pennsylvania.[15] He traded in the Ohio region during the winter of 1775–1776, and in the summer of 1776, he was the American emissary who invited the Shawnees and Delawares to a peace treaty at Fort Pitt. During a trading venture in 1776, he was robbed by Seneca Indians from Sandusky who said they were acting under orders of the British at Fort Detroit. Elliott spent the winter of 1776–1777 at the Shawnee towns, and in the spring of 1777, he decided to go to Fort Detroit. He pleaded his case in an attempt to retrieve his seized goods and his slave. The trunk that was taken from him contained letters from George Morgan and William Wilson, who were known as American Indian agents. Elliott was arrested at Fort Detroit in March 1777 as an American spy because of his association with Morgan and Wilson. Lieutenant Governor Hamilton sent Elliott to Quebec under suspicion of being an American spy. At Quebec it was decided there was no proof of Elliott's being a spy, and he was allowed to return to Pittsburgh on parole. He traveled by sea to New York and then to Philadelphia, both cities under British control at the time. He returned to Pittsburgh early in 1778. He was unable to recoup his loses, and the American prospects looked dim. He decided that his own prospects looked better at Fort Detroit than at Fort Pitt.[16]

Alexander McKee was the son of Thomas McKee, who ran a trading post. Alexander's mother was a member of a Shawnee tribe, but it is unknown if it was by birth or adoption. He was a trader and married a Shawnee woman. His sons either became Shawnee chiefs or officers in the British military. He fought in the French and Indian War. He was British assistant agent for Indian affairs from 1759 until 1772, when Sir William Johnson appointed him deputy Indian agent at Pittsburgh. At the outbreak of the American Revolution, he tried to keep the Shawnee neutral and was held in regard by the American military for his actions. Beginning in 1777, with the increase in Indian attacks in western Pennsylvania, the military leaders at Fort Pitt considered him suspect. A person named Grenadier Squaw accused McKee of regularly exchanging correspondence with the British in Fort Detroit. It was rumored that a conspiracy of loyalists was in the works to murder the Whigs in the west, and the loyalists would accept the terms offered in a proclamation by Royal Lieutenant Governor Hamilton at Detroit. American General Edward Hand did not believe the charges against McKee and eventually was forced to place McKee under house arrest at McKee's home outside of Pittsburgh.

Simon Girty was arrested as one of the conspirators and sent "to the common guard-house."[17] Girty was born in Pennsylvania in 1741. He, his three brothers, his half-brother, his mother, and his stepfather were captured by the French-led Shawnee and Delaware Indian forces who, on August 3, 1756, captured the military stockade known as Fort Granville near Lewistown, Pennsylvania. Simon Girty was taken by western Senecas to a village near the eastern shore of Lake Erie. He was adopted and trained as an interpreter and learned eleven languages. He left the Senecas in 1764, and was hired into the British Indian Department headquartered at Fort Pitt, to serve as an interpreter to the Six Nations.

George Morgan ran spies and was himself a spy on the western frontier during the American Revolution. (*Lamb's Biographical Dictionary of the United States*)

During the night of March 28, 1778, Alexander McKee; Simon Girty and his brothers George and James; Matthew Elliott; Robert Surphlitt (sometimes spelled Surphit), who was McKee's cousin; and John Higgins escaped from Pittsburgh.[18] They traveled to the Shawnee towns. In May they continued on their way to Detroit and arrived there by the middle of June.[19] They stirred up the Indians by spreading rumors that the Americans were defeated in the east and the Americans on the frontier were going to kill all the Indians.

Heckewelder told the Delawares they had been deceived. He wrote from Coshocton to Colonel Daniel Brodhead, commandant of the Western Department at Fort Pitt, that Simon Girty had gone to Detroit.[20] McKee was welcomed at Detroit and given the rank of captain and the job of an interpreter.[21]

At Detroit, Simon Girty was made an interpreter to the Six Nations, and he was sent on a mission there. He returned on February 4, 1779, with messages.[22] He also brought information on American troop strength and movements in western Pennsylvania.[23]

The eldest of the Girty brothers, Thomas, lived in Pittsburgh during the entire Revolutionary War. He was always a suspected person because of the activities of his three brothers.[24] Thomas and his half-brother, John Turner, in August 1783 left Redstone Creek (now Brownsville, Fayette County, Pennsylvania) and visited with their brother Simon in Detroit to determine "what kind of encouragement they will meet [with] if they settle under the British government."[25]

Simon Girty operated in the Ohio country, but he had a major handicap: he could neither read nor write. Secret messages from loyalists in the area of Fort Pitt were collected (possibly by Thomas Girty) and placed in a hollow tree. On July 8, 1779, Heckewelder wrote to Brodhead that Simon Girty "had a packet of letters supposedly taken from a hollow tree. It is desirous that [Alexander] McCormick should read them for him."[26] McCormick had been a trader at Fort Pitt and in the Indian country from before the American Revolution. In 1777, he had a trading post at the Wyandot Indians' Half King's village near Upper Sandusky, Ohio.[27] McCormick, who was really working for the Americans, helped Girty read his secret mail, then advised Brodhead of what he had read. One of McCormick's reports confirmed that Girty used a dead drop, in which one agent leaves a message hidden somewhere (such as the hollow of a tree or under a rock) for a second agent to pick up. The report said that Girty and eight Mingo Indians had gone to get a packet of letters from a hollow tree somewhere near Fort Pitt.[28]

Girty was known as the "White Savage," because he fomented Indian resistance to white settlers. Although he could neither read nor write, he still could carry messages. On February 7, 1779, he arrived at Detroit with messages from the Six Nations, the Shawnees, the Delawares, and the Wyandots. This was just after a raid he led against Fort Laurens, which had been built under the direction of American General Lachlan McIntosh in the fall of 1778.[29] On July 8, Heckewelder reported to Brodhead that Girty had been at Coshocton sometime shortly before and had gotten away, and that he had a packet of letters, supposedly taken from a hollow tree.[30]

The Americans decided it was time to shut down Girty's operation. On July 1, Brodhead, at headquarters in Pittsburgh, wrote
to Lieutenant Colonel Stephen Bayard of the 8th Pennsylvania
Regiment, who was at Kittaning, Pennsylvania, building a stockade fort to be known as Fort Armstrong, "Captain Brady and John
Montour have gone with a party to capture Simon Girty, who is
reported to be lucking with seven Mingo Indians near Holliday's
Cove. Express to Coshocton to seize Girty if he returns there." [31]
This effort to capture Girty was also mentioned in a letter from
Colonel George Woods at Bedford, Pennsylvania, about one hun-
dred miles east of Pittsburgh.[32]

When you're a suspect, you can get into trouble without doing
anything. Thomas Girty really got into hot water, as Brodhead
explained in a letter to Washington dated March 27, 1781:

> Since my last a small paper was brought to me by some faithful
> Indians who found it neatly rolled up in a powder horn which a dis-
> affected person had lost near the waters of Sandusky. I take the lib-
> erty to enclose a copy of it. I have discovered the writer and put him
> in irons, but . . . some of the garrison is concerned that he may
> escape before he meets the reward of his demerit. Indeed this place
> is infested with such a set of disaffected inhabitants.[33]

The "small paper," from Pittsburgh and dated January 21, 1781,
was signed "Thomas Girty."[34] However, it was actually sent by
Myndert Fisher, who confessed to having written it and sent it by
a Mr. Graverod, who was a merchant at Detroit. Fisher was previously a merchant in partnership with Elbert Graverod at Detroit
and in 1781 was a civilian who was employed as a guide for the
Continental Army at Fort Pitt. Girty knew nothing of the letter but
was an easy target because he was a known loyalist. A court-martial was held on July 26, 1781, with Lieutenant Colonel Bayard presiding. Fisher received a death sentence, which was sent to General
Washington for confirmation.[35]

But John Dodge, a trader at Sandusky, Ohio, and at Fort
Detroit who had been taken prisoner by the British, attempted to
intercede on Fisher's behalf. While Dodge was a prisoner in
Canada, Fisher helped him with "necessaries of life." Dodge wrote
to Washington that a one-hundred-dollar reward had been offered

for Fisher's scalp after the British discovered Fisher helping the Americans held prisoner. Dodge also wrote that when Fisher left Fort Detroit, he brought a large cargo to Pittsburgh, which he sold for the public good and accepted Continental currency, which depreciated quickly. Dodge begged Washington to postpone Fisher's execution.[36]

Washington wrote to William Irvine, the new commandant at Fort Pitt, "I have to inform, that the sentence of Myndert Fisher . . . is not approved, and that upon application of his friends, and some particular information respecting him, I have to request that he be liberated from his confinement."[37].

Both Pennsylvania and Virginia claimed Pittsburgh as a part of their colony. Dr. John Connolly was born about 1750 and raised near Wright's Ferry, now Columbia, Lancaster County, Pennsylvania. He lived in Pittsburgh, where he was captain and commander of the Virginia militia at Fort Dunmore, as it was known to the Virginia faction, or Fort Pitt to the Pennsylvanians. Connolly hoped to make money in land that he was granted by John Murray, Lord Dunmore, who was the royal governor of Virginia; therefore, he sided with Virginia.

In 1774, the Colony of Virginia split off the district of West Augusta from the county of Augusta. The district was composed of the counties of Monongalia, Ohio, and Yohogania. Dunmore traveled to Pittsburgh to appoint local officials. Connolly was appointed magistrate of West Augusta, and he suggested to Dunmore a plan to stir up the Indian tribes against the colonists opposed to British rule. In 1774, he was seized by Pennsylvania authorities while at the head of an armed party and was imprisoned.

After the first military engagement of the war, the Battles of Lexington and Concord in April 1775, Connolly and William Cowley, his servant, fled Pittsburgh for Portsmouth, Virginia. Cowley had become Connolly's servant in 1773. At Portsmouth they met with Dunmore, who authorized Connolly to raise in the west and Canada a regiment of loyalists and Indians to be called the Loyal Foresters. Dunmore sent Connolly with dispatches to British General Thomas Gage at Boston, and Cowley accompanied him. After they arrived in Boston, Cowley slipped out and went to the American forces surrounding the city. It was decided that Cowley would go back to Boston as a spy and continue as Connolly's servant. After a ten-day stay, Connolly left Boston on September 14 or 15 and returned to Virginia to see Dunmore. Cowley escaped and on October 12, 1775, provided a very accurate report on Connolly's plans.[38] On that day, Washington wrote to John Hancock, advising the president of the Continental Congress that Connolly's plan was to stir up the western Indians against the Colonies and descend on Fort Pitt from Fort Detroit.[39]

After Connolly returned to Virginia, Dunmore commissioned him a lieutenant colonel in the Queen's Royal Rangers on November 5, 1775. He left Williamsburg, Virginia, in the company of First Lieutenant Allan Cameron, also of the Queen's Royal Rangers, and Dr. John Ferdinand Dalzial Smith, the rangers' surgeon. They headed for Detroit to raise the forces for an attack on Pittsburgh, after which the force would continue onto Alexandria, Virginia.[40] Smith first met Connolly on Dunmore's ship, *William*.[41] They went up the Chesapeake Bay and the Potomac River. They stopped at Smith's house in Port Tobacco, Charles County, Maryland. They planned to split up, with Connolly and Cameron traveling to Detroit by the shortest route avoiding Pittsburgh, while Smith traveled through Pittsburgh.

Before they split up, Connolly and his party reached the house of a Dr. Snavely on Conococheague Creek about five or six miles from Elizabethtown (now Hagerstown), Maryland, where they spent the night of November 19. Somewhere, Connolly was seen by a hatter who knew him in Pittsburgh.[42] The hatter informed the locals, and Connolly and his band were arrested in their beds about midnight by a party of riflemen. They were questioned in Elizabethtown and then taken to Frederick Town.

At Frederick Town, Smith wrote, they "were stripped and searched, and examined again separately" before the Committee of Frederick County. Congressman Samuel Chase was in command of the committee. "By some neglect of Col[onel] Connolly's servant, an old torn piece of paper was found in his portmanteau, which discovered part of our design, and Col[onel] Connolly, to prevent our falling immediate sacrifices to a frantic mob, acknowledged our commissions." Smith said their money was taken except for a pound and one shilling each, they were confined in a third-story room with the windows nailed down, and no one was allowed to speak to them. They were also denied the use of pen, ink, and paper. They were kept under these conditions until Congress sent for them to be brought to Philadelphia.[43]

George Washington wrote in December 1775 that Connolly carried false documents that were "intended to deceive if he should be caught." Washington thought the real instructions were hidden "in the tree of his saddle and covered with canvass so nicely that they are scarcely discerned."[44]

Washington wrote to Congress on January 30, 1776, that the documents were concealed in the two pieces of wood that were on the mail pillion of Connolly's portmanteau saddle. They were first covered with tin and then a waxed canvas cloth. "Connolly probably has exchanged his saddle, or with drew the papers when it was mended as you [John Hancock] conjecture; those that have been discovered are sufficiently bad, but I doubt not of the others being worse and containing more diabolical and extensive plans." He added in the letter that he had just seen John Eustice, who was a member of Dunmore's family. Eustice said that he and another man saw the documents encased in tin, placed in the saddle tree, and covered over.[45]

Connolly said that his servant was not confined and had seen the saddle and accessories hung in a shed. A committee had searched the saddle and found nothing, so it was unguarded. During the night, the servant opened the pillion sticks just as Washington thought and destroyed all the documents except Connolly's commission. He then had a black girl, who would have been ignored by the guards, convey to Connolly a sealed message of what he had done.[46]

In December, Smith escaped from the log jail there. He was recaptured in January near Little Meadows and brought back before the committee on January 10, 1776. He was found to have been carrying letters written by Connolly to British officers in the backcountry. Smith was sent to Congress in Philadelphia via the jail in York Town, Pennsylvania. When Congress moved to Baltimore, he was sent to the jail there in December 1776. Smith escaped across the Chesapeake in a small boat and was hidden by Tories in the woods near Princess Anne. He went north into Sussex County, Delaware. On March 12, 1777, he, along with Simon Kollock, a cooper from Sussex County, Delaware, and others rowed out of the Indian River to the British man-of-war *Preston,* which was in the Atlantic Ocean south of Cape Henlopen.[47] Smith went to London around 1780.[48]

Connolly was examined by the Pennsylvania Council of Safety on January 30, 1776, and sent to jail at York Town, Pennsylvania.[49] In April 1777, Connolly was in jail in Philadelphia, and the Pennsylvania Committee of Safety offered him a parole for a two-thousand-pound bond and two freeholder posting bonds of one thousand pounds each.[50] Connolly wrote to the Board of War petitioning that he be released because several doctors said he would not recover his health if he remained in jail.[51]

Thomas Bradford, American commissary general of prisoners, was sent instructions from Congress that Connolly was to be moved to the new prison and its yard in Philadelphia. Also, a congressional committee consisting of John Armstrong, Richard Henry Lee, and Roger Sherman would prepare a report on Connolly's health.[52] Connolly was transferred to the new Philadelphia prison.[53] Brigadier General James Ewing of the Pennsylvania state troops advised Connolly that he signed a bond for him to be put on parole.[54] American General Alexander signed a pass that allowed Connolly's wife to come from New York with clothes and money. She was to be allowed to live with him in the jail.[55]

Connolly and his servant, James Sullivan, were paroled to Germantown on November 21, 1779, and Connolly's son was allowed to travel with him there.[56] In April, the limits of his confinement were eased to allow him the use of the mineral springs at Abington, which were ten miles away.[57] On July 3, 1780, in Philadelphia, Connolly signed his parole, which allowed him to travel directly to Elizabeth Town, New Jersey, and to cross over to New York for one month to arrange his exchange for Lieutenant Colonel Nathaniel Ramsey of the 3rd Maryland Regiment. He was allowed to take Timothy Mulloney, a naval prisoner, with him to New York and arrange to send back in exchange James Boodley or some other naval prisoner of war from a prison ship in Wallabout Bay, later the site of the Brooklyn Navy Yard.[58] Connolly deviated from his parole and on July 6 was at Bristol, Pennsylvania, claiming to Thomas Bradford that some fiscal concerns took him there to meet with a Major Spier.[59] Connolly eventually was exchanged in 1780.

On November 25, Connolly submitted a plan to General Clinton for an attack on the western Pennsylvania frontier. He said Alexander McKee, British deputy agent for Indian affairs, would assemble the Shawnee and the Lake Indians to meet him at Presque Isle whenever he needed them.[60]

On April 20, Connolly sent a letter to Clinton advising him that he had secretly negotiated with the residents of Northumberland County and with all the other loyalists on the east side of the Allegheny Mountains and was planning to raise troops at Pittsburgh. Connolly planned to take over western Pennsylvania and Virginia with these troops.[61] Clinton wanted Lord Cornwallis to assist Connolly after he secured the southern colonies. Clinton provided Connolly with a letter of introduction, dated June 9, 1781, to Cornwallis in Virginia. Clinton advised that Connolly was well acquainted with the frontier country and the Indians, and that he would provide Cornwallis with whatever information he wanted in those areas.[62]

Connolly was captured again, taken to Philadelphia, and put on parole. He was living at one of Philadelphia's many taverns, but because of the noise and turbulence of the public house, and because he had become ill, he moved to private lodgings at a Mrs. Ludlowe's on Fourth Street.[63] Because of his illness, he was allowed to go to England while on parole. On March 11, 1784, in London, he wrote to Lord Sydney, secretary of state, and offered his services to command at Fort Detroit or Fort Niagara.[64]

Other spies operated on the Pennsylvania frontier. William Gallaher, formerly a peddler, went to Fort Pitt from Fort Detroit. On searching him, the soldiers at Fort Pitt found a list of contacts at Fort Pitt and in the surrounding area who were considered loyal to King George. Gallagher escaped, and a reward was offered for his capture.[65]

Henry Bawbee was another British spy. Colonel Brodhead wrote form Fort Pitt on November 19, 1780, to the Delaware chiefs that "Henry Bawbee who lately came from Detroit says he belongs to the English and is paid by them to observe the conduct of you who live at Coochocking and to let the commanding officer know if any are friends to the Americans."[66] Bawbee threatened to kill Killbuck, a tribal leader of the turtle clan of the Delawares, and John Monture, a Delaware half breed, because he blamed them for his being imprisoned.[67] By May 1779, Monture was an outcast from the Delaware and was living at Detroit with the Wyandot Indians.[68]

TWELVE

European Adventures

Intrigue was a game everyone played in Europe, and Pennsylvanians were part of the action. Although most of Benjamin Franklin's activities in Europe were political, the quintessential Philadelphian did not miss playing in the game of espionage. At Franklin's request, Charles W. F. Dumas, a Swiss journalist at The Hague in neutral Holland, became an agent for the Committee of Secret Correspondence in 1775. He continued in that line of work after the war ended.[1] Some of his letters to Franklin were sent via Robert and Cornelius Stevenson at the Caribbean island of Saint Eustatius, where the Stevensons had been residents since the 1750s.[2]

Franklin was clandestinely in contact with a number of people in England. Samuel Wharton was born in Philadelphia in 1732, and was a member of the trading firm of Baynton and Wharton, later reorganized as Baynton, Wharton, and Morgan when George Morgan joined the firm. Wharton moved to England in 1769. While in London, he sent information on the British ministry to Franklin at Paris. Dr. Edward Bancroft and Major John Thornton, who used the alias J. Dumeneg, were couriers of some of his letters, and both were British spies. Some of the letters were in a dictionary code that Wharton explained to Bancroft and Bancroft was to explain to Franklin. Wharton warned Franklin that all Wharton's mail that went through the postal system was intercepted.[3]

On January 10, 1776, he advised Franklin that Bancroft's letter of December 30, 1775, was open when it was brought to him.[4] Wharton had been providing Franklin with accounts of events in

London. He also advised that the British government was being supplied with intelligence from someone Jewish who had lived "in Peter Evans's large House in Second Street," Philadelphia. The spy pretends to be a "friend to the views of the Congress, in order to acquire the best intelligence."[5] Wharton reversed his initials and signed the letter W. S. in an attempt to hide his identity.[6]

Wharton wrote to Bancroft in November 1778, "I am watched, I dare not write more."[7] Wharton left England for France in 1779, and he continued to send information to Franklin in France until he returned to America in 1780.

Juliana Ritchie, originally from the Philadelphia area, wrote to Franklin on January 12, 1777, from her convent in Cambray, France:

> I proceed to the purpose of this letter, which is to inform you Sir, that you are surrounded with spies, who watch your every movement who you visit, and by whom you are visited. Of the latter there are who pretend to be friends to the cause of your country but that is a mere pretence. Your own good sense will easily infer the motive of their conduct. One party assures that you are seeking aid and support from this Kingdom the other party insinuate that you have given up that cause and are making the best terms you can for the private advantage of your own family connections &c. I dare not be more explicit for weighty reasons to my self, but of the truth of what I inform you, you may strictly rely.[8]

Franklin was not concerned with who was a spy or what the spies were reporting, and responded, "If I was sure therefore that my Valet de Place was a spy, as probably he is, I think I should not discharge him for that, if in other respects I liked him. The various conjectures you mention concerning my business here, must have their course. They amuse those that make them, and some of those that hear them; they do me no harm."[9]

John Horne was forever the agitator. He was a member of the Constitution Society that campaigned for parliamentary reform, and in 1775, after the Battles of Concord and Lexington, he raised money in England for the Americans.

At 8 p.m. one evening in 1777, Horne and a John Bridges met with Israel Potter at the house of Charles Woodcocke in Brentford, England. After they met, Potter went to hide out at White Waltham Town, about twenty-five miles away, while preparations were made for him to carry a message to Franklin in Paris. When Potter returned on February 14, 1777, Bridges, Horne, and Woodcocke gave him a pair of boots with a false heel that held a letter for Franklin. He then traveled to Charing, in Kent, southeast of Maidstone, where he boarded a post coach to Dover. At Dover he took a packet to Calais, and fifteen minutes after landing in France, he was on his way to Paris.[10] He never knew the contents of the letter but believed it contained the views of the British cabinet on American affairs. The letter was an introduction to Franklin.[11] Potter delivered the letter to Franklin and remained with him for an hour. Potter stayed in Paris two days before Franklin sent him back with a message concealed in the heel of the boot. Potter left Paris accompanied by an Edward Griffis, posing as his servant on their way to Nantes. Potter made his way back to Woodcocke's house and remained there in hiding. He made another round-trip to Franklin in Paris. In 1778, on his third mission, he found out three hours before his arrival in Dover that all communications with France were prohibited, and he would be unable to cross.[12] This ended Israel Potter's career as a courier.

Peter Allaire, of Huguenot ancestry, was born in 1740 at Mamaroneck, New York, and his family settled at New Rochelle. He was a New York merchant who sold "wheat and rice to the French troops in Guiana; cannon and cloth in Morocco; traded on the Barbary Coast, in Spain and Jamaica; and traveled to Russia more than once."[13] He was based in London in 1775–1776. He sent a letter from London dated August 26, 1777, to Franklin that was signed "An American whom you have seen at Paris." In the letter he reported intelligence supposedly gathered from one of Lord George Germain's secretaries on military matters.[14] The information was not very accurate. Allaire crossed over to Calais, France, on May 22, 1778, and wrote to Franklin, telling him a British fleet had set sail from the Downs, off the east coast of Kent. He believed another fleet of twelve ships had departed from a place called Saint Helens. Allaire advised that he was going to stay in Boulogne, a major fishing port near Calais, France.[15]

On January 26, 1780, Allaire was staying at the Hotel de Chatre Rue de Richelieu in Paris. He wrote to William Temple Franklin grandson of Benjamin Franklin and secretary to the American delegation to France, and cited illness for not making himself available.[16] On the thirty-first, Allaire sent a note addressed from the Hotel de Saxe Rue Colombier to Benjamin Franklin along with a bottle of Old Madeira and a letter Franklin had not seen, which was William Eden's letters to Carlisle on the failed mission to America.[17]

On February 14, 1780, Allaire asked William Temple Franklin to provide him with a passport because he wanted to leave the next day for Brussels.[18] William Temple Franklin advised him that Benjamin Franklin chose not to provide the document.[19] The next day, Allaire was arrested by the French for being a spy and attempting to poison Benjamin Franklin. He was held for six weeks and then released because of lack of evidence.[20] At some point, Allaire began playing both sides. On August 1, 1782, the British government paid him one hundred pounds to set up a channel of intelligence.[21] In 1784, he was in New York City and working for Sir George Yonge, British secretary at war, sending intelligence reports to the British. By 1786, the reports were being sent monthly.[22]

Patience Lovell was a Quaker born in Bordentown, New Jersey, in 1725. She moved to Philadelphia when she was twenty. In 1748 she married Joseph Wright, and they settled back in Bordentown.[23] After Joseph's death in 1769, Patience Wright took up sculpting, creating portraits in wax in New York and Philadelphia. In 1772, she and her son, Joseph, moved to London and opened a studio. Her circle of clients included many powerful people.[24] She was an eccentric who called King George III "George" when he visited her studio. She claimed to have passed useful information to Franklin and Congress by putting messages in wax heads that she periodically sent to her sister's shop in Philadelphia.[25] However, a comparison of two of her letters dated September 3, 1774, that probably arrived on the same ship indicated that her ability to gather information accurately needed much improvement. In one letter she reported that Sir William Draper was coming to America, while the other letter indicated he was only offered a position as a governor.[26]

The British had discovered that she used Edward Bancroft's mistress to carry her letters to Franklin in Paris. Some historians have speculated that she may have been duped by the British to pass along misinformation. In 1781, she moved to Paris to open a shop. After a year she returned to London and was preparing to return to America when she died on March 23, 1786.[27] Her operation appears to have been driven by her patriotic initiatives rather than Benjamin Franklin directing her activities.

David Salisbury Franks was born in Philadelphia around 1740 and raised in Canada. He had been Benedict Arnold's aide-de-camp and was absolved of any complicity in Arnold's treachery. He was sent to Europe in 1781 to deliver dispatches to John Jay in Madrid and to Benjamin Franklin in Paris. With his assignment completed, he traveled from Passy, just outside of Paris, to Brest, looking for a sailing to America. On December 9, he was arrested by a private sentinel on a public walk on suspicion of being a spy. When the French commandant at Brest was able to document who he was, he was released.[28] Later that month he was attending a play, apparently accompanied by a prostitute, when he was arrested at the theater on suspicion of being a spy.[29]

THIRTEEN

More British Intrigues in Congress

Ever since the French had entered the war in 1778, British troops were spread over the globe to protect their colonies. The number of soldiers available for service in North American was dropping as the soldiers were needed elsewhere, and the situation was growing worse. With fewer soldiers to conduct the war in North America, it became more doubtful the British would win a military victory there. So the British began looking to win the political game for the control of territory at the peace negotiations.

On September 27, 1779, General Clinton sent Lord George Germain, secretary of state for the American Department, a letter marked "SECRET" that stated, "I have heard from Captain Dixon, that the dissentions and jealousies among the members of the Congress continue to increase."[1] The British had been hearing reports of unrest in the Continental Congress and decided to try to exploit the situation by attempting to entice a member of Congress to provide them with intelligence. Oliver De Lancey, who had become head of British intelligence in New York in 1780, ordered Captain Stephen Holland of the Prince of Wales Regiment to send someone to Philadelphia to contact Samuel Livermore, a member of Congress from New Hampshire from 1780 to 1782.[2] In London after the war, De Lancey wrote that Holland was recommended to him "as a person very capable of procuring intelligence and in whom I might confide. I accordingly did employ him and had much reason to be satisfied with his zeal and fidelity."[3]

On September 24, 1780, Holland sent Isaac Cotton, a refugee from Massachusetts, to procure intelligence on the French forces in

Rhode Island. He left from New York by way of Lloyd's Neck, Long Island, and crossed over to Connecticut. As Cotton neared Rhode Island, he employed two unidentified people to go to Aquidneck Island in Narragansett Bay. One went by Conanicut Island, which is due west of Newport, and the other by the Bristol Ferry, which is north of Aquidneck Island.[4] Cotton's spies accomplished their mission. He returned to Holland in New York with the information from the two spies and additional intelligence he collected.[5]

Stephen Holland was born in Northern Ireland around 1733, and was a veteran of the French and Indian War. He had been a lieutenant and adjutant of Goreham's Rangers.[6] He retired in 1762, settling in Londonderry, New Hampshire. On March 9, 1770, the king granted him two thousand acres in Londonderry for his service in the French and Indian War.[7] He was a tavern keeper and merchant, as well as a colonel of a regiment of militia and a member of the New Hampshire General Assembly for many years. He was also clerk of the peace and of the common pleas in Hillsborough County, and a justice of the peace.

In 1774, Holland sent word to General Gage in Boston of four British deserters who were in Londonderry. The deserters were seized by a detachment of British soldiers but were freed by a group of local Whigs. Holland, using the alias of Stephen Ash of Londonderry, was sending intelligence to New Hampshire Royal Governor John Wentworth. At the outbreak of the revolution, Wentworth persuaded Holland to stay in New Hampshire.[8] Holland had received and was distributing counterfeit New Hampshire currency. His correspondence with Wentworth was discovered. He was arrested and held in the Exeter, New Hampshire, jail. Holland quickly escaped but was soon recaptured in Boston and brought back to Exeter. The New Hampshire Committee of Safety spent much of an afternoon and evening interrogating him. He was convicted but escaped later that evening from the jail. On March 11, 1777, the New Hampshire Committee of Safety issued a warrant to Colonel Enoch Poor to arrest Colonel Stephen Holland. He was quickly captured. On March 15, he was examined by the New Hampshire House of Representatives and was "discharged and dismissed with honor."[9] In April, the New

Hampshire Committee of Safety spent ten days trying to determine the source of counterfeit money being passed in New Hampshire. Holland was suspected of having passed the counterfeit money. The committee sent officers searching for Holland in New Hampshire. On April 23, it sent a letter to Brigadier General Oliver Prescott of the Massachusetts militia to arrest Holland, as it believed he had fled to Massachusetts.[10] In April 1777, Holland was captured in Boston, where he was held in a "dungeon loaded with irons till his life was despaired of, he was sent off [on June 11, 1777] in the most ignominious manner to the province to which he belonged [New Hampshire], and once more committed to Exeter jail."[11] He was brought back by Colonel Samuel Folsom of the Exeter Corps of Independent Cadets.[12]

On June 11, 1777, Folsom was instructed to form a detachment of sixteen men to guard the jail day and night with no fewer than eight men on duty at any time. The men were to stay on this duty for three months.[13] In October 1777, Holland requested to be released from jail by posting a bond.[14] He escaped in the fall of 1777, it was suspected with the help of Captain William Vance.[15] Leaving his wife and family in Londonderry, Holland fled to Newport, arriving there in March 1778.[16] By May he was in New York City looking for employment.[17] He joined the Prince of Wales American Volunteers, and on December 12, 1778, General Clinton issued him a warrant to recruit for the corps.[18] He went to Newport with the appointment of town major, or chief administrative clerk. He was unable to complete recruiting for the corps because of the British evacuation of Newport.[19] His property in New Hampshire was confiscated. When a group of selectmen attempted to take possession of the property, they found Holland's wife, Jane, and most of the family still living there. Jane Holland reportedly cursed them in such gross manner that they did not want to write the curses in their report.[20]

Samuel Livermore was born on May 14, 1732, in Waltham, Middlesex County, Massachusetts. He graduated from the College of New Jersey in 1752, was admitted to the bar in 1756, and moved to New Hampshire two years later. He was judge advocate in the Admiralty Court and attorney general of the colony from 1769 to 1774. He became a member of the Continental Congress in 1780.

The British thought that because of his past royal jobs, Livermore might still be sympathetic to England.

Holland picked Captain Vance, who was also from Londonderry, to contact Livermore. Vance had been arrested on July 19, 1777, for loyalism to the crown, so Holland thought he was trustworthy. But Vance played both sides to his advantage, professing his loyalty to each whenever it was in his best interest.[21] Vance left New York on July 25, 1781, with instructions from Holland

> to wait upon Samuel Livermore Esq[ui]r[e] a member of Congress in order to procure what intelligence he could of the state and situation of affairs there. On the 30th he met with Mr. Livermore and informed him that Capt[ain] Holland had as[s]ured the Commander in Chief [General Clinton] that he was a friend to government and that he would render the Commander in Chief every service in his power. Vance reported that Mr. Livermore received him very affectionately and said he would be happy to render any service to the Commander in Chief in his power. He informed him, that Congress for some time past were almost wholly taken up about the State of Vermont that they were much divided but he imagined it would be determined in favor of Vermont being a state. That Congress had received from France an intercepted letter from Lord George Germain to Sir Henry Clinton informing him that Col[one]l. Allen of Vermont has joined government. Mr. Livermore further told him that there were no French fleet on the coast nor any expected, & that it was impossible for the people to pay their taxes and at last they would be obliged to make peace with Great Britain.[22]

Vance sent a report to the British in New York on September 8, 1781. He reported that Washington had arrived in Philadelphia on August 30, in the company of sixty light horses and a great number of rebel and French officers, and he dined with the French ambassador the next day. A frigate had arrived from France a few days earlier, but no one could board it. Vance also reported that some soldiers were sent off to Trenton.[23] It appears that Vance had talked to Bill Livingston, the son of New Jersey Governor William Livingston.[24] Vance left Philadelphia about eleven o'clock on September 8.[25]

Vance visited Philadelphia again, and he returned to New York on the evening of the twenty-fifth. The next day he reported to De

Lancey that he had met with Livermore, who had advised him that Washington was on his way to Virginia with Continental and French troops. Also, the French fleet had provided three thousand more troops. Livermore advised that Congress was very apprehensive that General Henry Clinton would visit them at Philadelphia because there were no troops at Philadelphia. Congress "had ordered the militia of that province [Pennsylvania] to the Jerseys but not any of them had arrived the 19th."[26]

Samuel Livermore of New Hampshire was a member of the Continental Congress 1780–1782 and 1785–1786. The artist is unknown but the print was made from an original by John Trumbull. (*Collections of the State of New Hampshire*)

After the British surrender of approximately seven thousand five hundred men to the combined American and French forces at Yorktown, Virginia, on October 19, 1781, De Lancey again ordered Holland to send someone to Philadelphia to contact Livermore. This time Holland chose John Stinson of Dumbarton, New Hampshire. The letter, which Stinson delivered on December 4, said that because of all the British and Hessian soldiers surrendered at Yorktown, the British would not have enough American and French prisoners to exchange on a one-to-one basis. Prisoner exchanges were accomplished by exchanging soldiers holding equal military rank, such as a captain for a captain. The British wanted Congress to propose an exchange that also assigned a financial value to soldiers where soldiers of equal rank could not be exchanged. The letter stated a precedent for such a procedure in the previous British war. The letter claimed the expense in maintaining British prisoners would induce Congress to propose some measures in the end.[27]

Livermore told Stinson to reply that he had received the letter and instructed Stinson to return as quickly as possible to New York.[28] No such motion for financial compensation was found in the Journal of the Continental Congress prior to Livermore's resignation from Congress on April 30, 1782.

Holland tried to bring another member of Congress from New Hampshire, John Sullivan, to the British side. Sullivan was from Durham, and early in his life he had studied law with Livermore. He had been a delegate to the Continental Congress in 1774 and 1775, and served in the Continental Army from 1775 to 1780, rising to the rank of major general. He resigned from the army because of ill health. New Hampshire returned him to Congress, where he took his seat on September 11, 1780, and continued in 1781.[29]

The British had intercepted some of Sullivan's letters, and they indicated his bad financial condition. These letters were published in James Rivington's *Royal Gazette* on December 18, 1780, and April 25, 1781. Holland wrote to Sullivan, stating that a union with England was better for Americans than a union with France.[30]

The British had captured Sullivan's older brother, Captain Daniel Sullivan, in February 1781 in Maine. Daniel Sullivan lived in New Bristol (now Sullivan) at the head of Frenchman's Bay. A detachment of sailors and marines from the British frigate *Allegiance* under the command of Captain Henry Mowatt woke him in his bed at night. His house, at the southern end of Waukeag Point, was torched, and his wife and children barely escaped.[31] He was taken to New York and placed in the prison ship *Jersey*. To win John Sullivan's favor, Holland had Daniel Sullivan removed from the *Jersey* and placed on parole on Staten Island.[32]

In the beginning of May, De Lancey sent Captain Sullivan on parole to Philadelphia, ostensibly to see his brother and attempt to make an exchange for himself. But the real purpose of the visit was to try to entice his brother to the British cause. Captain Sullivan was sent with a letter, and he arrived in Philadelphia on May 6, when there were public demonstrations of discontent with the depreciation of Continental currency. Over dinner he gave his brother the letter from Holland. The contents of the letter are unknown, but part of it would have discussed a prisoner exchange of someone for Captain Sullivan.[33]

He left Philadelphia on May 7, returned to New York, and wrote a report on May 17 with De Lancey and Holland.[34] In the report, Sullivan said that he saw his brother and gave him the letter, which his brother read "not less than thirty times and made him shed tears he said he [John] wished he had received it sooner, he desired Mr. Sullivan not to forget to say he would do everything in his power to comply with the letter. He said above a hundred times he wished from his heart to bring about a reconciliation." (The references to his brother having read the letter "not less than thirty times" and saying "above a hundred times" he wished for a reconciliation sound like some bad overacting by Captain Sullivan.) John Sullivan told his brother that he would not give him a letter in response because, if it was found, it would endanger his life, and that he would find another means of communication. Captain Sullivan reported that he thought the information would come from someone named Noble or Smith.[35]

Captain Sullivan was back in Philadelphia on June 12, saw his brother, and delivered a letter from Captain Holland. On July 4, Captain Sullivan wrote a deposition of his brother's response that "Captain Holland might assure the person [General Clinton] which he mentioned in his letters to him, in whose full confidence he was, that he would do everything in his power to serve him."[36]

John Sullivan contacted Chevalier de La Luzerne, the French minister to the United States, at Philadelphia, told him of the proposal he had received, and said he had thrown Holland's letter into a fire and rejected the offer. He claimed that he had kept silent about this overture in order to protect his brother. He also said he did not tell Congress about the offer in case some members might be interested in the offer. He proposed to use the ploy previously tried by Major General Philip Schuyler in upstate New York in 1777, when a fake positive response was sent to a British inquiry. The British discovered that their original letter had been found, and Schuyler's plan failed. Sullivan's plan was to advise four trusted members of Congress that he was going to send a messenger to New York to find out General Clinton's "plan of corruption." La Luzerne disapproved of Sullivan's plan.[37] He asked Sullivan if he thought there were members of Congress who would take advantage of the British overtures. Without naming them, Sullivan indicated he was concerned about two delegates.

Luzerne sent a lengthy report about the British attempt on John Sullivan to France's foreign minister, Charles Gravier comte de Vergennes. Luzerne mentioned that after he discovered Sullivan's financial problems, he gave Sullivan seventy-two pounds in the disguise of a loan during the previous year. Luzerne also wrote that John Sullivan told his brother to tell the people "who sent him that their overture had been received with the deepest scorn." Luzerne said that John Sullivan's report was basically true but that he did not believe he had sent "a message so haughty and so insulting to the English." Luzerne added that John Sullivan had a good reputation, and that he did not think and did not suspect that Sullivan's plan of correspondence was a cover for a clandestine adventure. Vergennes wrote back on July 27, 1781, that he approved the payments to John Sullivan as long as he was a member of Congress. The payments were to be recorded as "extraordinary expenses" without Sullivan's name.[38]

Captain Sullivan was sent back to Philadelphia, where he arrived on July 12, with a letter for his brother from Holland dated June 9.[39] Holland was asking for a response to his original letter and indicated the eagerness of British headquarters due to the response his brother had brought back. Holland advised him to have the bearer of his response "inquire for me at Messrs. Mills and Hicks, No. 2, Queen Street, New York." The letter played on his emotions: "For God's sake, for the sake of your family say you will assist; I have too much reliance on your honor to doubt it, and reflect, in how exalted a station a grateful nation will put the man, most instrumental in restoring it to peace and happiness; your own terms when you name them shall be scrupulously adhered to." To ensure secrecy, only his brother would carry the communications.[40]

Holland claimed to be in full confidence with General Clinton, who he said urged him to write the letter. Holland said that once John Sullivan agreed to the proposal and determined a means to communicate, they would stop using his brother. Sullivan was trying to do what he could to protect his brother and get him exchanged. John Sullivan arranged with Holland to exchange his brother, but Captain Sullivan died unexpectedly while he was waiting to be exchanged.[41]

On September 10, 1782, General Sullivan, in order to repay the favors Holland provided, wrote John Langdon, speaker of the New Hampshire House of Representatives. Some of the favors Holland had provided were having Captain Sullivan released from the

prison ship and placed on parole, and
notifying General Sullivan of his brother's death and arranging for his burial.
Sullivan requested that Holland's wife,
Jane, be allowed to come from New
York to visit her children at
Londonderry, under whatever restric-
tions the New Hampshire legislature
felt were necessary.[42] On September
12, the New Hampshire General
Assembly sent the request to committee.[43] General Sullivan wrote a follow-
up letter November 15 requesting an
answer.[44] The General Assembly
granted her permission to come to
Londonderry with her two daughters
who were with her and for her to stay
in the state to visit her children till the
last day of March 1783.[45] When word
that she could return was made public,

French print of Major
General John Sullivan from a
painting by Alexander
Campbell of Williamsburg,
Virginia. He was a member
of the Continental Congress
1774–1775 and 1780–1781.
(*William L. Clements Library*)

there was concern that other loyalists would return. On December
26, the legislature rescinded its vote and forbade her entering the
state.[46] Meschach Weare, president (or governor) of New
Hampshire, notified Sullivan of the change.[47] Sullivan then wrote
to Holland and his wife to let them know. He sent them to
Washington to send to New York.[48] Washington indicated they
were sent by the first flag of truce.[49] This ended the correspondence between Holland and Sullivan. Nothing further has been
found concerning the attempt to turn John Sullivan to the British
side. No documentation was found that he supplied the British
with any military intelligence.

In September 1781, the British military had been able to discover
through William Rankin, a loyalist from York, Pennsylvania, who
was involved in several local plots and raising troops, that the
secret records of Congress were with Thomas McKean of

Delaware, the president of Congress, who lived at the house formerly belonging to Israel Pemberton, Jr. at 312 Chestnut Street west of South Third Street, Philadelphia. Pemberton, a merchant known as the "King of the Quakers," had been treated as a Tory for his strong stand against the Revolutionary War.[50]

Rankin's informant said there are always two soldiers on guard at the president's house, as well as a body of militia constantly in the city. He indicated that any attempt to steal the records would be dangerous and said placing someone on the president's staff was the best method to secure the secret documents.[51] Despite the risk, the British command decided to try to steal the documents. Captain George Beckwith, an assistant to Major De Lancey, gave the assignment to Lieutenant James Moody, the best field agent the British had. Moody was born in Little Egg Harbor, New Jersey, in 1744. His family moved to Sussex County, New Jersey, where Moody, a Newton farmer, had been trying to be a neutral. But Moody was pressured by rebels to take a side, and he chose the king. Moody enlisted in the New Jersey Volunteers under the command of General Cortland Skinner in 1777. Skinner made him an ensign (third lieutenant) in 1778, explaining the promotion by saying he preferred Moody over another soldier because he "has behaved well and has recruited 17 Men."[52] In 1777, the state of New Jersey had ordered that Moody be arrested on sight, and in 1778, it ordered that his property in Sussex County be confiscated.

One American army officer described Moody as "an artful and enterprising fellow employed by the British [who has several times] succeeded in taking our mail from the post rider on the road, though he has had some very remarkable escapes."[53] He had spied on troop movements of Generals Washington, Sullivan, and Gates. He was able to steal the dispatches to Congress and the Continental Army concerning the council of war between Generals Washington and Rochambeau held at the Joseph Webb house in Weathersfield, Connecticut. His escapes would have made Houdini proud: he and his comrades were once cornered on three sides in the Palisade Highlands on the New Jersey side of the Hudson River and made their escape by jumping off a high cliff.

Lieutenant Moody; his brother, John; and a Thomas Addison left for the village of Cooper's Ferry (now Camden), New Jersey, opposite Philadelphia. On the morning of November 7, 1781, John Moody and Addison went to Philadelphia to steal congressional documents. There Addison turned John Moody over to the Americans. The Philadelphia Light Horse was sent to New Jersey to search for Lieutenant Moody from Cooper's Ferry to Egg Harbor, which is forty-five miles to the east. It was thought that Moody would spend the night at Egg Harbor.[54] But he hid in a haystack that had been searched before he entered it and was not discovered.

Newspapers reported that the court-martial of two spies— Corporal Lawrence Marr of the 1st Battalion, New Jersey Volunteers, and John Moody—began on November 8 at Philadelphia, presided over by the Marquis de Lafayette. It continued for two days, and the verdict—guilty of spying—was delivered on November 11. Marr and Moody were sentenced to be executed.[55]

A person from Philadelphia sent a local newspaper account to British headquarters in New York City. The most damaging news was that Addison had provided the names of many people to the Americans.[56] British headquarters received a report on November 15 from Lieutenant William Digby Lawler of the Queen's Rangers, who was returning from Yorktown, Virginia, that Lieutenant James Moody had not been captured but his brother John had.[57] He reported that John Moody and Marr had been found guilty and were to be executed.[58]

Major Daniel Isaac Browne of the 4th Battalion of New Jersey Volunteers and a Joseph Hayden proposed to take six men to Philadelphia and "by contrivance or force or both" set Moody free. If that could not be done, then they wanted to capture Governor Livingston of New Jersey or some member of Congress, bring him near the British lines but not in them, and do to their captive whatever was done to Moody. They wanted arms, rations for seven days, thirty-one pounds and ten shillings for expenses, and fifty-two pounds and ten shillings for everyone involved when the mission was completed. On April 25, 1778, Browne had been placed on half pay, or retired status, because of a reorganization of the army that reduced the number of officers needed. Browne would have looked at this venture as his chance to return to a field command and full pay.[59] But Browne and Hayden's proposals were never enacted, and Browne's status remained unchanged for the balance of the war.

The *Pennsylvania Gazette* of November 14 and the *Philadelphia Packet* of November 15 reported that John Moody was executed on the commons on November 13 between 11 a.m. and noon.[60] The *Packet* further stated that the plot to steal the secret records of Congress was the idea of Benedict Arnold and that the men were to receive five hundred and twenty-five pounds if successful.[61] The Boston newspapers incorrectly reported that Marr was executed on November 23.[62] He was never executed.

In a letter written to Livingston January 12–13, 1782, Washington expressed his frustration at not being able to execute James Moody as a spy:

> It is a pity that villain Moody could be apprehended lurking in the country, in a manner which would bring him under the description of a Spie. When he was taken before [at Liberty Pole, New Jersey], he was in arms in his proper uniform with a party, and had his commission in his pocket. It was therefore a matter of great doubt whether he could have been considered otherwise than a prisoner of war. It was said he had been inlisting men in the country but no proof of the kind ever appeared.[63]

Conclusion

Espionage activity in Pennsylvania during the American Revolution was widespread across the state and was crucial to the outcome of the war. As we have read, out west, at Pittsburgh, American intelligence was concerned with the British and loyalists at Fort Detroit, the Indians who remained friendly to the British, and the local Pennsylvania residents who were pro-British. The British had suspected the Moravian missionaries who lived among the Indians in the Ohio country were also working as spies for the Americans. Having detained missionaries suspected of espionage, however, each time the British were forced to release them for lack of evidence. The surprise discovery was finding a letter from John Heckewelder, a Moravian missionary, who admitted to working as a spy for the Americans.[1] Espionage would also play a role in the Indiana and Illinois country during the American Revolution. It did not provide any great military advantage to either side on the critical Pennsylvania frontier, but it helped to maintain the status quo.

The British had an interest in loyalist activities at Lancaster and York, Pennsylvania. They maintained contact with Dr. Henry Norris and Colonel William Rankin, the loyalist leaders in the area, through Andrew Fürstner who was Rankin's brother-in-law. Rankin had proposed a general loyalist uprising. General Sir Henry Clinton considered the proposal important but did not make plans to execute it until 1781. Clinton, as he had done in the past with the Pennsylvania Line Mutiny, would not make a move without consulting his longtime confidant General William Phillips. However Phillips died on May 13, 1781, in Virginia before providing any analysis. The plan called for Lord Cornwallis to supply the troops who would assist the loyalists in central Pennsylvania. His surrender at Yorktown caused the plan to be cancelled. The uprising never happened due to Clinton's indecisiveness and bad timing. I found that the British spy network at Lancaster and York did provide assitance to the British cause by helping escaping British and Hessian soldiers, many of whom were prisoners from General John Burgoyne's "convention army," make their way across the state and into New Jersey, where British contacts would make arrangements to get the escapees safely back to British territory.

As expected, I found that espionage activity in Philadelphia changed as the war progressed. At the beginning of the war, the British were interested in simply gathering intelligence on the rebels. When the First Continental Congress met in Philadelphia, delegates pledged to keep their transactions secret. Before I started my research, I knew that Royal Governor William Franklin of New Jersey had been forwarding information on Congress to the British authorities. There were a couple of possibilities as to whom provided this intelligence from Philadelphia. I found that Governor Franklin confirmed his source as Joseph Galloway, a member of Congress. Royal Governor William Tryon of New York also had a spy who reported on Congress, James Brattle servant to James Duane, delegate from New York.

When General George Washington, commander in chief of the Continental Army, was forced to abandon Philadelphia, he instructed General Mifflin to set up a spy system in the city, something he had neglected to do in New York City. Washington's instruction included the recruiting of Quakers as spies. Because Quakers were considered pacifists, they were thought to be non-combatants and not a threat by the British. Some of the responsibility of developing this spy network was delegated to Major John Clark Jr.

Clark would successfully run a spy ring in Philadelphia that provided timely intelligence. He recruited Quakers as spies as instructed and they provided him with good intelligence. With information provided by his spy network, Clark had warned Washington that the British planned to attack the Continental Army in force in December 1777, several days in advance of its occurrence. General Howe came out of Philadelphia, as Clark had predicted, with 10,000 men in an attempt to crush and destroy the Continental Army. Because the Continental Army was prepared,

Howe was only able to engage in several skirmishes and was unable to engage Washington in a decisive battle. Howe broke off the attack and returned to Philadelphia without his victory. The Continental Army was intact and safely moved to Valley Forge for the winter. Washington had won a strategic victory based upon intelligence provided by Major Clark and his spies.

The papers of General William Howe, commander in chief of British forces from October 10, 1775, to May 18, 1778, were destroyed when a family seat at Westport, Ireland, burned in the early nineteenth century. Because of the lack of his papers, it is difficult to determine how successful the British intelligence activities were during his command. There were most likely other British spy activities which have not yet been discovered. Samuel Wallis a merchant from Philadelphia and Muncy, Pennsylvania, provided intelligence to the British throughout the war. Over the course of my research I discovered more of Wallis's activities; however, I suspect much of the early documentation on Wallis was destroyed with Howe's papers.

Despite not having Howe's papers, I was able determine how the British intelligence network in Philadelphia operated during their occupation. Information gathered by Philadelphians and other loyalists, including Joseph Galloway and Dr. Henry Stevenson, was provided to Ambrose Serle, confidential secretary to Admiral Howe and Nisbet Balfour, aide-de-camp to General Howe. While General Howe was in Philadelphia from September 1777 to June 1778, he used Nisbet Balfour to coordinate his secret service operation. He also employed Lieutenant John Doyle, and Francis, Lord Rawdon, of the 5th Regiment of Foot in this calling.[2]

Every discussion of American spies in Philadelphia always arrives, sooner or later, at Lydia Darragh. As I have related, Lydia and William, her husband, were American spies who lived in Philadelphia and operated during the British occupation. Their older son was a lieutenant in the 2nd Pennsylvania Regiment of the Continental Line.[3] Some have doubted that she could have gotten out of the city. However I found that on December 3, 1777, the highways from Philadelphia to Germantown and Frankford, and the road to Trenton by way of Jenkintown, were open to anyone who wanted. She or anyone else could have traveled out of

Philadelphia on those roads passed the British redoubts without being stopped. I discovered a letter dated December 4, 1777, from Frankford attributed to a "W. D."–William Darragh–who had been in Philadelphia. It was a report on the British army's preparations in Philadelphia to attack the Continental Army.[4] One of the embellishment to the story is that Lydia Darragh was the first to warn of the British attack on Philadelphia. This I found not to be true, as her intelligence would have only confirmed what General Washington already knew several days earlier from information provided by Major John Clark Jr.

After the British evacuation, both the British Army and the Continental Army would turn their espionage activities to New York City.

Ever since the French had entered the war in 1778, British troops were spread over the globe to protect their colonies. The number of soldiers available for service in North American dropped and the situation was deteriorating. With fewer soldiers to conduct the war in North America, it became more doubtful that the British would win a military victory there. The British began looking to win the political game for the control of territory at the peace negotiations. This, I related, manifested in the unsuccessful British attempt to turn congressmen Samuel Livermore and John Sullivan to their side. They also sent spies to steal the secret records of Congress which were with the president of Congress Thomas McKean. The plot was uncovered and the spy, John Moody, was hung.

Both the Americans and the British had their successes and failures with espionage in Pennsylvania, a key battleground in the intelligence war. As I have related in this book, the role of intelligence operations had a much more significant influence on the course of the war, particularly in Pennsylvania, than generally understood or appreciated. Without timely intelligence, Washington's army could have been destroyed on the outskirts of Philadelphia and history would have been altered.

APPENDIX A
Possible Loyalist Spy List

These are loyalists from Pennsylvania who, after the American Revolution, claimed to have spied or gathered intelligence for the British. I have been unable to totally confirm or reject their claims to have been spies. The word "spy" in the eighteenth century included doing reconnaissance at a distance. It should be noted that these people made these claims in an attempt to obtain money from the British government for their losses of property and businesses. In some cases their memorials, which we would call petitions, were complete fabrications; in other cases they were very factual.

Burns, Thomas, of Lower Providence, Chester County
De List, Frederick, resident of Philadelphia
Fox, Joseph, of Philadelphia, blacksmith
Henry, William, of Reading, Chester County, farmer[1]
Hood, Thomas, of Philadelphia, attorney[2]
Kirk, Samuel, of Philadelphia, merchant[3]
Loofbourrow, John, of Moreland Manor, Philadelphia County
Rice, James Jeremiah, of Philadelphia[4]
Sinclair, George, of Chester County, tanner and currier
Smithers, James, of Philadelphia, businessman
Snowden, Myles, of Philadelphia, brewer
Vernon, Gideon, of Susquehanna, farmer[5]
Walton, Jonathan, of Philadelphia[6]
Ware, Richard, of Philadelphia, sail maker[7]
Williams, John, of Gulf Road, Chester County, possibly a farmer[8]

1. William Henry claimed to have carried intelligence. 2. I think Thomas Hood's story is a fabrication. 3. Samuel Kirk claimed to be a spy who was not paid. Because he was not paid, he most likely was doing reconnaissance work. 4. James Rice claimed to have carried intelligence. 5. Gideon Vernon gathered intelligence about Valley Forge, but I was unable to determine if he went into the camp or collected his information from a distance. 6. Jonathan Walton appeared to have done reconnaissance. 7. Richard Ware appeared to have done reconnaissance. 8. I was unable to find evidence of the court-martial that John Williams claimed occurred. His claim as a spy is doubtful.

NOTES

ABBREVIATIONS

CP   Sir Henry Clinton Papers at the William L. Clements Library
GWP   George Washington Papers at the Library of Congress
HMC   Historical Manuscript Commission
JCC   Journals of the Continental Congress
Naval   Naval Documents of the American Revolution Series
PA Archives   Pennsylvania Archives Series, which includes the early volumes
              issued as *Hazard's Register of Pennsylvania.*
PBF   Papers of Benjamin Franklin Series
PCC   Papers of the Continental Congress

INTRODUCTION

1. *American Quarterly Review,* vol. 1, no. 1 (March 1827) (Philadelphia: Robert Walsh), 32–34.

2. William Duane, ed., *Extracts from the Diary of Christopher Marshall, Kept in Philadelphia and Lancaster during the American Revolution, 1774–1781* (Albany, NY: Joel Munsell, 1877), 179, May 10, 1778.

3. *Pennsylvania Magazine of History and Biography,* vol. 17, no. 3 (1893): 343. Christopher Marshall Jr. to Christopher Marshall at Lancaster on January 28, 1778.

4. A vedette is a sentinel on horseback.

5. Bernhard A. Uhlendorf, trans. and annotator, *Revolution in America: Confidential Letters and Journals 1776–1784 of the Adjutant General Major Bauermeister of the Hessian Forces* (New Brunswick, NJ: Rutgers University Press, 1957), 134.

6. *Pennsylvania Magazine of History and Biography,* vol. 23 (1899): 89-90. Charles Darragh was born on November 18, 1755, and died June 5, 1801.

7. John Blair Linn and William H. Egle, eds., *Pennsylvania in the War of the Revolution, Battalions and Line, 1775–1783* (Harrisburg, PA: L. S. Hart, State Printer, 1880), vol. 1: 400.

8. *Pennsylvania Magazine of History and Biography,* vol. 36 (January 1912): 39. A footnote on page 39 indicates that Lieutenant Charles Darragh became a supernumerary in 1778.

9. *Pennsylvania Magazine of History and Biography,* vol. 23 (1899): 89.

10. *Philadelphia Monthly Meeting Minute Book for 1782-1789:* 47 and 101-102, Haverford College, Haverford, PA.

11. GWP, General Correspondence, Charles Craig at Frankford to George Washington, December 2, 1777.

12. GWP, General Correspondence, Charles Craig at Frankford to George Washington, November 20 and 28, 1777.

13. GWP, General Correspondence, American Intelligence Report to George Washington, December 4, 1777, from "W. D."

CHAPTER ONE

1. Lieutenant Nicholas de Sarrebourse de Pontleroy de Beaulieu's name appears as both Pontleroy and Beaulieu in documents.

2. *American Historical Review* (Washington, DC: American Historical Association, October 1895 to present), vol. 31 (1925-1926): 25, Claude H. Van Tyne, French Aid Before the Alliance of 1778.

3. George Bancroft, *History of the United States from the Discovery of the American Continent* (Boston: Little, Brown, 1856-1874), vol. 6: 25.

4. Bancroft, *History of the United States*, vol. 4: 193, Claude Louis Francois de Regnier, Count Guerchy (French ambassador at London) to le Duc de Choiseul, October 19, 1766.

5. Thomas Willing Balch, trans., *The French in America during the War of Independence 1777–1783* (Philadelphia: Porter and Coates, 1891), 54. Laura Charlotte Sheldon, *France and the American Revolution 1763–1778* (Ithaca, NY: Andrus and Church, 1900), 5-6. Choiseul was secretary of state for foreign affairs from December 3, 1758, to October 13, 1761, and from April 10, 1766, to December 24, 1770. Arnaud de Maurepas and Antoine Boulant, "*Les ministres et les ministères du siècle des Lumières (1715-1789): étude et dictionnaire*" (Paris: Christian, 1996). Choiseul was also secretary of state for the navy from October 13, 1761, to April 10, 1766, and secretary of state for war from January 26, 1761, to December 24, 1770.

6. Balch, *The French in America*: 54. One source states Johann de Kalb reached the rank of lieutenant colonel in the French army.

7. *Archives Diplomatiques for the Foreign secretary, Mémoires et documents*, 1-37. Friedrich Kapp, *The Life of John Kalb, Major-General in the Revolutionary Army* (New York: H. Holt, 1884), 46, Choiseul to de Kalb, April 20, 1767.

8. Marshal of France is not a military rank but a mark of exceptional achievement.

9. Kapp, *Life of Kalb*, 46-47, Choiseul to de Kalb, April 22, 1767.

10. *Archives Diplomatiques for the Foreign secretary, Mémoires et documents*: 1-37. Kapp, *Life of Kalb*, 48, de Kalb to Choiseul, July 15, 1767. The letter in the French archives is actually dated July 18, 1767.

11. Kapp, *Life of Kalb*, 49, Choiseul at Compiègne to de Kalb, August 19, 1767.

12. The de Kalb family home was at Courbevoye northwest of Paris.

13. Kapp, *Life of Kalb*, 48-51, de Kalb to Choiseul, October 1, 1767.

14. Rachel Marks was the second wife of Alexander Graydon and the mother of Captain Alexander Graydon (1752-1818) of the Third Pennsylvania Regiment. After the death of her husband in 1761, she moved from Bristol, Pennsylvania, to Philadelphia and took in boarders.

15. Thompson Westcott, *The Historic Mansions and Buildings of Philadelphia: With Some Notice of Their Owners and Occupants* (Philadelphia: Porter and Coates, 1877), 37-38. The main portion of the house had wings that projected to the street. The northern wall of the house was seventy to eighty feet long. The backyard was enclosed by a high wall.

16. Westcott, *Historic Mansions*, 48. A Mrs. Howells was the lessee in 1759.

17. Samuel Adams Drake, *Nooks and Corners of the New England Coast* (New York: Harper and Brothers, 1875), 387.

18. Adrien-Louis de Bonnières Comte de Guines had been a brigadier general in the French and Indian War and the French ambassador at Berlin in 1768-1769. He got his position as ambassador through the influence of Marie Antoinette.

19. Bancroft, *History of the United States*, vol. 8: 103.

20. *Naval Documents of the American Revolution Series* (Washington, DC: Government Printing Office, 1964 to present), vol. 4: 932, Notes on the Affairs Left Pending by Count de Guines and to be concluded by Mr. Garnier, February 23, 1776.

21. Ibid., vol. 3: 282. Achard de Bonvouloir to Count de Guines, December 28, 1775.

22. Ibid.

23. Paul H. Smith, et al., eds. *Letters of Delegates to Congress, 1774–1789* (Washington, DC: Library of Congress, 1976-2000), vol. 2: 542, Letter to Bonvouloir, late December 1775.

24. Leonard W. Labaree, ed., *The Papers of Benjamin Franklin* (New Haven, CT: Yale University Press, 1959 to present), vol. 22: 287, Benjamin Franklin to Charles-Guillaume-Frédéric Dumas, December 9, 1775. Reprinted from The Port Folio, 2 (1802), 236-237; extracts: American Philosophical Society; Archives du Ministère des affaires étrangères, Paris; Algemeen Rijksarchief, The Hague.

25. *Naval*, vol. 3: 279-285, Achard de Bonvouloir to Count de Guines, December 28, 1775.

26. James Parton, "Jefferson in the Continental Congress," *Atlantic Monthly*, vol. 29, issue 171, January 1872: 687. Carpenter's Hall is a two-story Georgian-style building fifty feet square with ten-foot cutouts at each corner. In 1774, it was the site of the first meeting of colonial delegates called the First Continental Congress.

27. *Naval*, vol. 3: 279-285, Achard de Bonvouloir to Count de Guines, December 28, 1775.

28. Archives du Ministere des Affaires Etrangeres, England supplement 18, folios 39-45.

29. Charles Forest was captain of the *St. John.*

30. *Naval*, vol. 3: 279-285, Achard de Bonvouloir to Count de Guines, December 28, 1775.

31. The only such correspondence that has been found appears in Carl Van Doren, *Benjamin Franklin* (New York: Viking, 1938), 539. It has been translated from Henri Doniol, *Historie de la participation de la France à l'établissement des États-Unis d'Amérique* (Paris, Imprimerie Nationale 1886-1892), vol. 1: 287-292. *Naval*, vol. 3: 279-285, Achard de Bonvouloir to Count de Guines, December 28, 1775.

32. Worthington C. Ford, et al., eds., *Journals of the Continental Congress, 1774-1789* (Washington, DC: Government Printing Office, 1904-1937), vol. 6: 986, June

12, 1776. Congress resolved that a committee of five should be appointed "by the name of the Board of War and Ordnance" to have a secretary and one or more clerks. On the following day, John Adams, Roger Sherman, Benjamin Harrison, James Wilson, and Edward Rutledge were elected commissioners, and Richard Peters, secretary. Before July 23, 1776, the Pennsylvania Council of Safety was known as the Committee of Safety. A Committee of Safety was a board established by patriot elements at the state or local level to oversee matters of defense and, sometimes, jurisprudence.

33. Samuel Hazard, *Pennsylvania Archives First Series* (Harrisburg, PA: Joseph Severns, 1852-1856), vol. 3: 138, Lord Loudoun at New York to Governor William Denny of Pennsylvania, April 19, 1757.

34. John Hay, *Answers to a Printed Libel Entitled A Representation to the Public of Affairs between Gilbert Barkly of Philadelphia and John Hay of Quebec* (Quebec: Brown and Gilmore, 1764). Barkly had brought John Hay from Scotland.

35. Gilbert Barkly, *A Reply to John Hay's Answer to Gilbert Barkly's Representation to the Publick* (Quebec: Brown and Gilmore, 1764), and Gilbert Barkly, *A Representation to the Public of Affairs between Gilbert Barkly of Philadelphia and John Hay of Quebec* (Quebec: Brown and Gilmore, 1764).

36. Francis Samuel Drake, *Tea Leaves: Being a Collection of Letters, and Documents Relating to the Shipment of Tea to the American Colonies in the Year 1773, by the East India Tea Company* . . . . (Boston: A. O. Crane, 1884), 199-202, Gilbert Barkly to directors of the East India Company, May 26, 1773.

37. Drake, *Tea Leaves*, 211-212, Grey Cooper to –- [Received by Henry Crabb Boulton], June 5, 1773. Grey Cooper was born circa 1726, was a native of Newcastle-on-Tyne, England, and died in 1801. He was a member of Parliament (1765–1784, 1786–1790), secretary to the treasury (1765-1782), and lord of the treasury (1783). He was a close friend of Benjamin Franklin's in London, but political differences resulting from the American Revolution seem to have damaged their relationship.

38. Drake, *Tea Leaves*, 215, William Settle for the Committee of Warehouses to Brook Watson et al., June 25, 1773.

39. Drake, *Tea Leaves*, 216-217, Gilbert Barkly, Lombard Street, to chairman and deputy chairman of the East India Company, June 29, 1773.

40. Drake, *Tea Leaves*, 239 and 238, William Settle for the Committee of Warehouses to Jonathan Clark et al., August 4, 1773. William Ross offered the security for Barkly.

41. The *Polly* was commanded by a Captain Samuel Ayres.

42. *Historical Magazine, and Notes and Queries Concerning the Antiquities, History, and Biography of America* (Boston: C.B. Richardson, 1857-1875), April 1864: 149. Captain Hazelwood is reputed to have been employed in constructing the chevaux-de-frise in the Delaware River and later assisted a Captain Machen in the construction of one in the Hudson River at Fort Montgomery.

43. A copy of this report is printed in the *Pennsylvania Magazine of History and Biography*, vol. 85: 34-37.

44. Peter Wilson Coldham, *American Migrations 1765-1799* (Baltimore: Genealogical Publishing, 2000), 450. Geoffrey Seed, "A British Spy in Philadelphia, Pennsylvania," *Magazine of History and Biography*, vol. 85 (1961): 3-37. In London in 1785, Barkly submitted a claim for his expenditures incurred in government service in Philadelphia.

45. The London Coffee House was at Front and High (present day Market) streets. It was opened for business in 1754, by printer William Bradford. It closed during the British occupation. In 1791, it was converted to a general store. It was later torn down.

46. Swan shot is made by melting lead and pouring it through a mesh or screen into a bucket of water. It is irregular in shape rather than round, like regular shot.

47. There were two people named Dr. John Kearsley in Philadelphia in the 1770s: the elder, who was the architect of the Pennsylvania State House and who died in 1772 at age eighty-eight, and his nephew, the Tory. Duane, *Extracts from the Diary of Christopher Marshall, Kept in Philadelphia and Lancaster during the American Revolution, 1774–1781*: 41, September 6, 1775. John F. Watson, *Annals of Philadelphia*, (Philadelphia: E. S. Stuart, 1877), vol. 2: 388.

48. Leonard Snowden emigrated from England to Carolina in 1767. After three years, his family moved to Burlington, New Jersey, and then to Philadelphia. In 1774, they entered a business partnership. His son Myles claimed to have collected valuable intelligence and was on his way to New York when he was betrayed by a servant, which caused him to be confined. Coldham, *American Migrations*, 486.

49. Samuel Hazard, *Pennsylvania Colonial Records Series* (Harrisburg, PA: T. Fenn, 1838-1853), vol. 10: 358-359, October 7, 1775.

50. Duane, *Extracts from the Diary of Christopher Marshall*, 46, October 6, 1775.

51. Ibid.

52. Hazard, *Pennsylvania Colonial Records*, vol. 10: 358-359, October 7, 1775. James Brooks is listed in the records as I. Brooks, J. Brooks, and John Brooks. John Kearsley had written to Lieutenant Robert Douglas, Royal Artillery at Boston.

53. Richard M. Lederer Jr., *Colonial American English* (Essex, CT: Verbatim Books, 1985), 166. Parole is a shortened form of the French *parole d'honneur*, which when translated means "word of honor."

54. Hazard, *Pennsylvania Colonial Records*, vol. 10: 361, October 8, 1775.

55. Duane, *Extracts from the Diary of Christopher Marshall*: 46, October 8, 1775.

56. Hazard, *Pennsylvania Colonial Records*, vol. 10: 361, October 8, 1775.

57. Duane, *Extracts from the Diary of Christopher Marshall*, 46, October 9, 1775.

58. Hazard, *Pennsylvania Colonial Records*, vol. 10: 362, October 10, 1775.

59. Francis Randolph Packard, ed., *Annals of Medical History* (New York: Paul B. Hoeber, 1918-1942), vol. 3: 401.

60. Hazard, *Pennsylvania Colonial Records*, vol. 10: 365-367, October 14, 1775, and 698, August 24, 1776. It was not until August 24, 1776, that Brooks was permitted to walk in the prison yard.

61. Ibid., 371, October 18, 1775.

62. Duane, *Extracts from the Diary of Christopher Marshall*, 238, March 29, 1780. There is a Carter who in March 1780 is banished from Pennsylvania. It is unknown if this is the same Carter. Hazard, *Pennsylvania Colonial Records*, vol. 10: 371-372, October 18, 1775.

63. Hazard, *Pennsylvania Colonial Records*, vol. 10: 381, pay order dated October 23, 1775 at Philadelphia.

64. Ibid., 403, November 15, 1775.

65. Ibid., 502-503, March 4, 1776, and 408-409, November 23, 1775.

66. Ibid., 373-374, and 380-381, October 19 and 24, 1775. US Naval Observatory, http://aa.usno.navy.mil/data/docs/RS_OneDay.php, for October 24, 1775, at Philadelphia. Dawn was at 6:21 a.m.

67. Hazard, *Pennsylvania Colonial Records*, vol. 10: 385, October 30, 1775. On October 28, 1775, the Pennsylvania Committee of Safety in Philadelphia received a letter written October 24, 1775, from the Lancaster Committee of Safety. It reported that Brooks and Kearsley had arrived safely and were confined in their jail.

68. Ibid., 773, October 31, 1776.

69. Duane, *Extracts from the Diary of Christopher Marshall*, 143-144, November 4, 1777. James Kearsley was buried at the church in Carlisle, which infuriated some parishioners.

70. Duane, *Extracts from the Diary of Christopher Marshall*, 131-132, October 4, 1777, and 152, December 27, 1777.

71. *Proceedings of the Massachusetts Historical Society*, vol. 50 (1917): 493-494, William Lee at London to Josiah Quincy Jr.

72. Mary D. McConaghy, Michael Silberman, and Irina Kalashnikova, "Penn in the 18th Century," University Archives and Records Center (Philadelphia: University of Pennsylvania, 2004), http://www.archives.upenn.edu/histy/features/1700s/penn1700s.html. General Alumni Catalog of the University of Pennsylvania. The name was changed from College of Philadelphia to University of Pennsylvania in 1779.

73. Ibid., http://www.archives.upenn.edu/people/1700s/smith_wm.html.

74. *Proceedings of the Massachusetts Historical Society*, vol. 50 (1917): 494, William Lee at London to unknown but probably Josiah Quincy Jr.

CHAPTER TWO

1. JCC, vol. 1: 26, September 6, 1774. "Resolved, That the doors be kept shut during the time of business, and that the members consider themselves under the strongest obligations of honour, to keep the proceedings secret, until the majority shall direct them to be made public."

2. Historical Manuscript Commission, Manuscripts of the Earl of Dartmouth, American Papers, vol. 2: 275, Secret Intelligence, endorsed correspondence between Governor Franklin and Mr. Galloway in February and March 1775. A copy is also in the British National Archives, America and West Indies, vol. 195,

folio 233, and Bancroft, *History of the United States*, vol. 7: 126. Oliver C. Kuntzleman, who wrote his biographical dissertation on Galloway, was also of the opinion that Galloway was the source of the leaks from the First Continental Congress to the British ministry. William Franklin, the royal governor of New Jersey, reported to the Royal Commission on the Losses and Services of American Loyalists on February 18, 1784, that Galloway sent his reports to London through him. Joseph Galloway was born at West River, Anne Arundel County, Maryland, in 1731. His family moved to Pennsylvania in 1740. He practiced law in Philadelphia. Galloway's home is known as Trevose Manor and is at 5408 Old Trevose Road, Bensalem Township, Pennsylvania. It is said to have been built between 1681 and 1685. See Coldham, *American Migrations*, 461, for a list of Galloway's vast land holdings.

3. Ford, *Letters of William Lee*, vol. 1: 127, Benjamin Franklin to Joseph Galloway, February 25, 1775. Bigelow, *The Complete Works of Benjamin Franklin*, vol. 5: 435.

4. Ibid., 127-128, William Lee at London to Richard Henry Lee, February 25, 1775.

5. John Jay Papers, Public Records Office, Image Library, National Archives, United Kingdom, John Jay to [Reverend John] Vardill, September 24, 1774.

6. Bancroft, *History of the United States*, vol. 7: 126.

7. Peter Force, *American Archives*, reprint of 1837-1853 editions (New York: Johnson Reprint, 1972), series 5, vol. 1: 1193, Ben Franklin to General Gates, August 28, 1776.

8. JCC, vol. 5: 653-655. On August 27, 1776, Congress adjusted the offer of land according to rank (see pp 705-709). George Washington Papers, Varick Transcripts, Letterbook 10: 157-158, George Washington to Continental Congress, August 18, 1776.

9. GWP, Varick Transcripts, Letterbook 1: 369, General Orders, August 25, 1776. JCC, vol. 6: 971-972, Resolve of November 22, 1776.

10. Christopher Ludwick was born in Geissen, Germany, on October 17, 1720. He became a baker like his father. He served in the military from 1737 to 1741. About 1746, he went to sea. After seven years as a sailor, he immigrated to Philadelphia in 1754 and made a living as a baker. In May 1777, Congress appointed him superintendent of bakers. He died on June 17, 1801, in Philadelphia. Samuel Hazard, *Hazard's Register of Pennsylvania Devoted to the Preservation of Facts and Documents and Every Other Kind of Useful Information Respecting the State of Pennsylvania* (Philadelphia: William F. Geddes, 1828-1836), vol. 9, no. 11: 161. He owned nine houses in Philadelphia and a farm near Germantown.

11. Carl E. Prince, ed., *The Papers of William Livingston* (1774-1988), (Trenton, NJ: New Jersey Historical Commission, 1979), vol. 1: 119, Joseph Reed at New York to William Livingston, August 19, 1776.

12. GWP, General Correspondence, Hugh Mercer to George Washington, July 16, 1776.

13. Prince, *Papers of William Livingston*, vol. 1: 124, William Livingston at Elizabeth Town to Hugh Mercer, August 23, 1776.

14. GWP, Varick Transcripts, Letterbook 10: 183-184, George Washington to Continental Congress, August 26, 1776.

15. John C. Fitzpatrick, ed., *Writings of George Washington from the Original Manuscript Sources, 1745-1799* (Washington, DC: Government Printing Office, 1931-1944), vol. 5: 496.

16. Uhlendorf, *Revolution in America*, 41.

17. Parliament of Great Britain, *The Examination of Joseph Galloway, esq. Late Speaker of the House of Assembly of Pennsylvania before the House of Commons in a Committee on the American Papers with Explanatory Notes* (London: J. Wilkie, 1779), 14. Joseph Galloway died in Watford, Herts, England, on August 29, 1803.

18. Oswald Tilghman, *Memoir of Lieutenant Colonel Tench Tilghman: Secretary and Aid to Washington* (Albany, NY: J. Munsell, 1876), 147-148, Tench Tilghman at Coryell's Ferry to James Tilghman, December 16, 1776. Tench Tilghman does not provide the source of the letter. Several Philadelphians are possible sources, such as Andrew, John, and William Allen. They were seen at Trenton by Captain Francis Murray. Andrew Allen was also seen by someone named McPherson. Tilghman, *Memoir of Lieutenant Colonel Tench Tilghman*, 151-153, Tench Tilghman to James Tilghman, February 22, 1777.

19. John Hill Martin, *Martin's Bench and Bar of Philadelphia* (Philadelphia: Rees Welch, 1883), 131. William H. W. Sabine, ed., *Historical Memoirs of William Smith 1763-1778*, vol. 2 (New York: New York Times and Arno Press, 1969), vol. 2: xii and 103-104. John Patterson had been the royal customs collector in Philadelphia in 1772, and deputy collector in 1774. His tombstone in Christ Church graveyard says he was born in Ireland and was a former officer in the British army. He died on February 24, 1798.

20. Christopher Marshall was born in Dublin, Ireland, in 1709, and was educated in England. He was a Quaker and had three sons. He was disowned by his family for emigrating to the American colonies without his parents' approval.

21. McConaghy, et al., "Penn in the 18th Century," http://www.archives.upenn.edu/people/1700s/fooks_paul.html. Duane, *Extracts from the Diary of Christopher Marshall*, 53, December 10, 1775. Paul Fooks lived on Second Street until 1775, when he moved to Arch Street. Marshall had given Fooks a window blind for his library room, two quarts of old French brandy, and a plate of choice red herring for the feast of Saint Nicholas on December 6.

22. *The (Philadelphia) Freeman's Journal, or, the North American Intelligencer*, August 15, 1781. In a newspaper article written in 1781, John Bayard, John Cox, and Joseph Reed had a lapse of memory and stated the date was January 7, 1776, and referred to Brattle as Rattle.

23. Bancroft, *History of the United States*, vol. 7: 215.

24. Duane, *Passages from the Diary of Christopher Marshall*, 63.

25. Sabine, *Historical Memoirs of William Smith 1763-1778*, vol. 2: 103-104. William Smith, royal chief justice of New York, said in his memoirs that the information was passed to the keeper of the Tryon Arms on Broadway and then to

Governor Tryon on the British warship *Asia*. Neither the keeper nor the Tryon Arms have been identified. The Tryon Arms was probably a tavern or inn, and the keeper would be the owner or manager of the business.

26. Norris Stanley Barratt and Julius Friedrich Sachse, *Freemasonry in Pennsylvania, 1727-1907, as Shown by the Records of Lodge No. 2, F. and A. M. of Philadelphia from the Year A.L. 5757, A.D. 1757* (Lancaster, PA: New Era Printing, 1909), 55n3. Joseph Dean was the son of Reverend William Dean, a Presbyterian clergyman. He was born August 10, 1738, at Ballymenagh, County Antrim, Ireland. He signed the Nonimportation Agreement. In December 1776, the Pennsylvania Assembly appointed him to the Committee of Safety.

27. In 1775, Joseph Reed was president of the Pennsylvania Convention, which was setting up a state government, and aide-de-camp to General George Washington. Later he would become governor of Pennsylvania.

28. Hall and Seller's was owned by David Hall Jr., William Hall, and William Sellers from 1772 to 1804.

29. Duane, *Passages from the Diary of Christopher Marshall*, 63-64.

30. Francis B. Heitman, *Historical Register of Officers of the Continental Army during the War of the Revolution, April, 1775, to December, 1783* (Washington, DC: Rare Book Shop Publishing, 1914), 118, indicates Abraham Brasher was a second lieutenant in the 1st New York Regiment. E. B. O'Callaghan, *Documents Relative to the Colonial History of New York* (Albany, NY: Weed, Parsons, 1857), vol. 8: 601, indicates he was a second lieutenant in a grenadier company of New York, which wore blue uniforms with red facings.

31. Force, *American Archives*, series 4, vol. 5: 44-45, Christopher Marshall's report, January 9, 1776, Philadelphia. *Freeman's Journal*, August 15, 1781; and *Naval*, vol. 3: 699-700.

32. O'Callaghan, *Documents Relative to the Colonial History of New York*, vol. 8: 645n1, Governor Tryon to Earl of Dartmouth, December 6, 1775.

33. "Extract of a Letter from New York," *Lloyd's Evening Post and British Chronicle*, London, April 17 to 19, 1776, March 2, 1776.

34. *Letters of Delegates to Congress*, vol. 2: 326, November 9, 1775, citing *Journals of New York Provincial Congress*, 2: 107.

35. British Archives, C.O. 5, 1107: 11 and 29.

36. *Naval* 2: 1050-1051, citing British National Archives, Public Record Office, Admiralty 1/484, which indicated that the letter was forwarded by Tryon and received in Vice Admiral Molyneux Shuldham's letter of January 19, 1776.

37. Sabine, *Historical Memoirs of William Smith 1763-1778*, vol. 2: 103-104.

38. HMC, *Manuscripts of the Earl of Dartmouth, American Papers*, vol. 2, 14th report, appendix, part 10, 1895 (reprint, Boston: Gregg Press, 1972, 401-402, Congress Minutes and Resolution.

39. James Duane married Maria Livingston, daughter of Robert Livingston. They had three children: James Chatham Duane, Mary Duane, and Adelia Duane.

40. Smith, *Letters of Delegates to Congress*, vol. 3: 297, James Duane to Mary Duane, February 22, 1776.

41. Ibid., vol. 3: 414-416, James Duane to Robert R. Livingston, March 20, 1776.

42. Robert R. Livingston (1746-1813) was recalled by New York before he could sign the Declaration of Independence. He was the first chancellor of New York, its highest judicial office, from 1777 to 1801, and was often called chancellor even after leaving office. He administered the presidential oath of office to George Washington at Federal Hall in New York City in 1789.

43. Smith, *Letters of Delegates to Congress*, vol. 3: 303, John Jay at Elizabeth Town, New Jersey, to Robert R. Livingston, February 26, 1776.

44. Joseph Alfred Scoville, *The Old Merchants of New York* (New York: Carleton, 1885), vol. 4: 294.

45. *Virginia Gazette*, John Dixon and William Hunter Jr. owners, (Williamsburg, VA: 1775-1778), November 22, 1776, no. 1320: p. 1, col. 1.

46. Papers of the Continental Congress, 1774-1789, published and on microfilm (Washington, DC: National Archives and Records Service, General Services Administration, 1971), vol. 2: 221, July 29, 1775.

47. CP: 13:13, James Robertson at Boston to Sir Henry Clinton, January 13, 1776. Samuel Wallis's name appears as both Wallis and Wallace in the Sir Henry Clinton papers at the William L. Clements Library.

48. CP 13:15, James Robertson to Sir Henry Clinton, January 14, 1776.

49. CP 63:3, Joseph Stansbury to John André, July 12, 1779.

50. GWP, Varick Transcripts, Letterbook 3: 299, George Washington to Continental Congress, April 25, 1778.

51. GWP, Varick Transcripts, Letterbook 5: 380-381, George Washington to John Sullivan, June 10, 1778.

52. Roger W. Moss and Tom Crane, *Historic Houses of Philadelphia: A Tour of the Region's Museum Homes* (Philadelphia: University of Pennsylvania Press, 1998), 34.

53. GWP, Varick Transcripts, Letterbook 1: 146-148, George Washington to Henry Laurens, September 12, 1778.

54. Ballagh, James Curtis. *The Letters of Richard Henry Lee, Volume 1, 1762-1778.* (New York: Macmillan, 1911), vol. 1: 414-415. Henry Laurens to the Peace Commissioners, June 17, 1778.

55. William B. Reed, *Life and Correspondence of Joseph Reed: Military Secretary of Washington, at Cambridge, Adjutant-General of the Continental Army . . . .* (Philadelphia: Lindsay and Blakiston, 1847), vol. 1: 382-383.

56. Ibid., 383-388.

57. JCC, vol. 11, 770-774.

58. Most letters at this time used the back or blank side of a letter for the address. The letter would be folded allowing only the address to be visible and was sealed closed with wax. De Gimat's covering envelope contained a letter in French which requested a response to Lafayette's letter, which was enclosed.

59. The Earl of Carlisle's original letters can be found in HMC, 15th report, appendix, part 6, The Manuscripts of the Earl of Carlisle Preserved at Castle

Howard: 374. Lafayette at Fishkill, New York, to Lord Carlisle at New York, October 5, 1778, in French; Lieutenant Colonel de Gimat at Bedfort [Bedford], New York, to Lord Carlisle at New York, October 8, 1778, in French; and Carlisle to Lafayette, October 11, 1778. An English translation of Lafayette's and Carlisle's letters can be found in James Grant Wilson, *The Memorial History of the City of New York from its Founding to the Year 1892* (New York: New York History Company, 1892), vol. 2, 568. No translation was published of de Gimat's letter. De Gimat was born in 1747 in Gascony, the son of a French military officer.

CHAPTER THREE

1. Mrs. McCoy was unable to write, which caused much confusion as to her name.

2. Hazard, *Pennsylvania Archives First Series*, vol. 5: 277-278, examination of Sarah O'Bryan [O'Brien], March 27, 1777.

3. Reed, *Life and Correspondence of Joseph Reed*, vol. 2: 32. Smith, *Letters of Delegates to Congress*, vol. 6: 512, John Adams to Abigail Adams, March 31, 1777. Jared Sparks, *Correspondence of the American Revolution: Being Letters of Eminent Men to George Washington, from the Time of His Taking Command of the Army to the End of His Presidency* (Boston: Little, Brown, 1853), 363. Sparks states that Galloway made the deal with Molesworth, but it was done by Admiral Howe who had promised Molesworth a commission if successful. Galloway only made an introduction.

4. Peter Wilson Coldham, *American Loyalist Claims,* vol. 1, abstracted from the Public Records Office, series 13, bundles 1-35 and 37 (Washington, DC: National Genealogical Society, 1980), 443, and Coldham, *American Migrations*, 484. William Shepard had settled at Seventh Street in Philadelphia seven years before the American Revolution. His house was occupied by the British army from November 1777 to June 1778.

5. *Pennsylvania Gazette*, October 31, 1765.

6. *Pennsylvania Magazine of History and Biography*, vol. 81, no. 1 (January 1957): 39-68.

7. Coldham, *American Loyalist Claims*, 443, and Hugh E. Egerton, ed., *The Royal Commission on the Losses and Services of American Loyalists, 1783-1785* (Oxford: H. Hart at the Oxford University Press, 1915, reprinted New York: Burt Franklin, 1971), 291, memorial of William Shepard, January 27, 1785.

8. Most likely the husband of Mrs. O'Brien.

9. Hazard, *Pennsylvania Archives First Series*, vol. 5: 270-271, statement from John Snyder about Higgons, March 27, 1777.

10. Ibid., 271-272, examination of John Eldridge, March 27, 1777.

11. Ibid.

12. Ibid., 272, examination of Andrew Higgons, March 27, 1777, and 273-275, examination of John Snyder, March 27, 1777.

13. Reed, *Life and Correspondence of Joseph Reed*, 32.

14. Hazard, *Pennsylvania Archives First Series*, vol. 5: 273-275, examination of John Snyder, March 27, 1777, and 276-278, examination of Joseph Molesworth, March 27, 1777.

15. Ibid., 280-281, Confession of James Molesworth, and Pennsylvania War Office to General Benjamin Lincoln, March 31, 1777.

16. Hazard, *Pennsylvania Archives First Series*, vol. 5: 272-273, examination of Andrew Higgons of Philadelphia, March 27, 1777.

17. Coldham, *American Migrations*, 484, and Egerton, *Royal Commission on the Losses*, 291, memorial of William Shepard, January 27, 1785.

18. Reed, *Life and Correspondence of Joseph Reed*, 32.

19. Massachusetts Historical Society, Adams Family Papers, John Adams to Abigail Adams, March 31, 1777.

20. JCC 7: 210, March 31, 1777.

21. Smith, *Letters of Delegates to Congress*, vol. 6: 514, John Hancock to Horatio Gates, March 31, 1777.

22. Massachusetts Historical Society, Adams Family Papers, John Adams to Abigail Adams, March 31, 1777, and Hazard, *Pennsylvania Archives First Series*, vol. 5: 270-282.

23. Reed, *Life and Correspondence of Joseph Reed*, 33.

24. Hazard, *Pennsylvania Archives First Series*, vol. 5: 290, War Office to Supreme Executive Council, April 2, 1777.

25. Ibid., 336, Supreme Executive Council to James Young, [undated] but sent May 9, 1777.

26. Ibid., 279 and 337-339, examination of Abigail McCoy, March 28, 1777, and May 13, 1777.

27. Ibid., 339-340, examination of Sarah O'Brien, May 13, 1777.

28. Ibid., 337, James Young to Timothy Matlack, secretary to the Supreme Executive Council, May 13, 1777.

29. Coldham, *American Migrations*, 449, and Gail Stuart Rowe, *Embattled Bench: The Pennsylvania Supreme Court and the Forging of a Democratic Society, 1684-1809* (Newark, DE: University of Delaware Press, 1994), 138. Israel Pemberton Jr. (1715-1779) was one of the managers of the Pennsylvania Hospital, along with Benjamin Franklin.

30. CP 231:28, Henry Stevenson Memorial to Sir Henry Clinton, September 13, 1780. John Graves Simcoe, *A History of the Operations of a Partisan Corps Called the Queen's Rangers* (New York: Bartlett & Welford, 1844), 56.

31. Coldham, *American Loyalist Claims*: 109-110. Smith, *Letters of Delegates to Congress*: vol. 6: 514, John Hancock to Horatio Gates, March 31, 1777.

32. Hazard, *Pennsylvania Archives First Series*, vol. 5: 279, examination of Abigail McKay [McCoy], March 28, 1777.

33. Ibid., 282, Pennsylvania Board of War to Israel Putnam, March 31, 1777, case of J. Molesworth.

34. Ibid., 281, Confession of James Molesworth, undated but March 30, 1777, and Pennsylvania War Office to General Banjamin Lincoln, March 31, 1777.

35. GWP, General Correspondence, George Washington to Joseph Reed and John Cox, April 7, 1777.

36. Archives of the State of New Jersey, series 2, vol. 1, *Documents Relating to the Revolutionary History of the State of New Jersey: Extracts from American Newspapers, 1776-1777* (Trenton, NJ: J. L. Murphy, 1901), 153, 334-335, and 344. Joseph Arrowsmith owned property in Hillsborough, Somerset County, New Jersey.

37. GWP, General Correspondence, Joseph Reed to George Washington, June 4, 1777.

38. *Bridgeton (NJ) Plain Dealer*, January 1776, 9.

39. GWP, Varick Transcript, Letterbook 3: 23-24, George Washington at Morris Town, New Jersey, to Joseph Reed and John Cox, April 7, 1777.

40. GWP, Varick Transcripts, Letterbook 2: 67-68, George Washington to Pennsylvania War Board, April 18, 1777, and GWP, Letterbook 2: 239-244, George Washington to Continental Congress, April 18, 1777. The individuals Washington identified may have been Robert Brown and Lawrence Hartshorne. Hartshorne was from the Hartshorne family of Black Point, New Jersey. Abraham Woodhull was part of George Washington's Culper spy ring in New York City. In one of his intelligence reports, he stated that Brown frequently had loyalist refugees at his house in Shrewsbury, New Jersey, and stayed in con-tact with them. John Hartshorne was born in 1725 and owned the Black Point Inn, which was at the northeast end of Rumson Neck, earlier known as Ramson's Neck. Rumson Neck was at Black Point, which previously was known as Passage Point. John Hartshorne had a brother Robert (1721-1805) and an older brother Hugh (1717-1777) who married Hannah Pattison, and they lived in Philadelphia. The Hartshornes were considered to be loyalist sympa-thizers. John's son John had run off and joined the British army.

41. GWP, Varick Transcripts, Letterbook 2: 76-77, George Washington to Pennsylvania War Board, April 26, 1777.

42. GWP, Varick Transcripts, Letterbook 2: 76-77, George Washington to Pennsylvania War Board, April 26, 1777.

43. There were two John Taylors. John Taylor (1751-1801) from Middlesex County, New Jersey, served in the Middlesex County militia. The other John Taylor (1716-ca. 1798) was from Middletown, Monmouth County, New Jersey, and was a loyalist who was held in the jail at Burlington, New Jersey.

44. W. S. W. Ruschenberger, *Obituary Notice of Dr. Robert Bridges* (read before the American Philosophical Society, February 15, 1884), *Proceedings of the American Philosophical Society*, vol. 21, No. 115, (Philadelphia: American Philosophical Society, 1884), 429. William Cliffton was born March 4, 1729, in Philadelphia and died February 24, 1802. He was a Quaker blacksmith who lived in 1785 on Water Street between Almond (renamed Kenilworth in 1897) and Catharine streets.

45. Prince, *Papers of William Livingston*, vol. 1: 330, John Taylor at Cranbury to William Livingston, May 10, 1777, and 281n7, John Taylor made lieutenant colonel on June 6, 1777.

46. *Minutes of the Council of Safety of the State of New Jersey* (Jersey City: J. H. Lyon, 1872), 44. The Council of Safety members present were Governor William Livingston, Silas Condict, Samuel Dick, Theophilus Elmer, William Paterson, Nathaniel Scudder, and John Cleves Symmes.

47. Prince, *Papers of William Livingston*, vol. 1: 331-332, William Livingston at Haddonfield to Philip Schuyler, May 13, 1777.

48. Prince, *Papers of William Livingston*, vol. 1: 332, Philip Schuyler at Philadelphia to William Livingston, May 15, 1777.

49. Prince, *Papers of William Livingston*, vol. 1: 333, William Livingston at Haddonfield to Philip Schuyler at Philadelphia, May 15, 1777. It is possible that Mrs. Thompson was an American spy operating in British-held New Brunswick, which would explain her return to the British.

50. JCC, vol. 7: 374, May 21, 1777.

51. JCC, vol. 8: 382-383, May 23, 1777.

52. GWP, General Correspondence, William Duer to George Washington, January 28, 1777, and Varick Transcripts, Letterbook 1: 409, George Washington to William Duer, February 3, 1777.

53. GWP, Varick Transcripts, Letterbook 2: 266, George Washington to Nathaniel Sackett, February 4, 1777.

54. GWP, Varick Transcripts, Letterbook 3: 31-33, George Washington to Thomas Mifflin, April 10, 1777.

55. GWP, Varick Transcripts, Letterbook 2: 318-320, George Washington to Israel Putnam, February 22, 1777 (two on the same date), and Letterbook 3: 31-33, George Washington to Thomas Mifflin, April 10, 1777.

56. GWP, Varick Transcripts, Letterbook 2: 245-246, George Washington to Continental Congress, April 23, 1777. PCC, George Washington at Morristown to Congress, April 23, 1777. Martinsburg is now in West Virginia.

57. PCC, r167 i152 V4: 103, General Adam Stephen at Chatham to George Washington at Morristown, April 23, 1777.

58. GWP, Varick Transcripts, Letterbook 2: 245-246, George Washington to Continental Congress, April 23, 1777, and General Correspondence, George Washington to John Hancock, April 23, 1777.

59. PCC r167 i152 V4: 95, George Washington at Morristown to Congress, April 23, 1777.

60. Robert Morris Letter, Rosenbach Museum and Library, Philadelphia, Robert Morris at Philadelphia to Jonathan Hudson, merchant at Baltimore, June 24, 1777.

61. National Archives, *Revolutionary War Pension and Bounty Land Warrant Application Files*, microfilm, no. 1151, William Hadar's pension claim deposition, October 23, 1832. Hadar was born on September 1, 1762, in Hunterdon County, New Jersey.

62. Ibid.

63. *New Jersey Archives Series*, 1880-1950 (Trenton: New Jersey Bureau of Archives and History), 2nd series, vol. 4, newspaper extract, November 9, 1779: 54.

64. *Proceedings of the New Jersey Historical Society*, vol. 7, nos. 1 and 2 (Newark: New Jersey Historical Society, 1922), vol. 7, no. 2: 168, citing John Smith Hatfield at Public Record Office, Foreign Office 4/1.

65. *Proceedings of the New Jersey Historical Society*, vol. 7, no. 1: 26.

66. Richard K. Showman, ed., *The Papers of General Nathanael Greene* (Chapel Hill: University of North Carolina Press, 1976-2005), vol. 2: 60, Nathanael Greene to Catherine Greene, April 27, 1777.

67. Ibid., 61, Nathanael Greene to General Benjamin Lincoln, April 27, 1777.

68. Robert F. Oaks, "Philadelphians in Exile: the Problem of Loyalty during the American Revolution," *Pennsylvania Magazine of History and Biography*, vol. 96, no. 3 (July 1972), 302-303, John Sullivan to John Hancock, August 25, 1777, and JCC, vol. 8, 688-689. Congress received Sullivan's letter on August 28, 1777, and sent it to a committee. Sullivan was a lawyer from New Hampshire who was elected to the First and Second Continental congresses. He resigned to join the army as a general. He led the American retreat from Canada in 1776. He was captured by the British at the Battle of Long Island and later exchanged. At the Battle of Trenton, he blocked the escape route, ensuring the capture of a large number of Hessians.

69. *Pennsylvania Magazine of History and Biography*, vol. 1: 289n1.

70. Coldham, *American Migrations*, 449.

71. John Montresor, *The Journal of Captain John Montresor* (New York: New York Historical Society, 1881), 451, September 11, 1777.

72. Winslow C. Watson, ed., *Men and Times of the Revolution, or, Memoirs of Elkanah Watson: Including Journals of Travels in Europe and America, from the Year 1777 to 1842: and His Correspondence with Public Men, and Reminisce* (New York: Dana, 1856), 29.

CHAPTER FOUR

1. *The Papers of George Washington, Revolutionary War Series (1775-1783)* (Charlottesville, VA: University of Virginia, 1985–present), vol. 11: 344, George Washington to Major John Clark, September 29, 1777, says "received yours [Clark's] of the 25th from Elizabeth Town," and William J. Casey, *Where and How the War Was Fought* (New York: William Morrow, 1976), 135. Several authors state that Major Clark was supervising the American spy network in Philadelphia when the British arrived, but Clark was at Elizabeth Town, New Jersey, eighty miles away at the time.

2. John Montresor, *The Journal of Captain John Montresor* (New York: Collections of the New York Historical Society, 1881), 132. Montresor estimated in the spring of 1778 that the population of Philadelphia was sixty thousand.

3. George Germain Papers, William L. Clements Library, University of Michigan, Ann Arbor, vol. 6, A State of the Circumstances of Philadelphia when the British Troops Took Possession.

4. Fitzpatrick, *Writings of Washington*, vol. 1, George Washington's Accounts of Expenses While Commander-in-Chief of the Continental Army 1775-1783.

5. Benjamin Tallmadge, *Memoir of Colonel Benjamin Tallmadge* (New York: Thomas Holman, Book and Job Printer, 1858), reprint (New York: New York Times and Arno Press, 1968), 26. The journal does not say at whose instigation this heroine visited Philadelphia.

6. General Howe later moved his headquarters to a home on the south side of Market Street east of Sixth Street–a home Washington later used when he was president. When Howe moved out of Cadwalader's house (which was 38 by 41 feet), Hessian General Wilhelm von Knyphausen took up residence.

7. *Pennsylvania Magazine of History and Biography*, vol. 23 (1899): 86. Lydia Darragh was born in Ireland circa 1750, and was the daughter of John Barrington.

8. Ibid., vol. 23 (1899): 86-91. John Darragh was born December 5, 1763.

9. Ibid., vol. 36 (January 1912): 39. A regimental court-martial of the 2nd Pennsylvania Regiment of the Continental Line was held on April 21, 1778, with Captain Peter Gosner as president and Lieutenant Charles Darragh part of the board.

10. *American Quarterly Review*, vol. 1, no. 1 (March 1827) (Philadelphia: Robert Walsh) 32-34. The explanation of the term "closet" is from Lederer, *Colonial American English*, 51.

11. W. A. Newman Dorland, "Second Troop Philadelphia City Cavalry," *Pennsylvania Magazine of History and Biography*, vol. 45, no. 4 (1921) (Philadelphia: Pennsylvania Historical Society), 381. The Old Swedes Mill in Frankford was popularly known as Lydia Darragh's Mill.

12. *American Quarterly Review*, vol. 1, no. 1 (March 1827): 33, says it was a Lieutenant Colonel Craig of the light horse. That would have been Captain Charles Craig, who was assigned to gather intelligence.

13. Robert I. Alotta, *Another Part of the Field: Philadelphia's American Revolution* (Shippensburg, PA: White Mane, 1991), 45-49.

14. John W. Jackson, *With the British Army in Philadelphia 1777-1778* (San Rafael, CA: Presidio Press, 1979), 109-110.

15. GWP, General Correspondence, John Clark Jr. at Mr. Turnbull's to George Washington, December 3, 1777, at 1 p.m.

16. GWP, General Correspondence, John Clark Jr. at Mr. Lewis's to George Washington, December 3, 1777, at 6 p.m.

17. Elias Boudinot, *Journal of Events in the Revolution,* ed. Frederick Bourquin (Philadelphia: H. J. Bicking Printer, 1894), 50. A commissary general of prisoners was responsible not just for enemy prisoners, but for supplying prisoners held by the enemy. The Rising Sun Tavern was at Germantown Road and Old York Road.

18. Uhlendorf, *Revolution in America*, 134.

19. "Narrative of Lieutenant Luke Matthewman of the Revolutionary Navy," *Magazine of American History with Notes and Queries*, vol. 2, pt. 1 (New York: A. S. Barnes, 1878), 177.

20. GWP, General Correspondence, American Intelligence Report to George Washington, December 4, 1777, identified as "D. W." but marked received

December 3, 1777, and American Intelligence Report to George Washington, December 4, 1777, from "W. D." The "D. W." is incorrectly attributed, as the signature is either an "I.W." or "J.W." and endorsed as coming from "Brigadier" and an unrecognizable name.

21. GWP, General Correspondence and Varick Transcripts, Letterbook 3: 117-119, December 10, 1777.

22. Christopher Sower (Christopher Saur III) was born on January 27, 1754, in Germantown, Pennsylvania. On January 8, 1775, he married Hannah Knorr. He eventually ran the family newspaper, the *Germantowner Zeitung.*

23. Heitman, *Historical Register of Officers of the Continental Army*, 165; James O. Knauss, *Christopher Saur the Third* (Worcester, MA: American Antiquarian Society, 1931), 8; and *Pennsylvania Magazine of History and Biography*, vol. 39: 394, Henry Hugh Fergusson, Commissary of Prisoners to Elias Boudinot, January 2, 1778. General Howe proposed the exchange.

24. *Pennsylvania Magazine of History and Biography*, vol. 23 (1899): 89.

25. GWP, General Correspondence, Lieutenant Colonel Adam Comstock at Red Bank to George Washington, October 27, 1777.

26. Duane, *Extracts from the Diary of Christopher Marshall*, 143, November 10, 1777.

27. Jeffrey M. Dorwart, *Fort Mifflin of Philadelphia: An Illustrated History* (Philadelphia: University of Pennsylvania Press, 1998), 39.

28. Amandus Johnson, *The Journal and Biography of Nicholas Collin 1746-1831* (Philadelphia: The New Jersey Society of Pennsylvania, 1936), 241.

29. Uhlendorf, *Revolution in America*, 131.

30. Historic Manuscript Report, *Report on American Manuscripts in the Royal Institution of Great Britain*, vol. 1 (London: Mackie, 1904), 160, General Sir William Howe's Proclamation of December 4, 1777.

31. The proclamation, which appeared in the *Pennsylvania Evening Post* on January 15, 1778, read, "No person or persons whatever presume to cross the river to the Jersies, or land from thence, at any other places than the above mentioned ferries, nor cross from these ferries but by virtue of a pass under the hand of one of the magistrates of which the ferrymen and all others are hereby directed to take notice, and govern themselves accordingly, on pain of imprisonment."

32. *Proceedings of the Massachusetts Historical Society* (Boston: Massachusetts Historical Society), vol. 44: 162n1.

33. Transcription, Audit Office Treasury of Great Britain, New York Public Library, 25: 250.

34. Ibid. When the British evacuated Philadelphia, Fürstner was sent with messages to Colonel Walter Butler in upstate New York.

35. CP 35:7, Account of moneys paid for Secret Service for the period January 13, 1778, to May 22, 1778.

36. HMC, *Report on American Manuscripts in the Royal Institution of Great Britain*, vol. 1: 168, William Knox to General Sir William Howe, December 12, 1777.

37. Miscellaneous Collection, papers, Historical Society of Pennsylvania, Philadelphia, Robert Proud at Philadelphia to John Proud.

38. Uhlendorf, *Revolution in America*, 150.

39. Duché lived at the northeast corner of Third and Pine streets.

40. Frederick Wampole (February 15, 1717, to February 13, 1800) had been a township supervisor in 1773 and lived on a 250-acre farm. His house that Washington used as his headquarters was torn down in 1881.

41. GWP, Varick Transcripts, Letterbook 3: 55-57, George Washington to Continental Congress, October 16, 1777.

42. Westcott, *Historic Mansions and Buildings*, 341.

43. Robert Morris occupied the house of Henry William Stiegel, ironmaster and glassmaker.

44. Duane, *Extracts from the Diary of Christopher Marshall*, 144, November 21, 1778. Christopher Marshall was at the hearing when Brown was ordered held at the Lancaster County jail.

45. Ford, *Journals of the Continental Congress*, November 18, 1777; and *Minutes of the Supreme Executive Council of Pennsylvania from its Organization to the Termination of the Revolution* (Harrisburg, PA: Theo. Fenn, 1852), vol. 11: 344-346, War Office at York, PA, to Council of Safety, November 19, 1777; and "Minutes of the Council of Safety," Hazard, *Pennsylvania Colonial Records*, November 21, 1777.

46. GWP, Varick Transcripts, Letterbook #3: 103-104, George Washington to Congress, November 23, 1777.

47. *Minutes of the Supreme Executive Council of Pennsylvania*, vol. 11: 347, Council of Safety, November 24, 1777.

48. Ibid., 347-349, Council of Safety, November 25, 1777.

49. Duane, *Extracts from the Diary of Christopher Marshall*, 146-147, December 2, 1777.

50. Ibid., 164, January 25, 1778.

51. Uhlendorf, *Revolution in America*, 134.

52. Jackson, *With the British Army in Philadelphia*, 142.

53 *Minutes of the Supreme Executive Council of Pennsylvania*, vol. 11: 472.

54. *Historical Magazine*, vol. 3, no. 2: 34, Colonel John Jameson at Wright's Tavern to George Washington, February 2, 1778.

55. James C. Neagles, *Summer Soldiers: A Survey and Index of Revolutionary War Courts-Martial* (Salt Lake City, UT: Ancestry Inc., 1986), passim.

56. *Minutes of the Supreme Executive Council of Pennsylvania*, vol. 11: 472.

57. *Archives of Maryland Online* (Baltimore and Annapolis, 1883-present), vol. 16: 348, http://www.aomol.net/html/volumes.html. A. Hall to Governor Johnson. The militia did capture Dr. Stevenson's horse, bridal, and saddle.

58. CP 231:28, Henry Stevenson Memorial to Sir Henry Clinton, September 13, 1780.

59. GWP, Varick Transcripts, Letterbook 4: 328-329, George Washington to Allen McLane, November 22, 1777. The letter was in the handwriting of Lieutenant Colonel John Laurens, a Washington aide-de-camp and son of Henry Laurens, president of the Continental Congress.

60. GWP, General Correspondence, John Clark Jr. to George Washington, December 21, 1777, and *Bulletin of the Historical Society of Pennsylvania* (Philadelphia: The Society, 1845-1848), 27.

61. Howard Henry Peckham, ed., *The Toll of Independence: Engagements and Battle Casualties of the American Revolution* (Chicago: University of Chicago Press, 1974), 46.

62. The Buck Tavern was the most popular tavern in Germantown. It was owned by Magdalena Hesser from the 1750s until 1826. It was across Germantown Avenue from Saint Michael's Lutheran Church. It was torn down in 1900 to make way for a street. "18th and Early 19th Century," *Crier*, vol. 55, no. 2 (2005) (Philadelphia: Germantown Historical Society), 45.

63. GWP, Varick Transcripts, Letterbook 4: 122-123, George Washington at Camp at Bucks Tavern to William Rumney, September 14, 1777; Letterbook 4: 121, George Washington headquarters near Germantown to Philemon Dickinson, September 14, 1777; and Papers of George Washington, "Washington's Revolutionary War Itinerary and the Location of His Headquarters, 1775-1783" (Charlottesville, University of Virginia), http://gwpa-pers.virginia.edu/documents/revolution/itinerary/all.html.

64. Andrew, Jacob, and John were sons of Abraham and Anna Levering, who had eight children.

65. John Levering, *Levering Family: History and Genealogy* (Albany, NY: Joel Munsell, 1887), 885-886; and GWP, General Correspondence, Stephen Moylan to George Washington, October 1, 1777.

66. T. A. Daly, *The Wissahickon* (Philadelphia: The Garden Club of Philadelphia, 1922), 30. A monument in memory of those Virginia patriots is in the Roxborough Baptist Church Graveyard.

67. GWP, General Correspondence, American Intelligence, December 11, 1777, Endorsed by George Washington: "Accusation of Captn. ____ Craig." Part of the document is missing.

68. GWP, General Correspondence, Charles Craig to George Washington, January 15, 1778.

69. GWP, General Correspondence, Charles Craig to George Washington, March 5, 1778.

CHAPTER 5

1. John B. B. Trussell Jr., *The Pennsylvania Line Regimental Organization and Operations, 1776-1783* (Harrisburg, PA: Pennsylvania Historical and Museum Commission, 1977), 165 and 172.

2. Heitman, *Historical Register of Officers of the Continental Army*, 157.

3. GWP, General Correspondence, John Clark Jr. to George Washington, October 6, 1777. Dunwoody's first name, William, appears only on the address side of a letter dated October 6, 1777. Cadwalader Jones's house is the oldest part of the Cadwalader Apartments community building, Route 100, Uwchlan Township, Pennsylvania.

4. Nathanael Greene Papers, William L. Clements Library, University of Michigan, Ann Arbor, and Showman, *Papers of General Nathanael Greene*, vol. 2: 249-251, Major John Clark Jr. at York, Pennsylvania, to Nathanael Greene, January 10, 177[8].

5. *The Papers of George Washington, Revolutionary War Series,* vol. 11: 344-345, George Washington at Pennybackers Mill to Major John Clark Jr. at Elizabeth Town, New Jersey (September 29, 1777).

6. Revolutionary War Military Abstract Card File, Cad'r Jones, Pennsylvania State Archives, Harrisburg. At least two Cadwalader Joneses were involved in the American Revolution, one from Uwchlan, Pennsylvania, and the other from Virginia, serving in the 3rd Continental Dragoons and later as aide-de-camp to General Lafayette. One source says the Cadwalader Jones from Pennsylvania used the name Cadwalader John. In 1780, he became a lieutenant in Captain Jacob Peterman's company of the 4th Battalion, Philadelphia County militia, Regiment of Foot.

7. *Pennsylvania Packet or General Advertiser* (Philadelphia, 1776-1781), September 10, 1776.

8. GWP, General Correspondence, John Clark Jr. to George Washington, October 6, 1777, at 5 p.m.

9. PA Archives, vol. 14: 758-759.

10. Revolutionary War Military Abstract Card File, William Dunwoody, Pennsylvania State Archives, Harrisburg. Trussell, *The Pennsylvania Line,* 27.

11. PA Archives, vol. 14: 88-89.

12. GWP, General Correspondence, John Clark Jr. to George Washington, October 6, 1777, at 10 p.m.

13. GWP, General Correspondence and Varick Transcripts, Letterbook 4: 175-177, George Washington to General John Armstrong, October 8, 1777.

14. GWP, Varick Transcripts, Letterbook 4: 222, and General Correspondence, Robert H. Harrison at camp near White Marsh to John Clark Jr., October 23, 1777.

15. *Minutes of the Supreme Executive Council of Pennsylvania,* vol. 11: 481-485, May 8, 1778. GWP, General Correspondence, Major John Clark at Goshen to George Washington, October 27, 1777, at 9 a.m. A note on the reverse says it was answered the same day, but the document could not be located.

16. GWP, General Correspondence, John Clark Jr. at Whiteland to George Washington, November 3, 1777. *Pennsylvania Magazine of History and Biography,* vol. 3: 157.

17. *Biographical Directory of the United States Congress, 1774-Present,* http://bioguide.congress.gov/biosearch/biosearch.asp. Philemon Dickinson was the brother of John Dickinson, a member of the Continental Congress's Committee of Secret Correspondence. Philemon was born April 5, 1739, at Crosiadore, near Trappe, Talbot County, Maryland. In 1740, his parents moved to Dover, Delaware, where he received his education from a private tutor. He graduated in the first class of what would become the University of Pennsylvania at Philadelphia in 1759, and superintended his father's estates in Delaware until 1760. He studied law in Philadelphia and was admitted to the bar but never practiced. In 1767, he moved to Trenton, New Jersey. He was a delegate to the New Jersey Provincial Congress in 1776. That year he was com-

missioned a brigadier general, and in 1777 a major general commanding the New Jersey militia, serving throughout the Revolution. He was a member of the Continental Congress from Delaware (1782-1783) and vice president of the Council of New Jersey (1783-1784). Philemon Dickinson was elected to the United States Senate from New Jersey to fill the vacancy caused by the resignation of William Paterson, and served from November 23, 1790, to March 3, 1793. He chose not to run again. He died at his home, the Hermitage, near Trenton, on February 4, 1809, and was buried in the Friends Meeting House Burying Ground at Trenton.

18. GWP, General Correspondence, Philemon Dickinson at Elizabeth Town, New Jersey, to George Washington, November 1, 1777.

19. GWP, General Correspondence, Philemon Dickinson at Elizabeth Town, New Jersey, to George Washington, November 2, 1777.

20. GWP, Varick Transcripts, Letterbook 4: 269-270, George Washington to Philemon Dickinson, November 4, 1777.

21. GWP, Varick Transcripts, Letterbook 4: 271-272, George Washington to Israel Putnam, November 4, 1777.

22. GWP, General Correspondence, Philemon Dickinson to George Washington, November 6, 1777.

23. GWP, General Correspondence, Philemon Dickinson to George Washington, November 15, 1777.

24. GWP, General Correspondence, Philemon Dickinson to William Livingston, November 7, 1777.

25. GWP, General Correspondence and Varick Transcripts, Letterbook 4, 277-278, George Washington to John Clark Jr., November 4, 1777.

26. GWP, General Correspondence and Varick Transcripts, Letterbook 4, pp. 277-278, George Washington to John Clark Jr., November 4, 1777, at 10 a.m.

27. Goshen Township during the American Revolution included present-day West Chester, East Goshen, and West Goshen townships in Chester County. GWP, General Correspondence, John Clark Jr. to George Washington, November 4, 1777.

28. GWP, General Correspondence, John Clark Jr. at Goshen to George Washington, November 4, 1777, at 6 p.m. Washington's response of the fifth has not been found.

29. Delaware County Planning Department, *Report of the Findings of the Delaware County Historic Resources Survey for Newton Township, June 1984*, Tax Parcel Number 30-00-00691-01 (page 63 of 151). General Potter's headquarters were at the Evan Lewis house, which is now at 330 Echo Valley Lane, Newtown Square. The earliest part was built in 1719, with major additions in 1818, 1880, and 1904. The 1719 section is a two-bay, two-story fieldstone house with walk-in fireplace and bake oven.

30. GWP, General Correspondence, John Clark Jr. to George Washington, November 8, 1777, at 11 a.m. (nineteenth century transcription).

31. GWP, General Correspondence, John Clark Jr. at Mr. Jacob's House to George Washington, November 12, 1777, at 8 a.m.

32. Delaware County Planning Department, *Report of the Findings of the Delaware County Historic Resources Survey for Newton Township, June 1984*, Tax Parcel Number 30-00-01080-02 (page 59-62 of 151). Nathan Lewis's house was built by his grandfather, William Lewis, in 1708. The original structure, its 1750 addition, and its barn are at 4109-4111 Goshen Road, Newtown Square. It is a two-and-a-half-story, five-bay fieldstone house. Lewis also owned a stone spring house, and based on archeological evidence, it is believed that a powder magazine was also operated on the property.

33. GWP, General Correspondence, John Clark Jr. at Newtown to George Washington, November 16, 1777.

34. GWP, General Correspondence, John Clark Jr. at General James Potter's quarters to George Washington, November 16, 1777, at 8 p.m.

35. For the history of the Provincial Corps of Pennsylvania Loyalists, see The On-Line Institute for Advanced Loyalist Studies at http://www.royalprovincial.com/military/rhist/paloyal/pallist.htm.

36. GWP, General Correspondence, John Clark Jr. to George Washington, November 17, 1777, at 10 a.m. Their first allowance was a quarter pound of beef and four and a half biscuits for three days. That was reduced to a quarter pound of salt pork and six biscuits for eight days.

37. *Biographical Directory of the United States Congress, 1774-Present*, http://bioguide.congress.gov/biosearch/biosearch.asp. Charles Humphreys was born September 19, 1714, in Haverford, Delaware County, Pennsylvania. He was a member of the Pennsylvania Assembly from 1763 to 1776, and a member of the Continental Congress from 1774 to 1776. He voted against the Declaration of Independence, as he was a Quaker and was opposed to war. He died in Haverford on March 11, 1786, and was buried in the Old Haverford Meeting House Cemetery. His house is at 2713 Haverford Road, Ardmore.

38. GWP, General Correspondence, John Clark Jr. at Mr. Charles Humphreys to George Washington, November 18, 1777, at 9 a.m.; and John Clark Jr. at Mr. Rees's to George Washington, November 22, 1777, at 10 a.m.

39. GWP, General Correspondence, John Clark Jr. at Newton [Newtown] Township to George Washington, November 18, 1777, at noon.

40. GWP, General Correspondence, John Clark Jr. at Mr. Lewis's at Newtown to George Washington, November 18, 1777, at 4 p.m.

41. Mrs. Withy's tavern was used as a meeting place for the Committee of Inspection of Chester County on March 1 and 2, 1776, and her house was used for an election in 1786. Gilbert Cope and John Smith Futhey, *History of Chester County, Pennsylvania, with Genealogical and Biographical Sketches*, vol. 1, original 1881 and reprint (Westminster, MD: Heritage Press, 1995), 63 and 225.

42. GWP, General Correspondence, John Clark Jr. at Mrs. Withy's at Chester, Pennsylvania, to George Washington, November 19, 1777, at 4 p.m.

43. Archibald Erskine became a captain of the 42nd Regiment of Foot, also known as the Royal Highland Regiment, in September 1771. In 1777, he was made an extra brigade major, a temporary appointment.

44. GWP, General Correspondence, John Clark Jr. at Mr. Rees's to George Washington, November 22, 1777, at 10 a.m.

45. John Thomas Schraf and Thompson Westcott, *History of Philadelphia 1609-1884* (Philadelphia: L. H. Everts, 1884), vol. 3: 1765 and 2064. GWP, General Correspondence, Nisbet Balfour to John Fox, November 21, 1777, printed pass.

46. GWP, General Correspondence, American Intelligence from Philadelphia, November 21, 1777, Report on British Military Operations. The report says "this morning" on November 21, 1777.

47. GWP, General Correspondence, John Clark Jr. at Mr. Rees's to George Washington, November 22, 1777, at 6:30 p.m.

48. Ibid.

49. Persifor Frazer had commanded Company A as a captain until he was promoted to major.

50. GWP, General Correspondence, John Clark Jr. at Mr. Rees's to George Washington, November 24, 1777, at 7 p.m.

51. GWP, General Correspondence, General John Armstrong at White Marsh to George Washington, November 25, 1777.

52. Private Collection, General Washington from Head Quarters to Major Clark, November 25, 1777.

53. GWP, General Correspondence, John Clark Jr. at Mr. Lewis's to George Washington, November 26, 1777, at 9 a.m.

54. Fitzpatrick, *Writings of George Washington*, vol. 10: 164, George Washington to Major John Clark Jr., December 16, 1777; and GWP, General Correspondence, John Clark Jr. at Mr. Lewis's to George Washington, November 26, 1777, at 9 a.m.

55. GWP, General Correspondence, John Clark Jr. at Radnor to George Washington, November 29, 1777, at 6 a.m.

56. GWP, General Correspondence, John Clark Jr. at Mr. Lewis's to George Washington, December 1, 1777, at 11 p.m.

57. GWP, General Correspondence, John Clark Jr. at Mr. Lewis's to George Washington, December 18, 1777.

58. GWP, General Correspondence, John Clark Jr. at Mr. Trumbull's to George Washington, December 3, 1777, at 1 p.m.

59. Ibid.

60. GWP, General Correspondence, John Clark Jr. at Mr. Lewis's to George Washington, December 3, 1777, at 6 p.m.

61. Ibid.

62. Ibid.

63. GWP, General Correspondence, John Clark Jr. to George Washington, December 18, 1777. Heitman, *Historical Register of Officers of the Continental Army*, 597. Major William Williams of the 2nd Pennsylvania Battalion was captured at the Battle of Germantown, October 4, 1777.

64. *The Papers of George Washington, Revolutionary War Series*, vol. 10: George Washington to John Clark, December 16, 1777.

65. GWP, General Correspondence, John Fitzgerald to John Clark Jr., December 16, 1777.

66. GWP, General Correspondence, John Clark Jr. at Mr. Lewis's to George Washington, December 18, 1777.

67. GWP, General Orders, George Washington, December 18, 1777.

68. GWP, Varick Transcripts, Letterbook 4: 352-353, George Washington to James Potter, December 21, 1777.

69. GWP, General Correspondence, John Clark Jr. at Mr. Lewis's at Newtown Square to George Washington, December 19, 1777, at 4 a.m.

70. GWP, General Correspondence, John Clark Jr. to George Washington, December 20, 1777, at 8 p.m.

71. Nathaniel Vernon, a Quaker who was well acquainted with the inhabitants, led the guards during the British occupation of the city. Vernon was on a list of people cited on May 8, 1778, by the Supreme Executive Council as being accused of being a traitor.

72. GWP, General Correspondence, John Clark Jr. to George Washington, December 21, 1777.

73. GWP, General Correspondence, John Clark Jr. at Newton to George Washington, December 22, 1777, at 2 p.m.

74. GWP, General Correspondence, John Clark Jr. at General [James] Potter's Quarters to George Washington, December 22, 1777, at twelve o'clock.

75. GWP, General Correspondence and Varick Transcripts, Letterbook 3: 135-142, George Washington to Continental Congress, December 23, 1777.

76. GWP, General Correspondence, John Clark Jr. at Newtown to George Washington, December 23, 1777, at 6 p.m.

77. GWP, General Correspondence, John Clark Jr. at Mr. Lewis's to George Washington, December 25, 1777, at 1 p.m.

78. GWP, General Correspondence, John Clark Jr. at Mr. Lewis's to George Washington, December 26, 1777, at 8 a.m.

79. GWP, General Correspondence, John Clark Jr. at Mr. Lewis's to George Washington, December 28, 1777, at 8 a.m.

80. GWP, General Correspondence, John Clark Jr. to George Washington, December 30, 1777.

81. GWP, General Correspondence, John Clark Jr. to George Washington, December 30, 1777, at 5 a.m.

82. Ibid.

83. GWP, Varick Transcripts, Letterbook 3: 152-156, George Washington to Henry Laurens, January 2, 1778, Letter of Introduction. Henry Laurens was president of Congress from November 1, 1777, to December 9, 1778.

84. GWP, General Correspondence, John Clark Jr. at York, Pennsylvania, to George Washington, January 13, 1778.

85. GWP, Varick Transcripts, Letterbook 5: 12-13, George Washington to John Clark, January 24, 1778.

CHAPTER SIX

1. His name was George Augustus Francis Rawdon, but he was known by the courtesy title of Francis, Lord Rawdon. He was born in Ireland on December 9, 1754. He became an ensign in the 15th Regiment of Foot on August 7, 1771. He purchased a lieutenancy in the 5th Regiment of Foot on October 20, 1773. After the Battle of Bunker Hill, he was made a captain in the 63rd Regiment of Foot. At the beginning of 1776, he was appointed aide-de-camp to General Henry Clinton. After Forts Clinton and Montgomery were captured on October 6, 1777, Clinton sent Rawdon to Philadelphia to inform General Howe. Rawdon arrived in Philadelphia on October 18, 1777.

2. CP 35:7, Account of moneys paid for Secret Service for the period January 13, 1778 to May 22, 1778.

3. *Collections of the New York Historical Society for the Year 1900*, vol. 32 (1901): 37n, Abstracts of Wills–Liber 31 and *New York Gazette and Weekly Mercury*, June 9, 1777. Samuel Burling's business was at 36 Wall Street, New York. Burling, a Quaker, owned the northwest corner lot at John and Pearl streets, and Burling Slip at John Street in New York City was named after him.

4. Parliament of Great Britain, *The Examination of Joseph Galloway*: 72n.

5. HMC, *Report on American Manuscripts in the Royal Institution of Great Britain*, vol. 4: 455, Samuel Burling at New York City to Sir Guy Carleton, November 14, 1783.

6. Sir William Howe, *The Narrative of Lieut. Gen. Sir William Howe* (London: H. Baldwin, 1780), 42-43.

7. HMC, *Report on American Manuscripts in the Royal Institution of Great Britain*, vol. 1: 194, George Thompson of the 63rd Regiment of Foot to John Potts, Magistrate of Police, February 16, 1778.

8. HMC, *Report on American Manuscripts in the Royal Institution of Great Britain*, vol. 1: 196, General Sir William Howe to George Washington, February 21, 1778.

9. HMC, *Report on American Manuscripts in the Royal Institution of Great Britain*, vol. 1: 196, General Sir William Howe to George Washington, March 21, 1778.

10. GWP, Varick Transcripts, Letterbook 1: 108-112, George Washington to William Howe, March 22, 1778.

11. James Parker married Margaret Elligood around 1760. He was captured in 1776 and 1781. In October 1780, he accompanied General Alexander Leslie to Virginia and secured intelligence in Portsmouth. Parkers Papers, March 3, 1783, Certification from General Alexander Leslie, London, England. Parker brought his wife to London in 1784, and returned to Glasgow. He died in 1815.

12. William Aitchison had represented Norfolk in the House of Burgesses in 1759-1761.

13. Parker Family Papers 1760-1795, Liverpool Public Library, Liverpool, England. David Library of the American Revolution, Washington Crossing, PA, microfilm, April 3, 1783, and November 24, 1785, Certifications from Lord Dunmore, London, England.

14. Henry Clinton Maps, William L. Clements Library, University of Michigan, Ann Arbor, Map no. 256, *Plan of Washington's position* [at Valley Forge, PA] by

James Parker. The map is annotated on the back that it was made by Parker. Parker is also believed to be the source of CP 78:10 and 78:11.

15. John F. Reed, *Valley Forge, Crucible of Victory* (Monmouth Beach, NJ: Philip Freneau, 1969), 52.

16. Sir John Hussey Delaval Papers, Northumberland Archives, Ashington, Northumberland, England, Delaval 2DE/12/5/1-74 (24), J. Wheatley at Cork to Sir John Hussey Delaval (March 17, 1728–May 17, 1808) of Delaval Hall.

17. Gruber, *John Peebles' American War*, 165, February 23, 1778.

18. GWP, General Correspondence, Anne Myers, Intelligence Report on Loyalist Refugees, February 23, 1778. She reported on the activities of John Robinson, of Sherman's Valley, Pa. to Major John Jameson of the 2nd Continental Dragoons. Robinson, who had left Philadelphia with letters was expected to return. He was collecting a force of loyalists north of Carlisle.

19. Gruber, *John Peebles' American War*, 165, February 23, 1778.

20. Delaval, Northumberland Archives, Delaval 2DE/12/5/1-74 (24), J. Wheatley at Cork to Sir John Hussey Delaval (March 17, 1728–May 17, 1808) of Delaval Hall.

21. Gruber, *John Peebles' American War*, 165, February 23, 1778.

22. Ibid., 168, March 10 and 11, 1778.

23. GWP, General Correspondence, William Maxwell to George Washington, June 1778. University of Pennsylvania, *Biographical Catalogue of the Matriculates of the College Together with Lists of the Members of the College Faculty and the Trustees, Officers and Recipients Of Honorary Degrees*, 1749-1893, (Philadelphia: Alumni Society, Avil Printing, 1894), 14. Jacob Bankson died on December 10, 1795.

24. Miscellaneous Collection Papers, Historical Society of Pennsylvania, Philadelphia, Box 9B. Bankson owned property in Moyamensing Township in 1749, and on June 20, 1755, he bought land in Passyunk Township from Sarah Stretch.

25. "General Alumni Catalog of the University of Pennsylvania," Penn in the 18th Century, http://www.archives.upenn.edu/histy/features/1700s/penn1700s.html. Norris Stanley Barratt, *Outline of the History of Old St. Paul's Church, Philadelphia* (Lancaster, PA: Colonial Society of Pennsylvania, New Era Printing, 1917), 32n23, which has biographical information about Jacob Bankson.

26. Martin, *Martin's Bench and Bar of Philadelphia*, xv and 242.

27. Princeton University, *General Catalog of Princeton University 1746-1906* (Princeton, NJ: Princeton University, 1908),398; and American Whig Society, *Addresses and Proceedings at the Celebration of the One Hundredth Anniversary of the Founding of the American Whig Society of the College of New Jersey* (Princeton, NJ: Steele and Smith, 1871), 41. The name was changed from College of New Jersey to Princeton University in 1896.

28. *Genealogies of Pennsylvania Families: From the Pennsylvania Genealogical Magazine*, vol. 1 (Baltimore: Genealogical Publishing, 1982), 29, 33, and 39. The Banksons had a daughter, Elizabeth Grant Bankson, born February 1, 1775, and baptized January 2, 1776, at the Second Presbyterian Church. 29, 33, and 39.

29. Barratt, *Freemasonry in Pennsylvania*, 270, 364, and 391.

30. GWP, Varick Transcripts, Letterbook no. 2: 277, George Washington at Valley Forge to William Livingston, March 25, 1778.

31. GWP, Varick Transcripts, Letterbook 5: 207-208, Alexander Hamilton to Stephen Moylan, April 3, 1778.

32. GWP, Warrant Book 2: 88R and 91R, Jacob Bankson Esq. for secret service. Fitzpatrick, *Writings of Washington*, vol. 1, George Washington's Accounts of Expenses While Commander-in-Chief of the Continental Army 1775-1783, annotation by John C. Fitzpatrick.

33. Prince, *Papers of William Livingston*, vol. 2: 333-334, William Livingston at Princeton to George Washington, May 17, 1778.

34. Ibid., 334n1, translated by Lord Stirling at Valley Forge.

35. Ibid., 339-340, William Livingston at Princeton to George Washington, May 20, 1778.

36. GWP, General Correspondence and Varick Transcripts, Letterbook 2: 317-318, George Washington to William Livingston, May 21, 1778.

37. Prince, *Papers of William Livingston*, vol. 2: 340, William Livingston at Princeton to George Washington, May 23, 1778.

38. John Edwin Bakeless, *Turncoats, Traitors and Heroes* (Philadelphia: J. B. Lippincott, 1959), 207.

39. GWP, Varick Transcripts, Letterbook 2: 327, George Washington at Valley Forge to William Livingston, June 1, 1778.

40. GWP, Varick Transcripts, Letterbook 5: 65-67, George Washington to John Lacey Jr., February 18, 1778. Lacey was encamped in the woods near the Gilbert Rodman property in the northern end of Warwick Township.

41. Ibid., 105-106, George Washington to John Lacey Jr., March 2, 1778.

42. Coldham, *American Migrations*, 467.

43. Ibid.

44. Ibid.; Hazard, *Pennsylvania Colonial Records*, vol. 12: 666, and Thomas Lynch Montgomery, *Pennsylvania Archives Sixth Series* (Harrisburg, PA: Harrisburg Publishing, 1906-1907), vol. 13: 152, 158, 160, 161, 163, 339, 355, 357, 440, 522, 534, 535, and 558. Blackford's claim for gathering intelligence is supported only by his statement. His property was confiscated because he joined the British army.

45. Coldham, *American Migrations*, 471-472.

46. Reed, *Valley Forge Crucible of Victory*, 65, quoted from John F. Reed manuscript collection, Lieutenant James Bradford to Captain Thomas Wooster, June 7, 1778.

47. GWP, Varick Transcripts, Letterbook 3: 235, General Orders, June 3, 1778. *Virginia Magazine of History and Biography* (Richmond, VA: Virginia Historical Society, 1893 to present), vol. 14, no. 3 (January 1907), 313. Neagles, *Summer Soldiers*: 12, record of the court-martial in the orderly book.

48. Ebenezer Wild, "Journal of Ebenezer Wild (1776-1781)," *Proceedings of the Massachusetts Historical Society*, 2nd series, vol. 6 (1890-1891), (Boston: Massachusetts Historical Society), 108.

49. Reed, *Valley Forge Crucible of Victory*, 65, quoted from John F. Reed manuscript collection, Lieutenant James Bradford to Captain Thomas Wooster, June 7, 1778.

50. Elijah Fisher, *Elijah Fisher's Journal while in the War for Independence, 1775-1784* (Augusta, ME: Badger & Manley, 1880), 143, June 4, 1778.

51. GWP, Varick Transcript, Letterbook 2: 207-209, George Washington to George Baylor, January 9, 1777.

52. GWP, General Correspondence, Richard K. Meade, Aid de Camp to George Washington, to Alexander Clough, May 23, 1778, and Allen McLane to Alexander Clough, May 23, 1778, nineteenth-century transcription by William B. Sprague.

53. GWP, General Correspondence, Alexander Clough to George Washington, June 2, 1778.

54. GWP, Varick Transcripts, Letterbook 5: 367-368, and General Correspondence, John Laurens to Alexander Clough, June 3, 1778.

55. GWP, Varick Transcripts, Letterbook 3: 88-89, George Washington, General Orders, March 5, 1778.

56. Ibid., 80-86, George Washington, General Orders, March 1, 1778. The execution was to be at 10 a.m. on March 3, 1778.

57. Ibid., 84, George Washington, General Orders, March 2, 1778.

58. Duane, *Extracts from the Diary of Christopher Marshall*, 170, March 7, 1778.

59. Ibid., 171, March 9, 1778; and Heitman, *Historical Register of Officers of the Continental Army*, 339.

60. GWP, Varick Transcripts, Letterbook 3: 184-188, George Washington, General Orders, May 5, 1778. Washington's after orders of May 5, 1778, instructed the celebration to be on May 6, 1778.

61. Fitzpatrick, *Writings of Washington*, vol. 11, General Order, May 6, 1778.

62. GWP, Varick Transcripts, Letterbook 3: 151-152, George Washington, General Orders, April 12, 1778; GWP, Varick Transcripts, Letterbook 3: 184-188, George Washington, General Orders, May 5, 1778; and GWP, Varick Transcripts, Letterbook 3: 188-189, George Washington, General Orders, May 6, 1778. William McMarth had been convicted of deserting to the enemy. John Morrel was convicted of deserting his post while on sentry.

63. James Thomas Flexner, *George Washington in the American Revolution, 1775-1783* (Boston: Little, Brown, 1968), 296.

64. John Laurens, *Correspondence of Colonel John Laurens in the Years 1777-1778* (New York: John B. Moreau, 1867), reprint (New York: Arno Press, 1969), 176.

65. Frederick Lewis Weis, *The Colonial Clergy of the Middle Colonies: New York, New Jersey, and Pennsylvania, 1628-1776* (Baltimore: Genealogical Publishing, 1978), 199.

66. Valley Forge Legacy, "The Muster Roll Project," http://valleyforgemuster-roll.org.

67. National Archives, *Revolutionary War Pension Applications*. David Library of the American Revolution, Washington Crossing, PA, microfilm, no. 27, S 2109,

McDonald Campbell. He died at Mount Gilead, Ohio, at age ninety-five and is buried in Mount Tabor Cemetery there.

68. Prince, *Papers of William Livingston*, vol. 333, William Livingston at Princeton to George Washington, May 17, 1778; and GWP, General Correspondence, William Livingston at Princeton to George Washington, May 17, 1778.

69. GWP, General Correspondence and Varick Transcripts, Letterbook 5: 302-303, George Washington at Valley Forge to Nathanael Greene, May 17, 1778.

70. The document says "J.T.," but others have interpreted it as "J.F." GWP, General Correspondence, American Intelligence Report from "J.T.," June 1, 1778, British on Champlain.

71. Coryell's Ferry was the name for Lambertville, New Jersey, and also for the ferry that connected the present-day towns of Lambertville and New Hope, Pennsylvania.

72. GWP, Varick Transcripts, Letterbook 5: 333-335, George Washington at Valley Forge to William Maxwell, May 25, 1778.

73. GWP, General Correspondence, William Maxwell at Mount Holly, New Jersey, to Major General Philemon Dickinson at Trenton, New Jersey, May 31, 1778.

74. GWP, General Correspondence, Philemon Dickinson to George Washington, June 1, 1778.

75. GWP, General Correspondence, William Maxwell at Mount Holly to George Washington, June 1, 1778.

76. Fostertown is at the intersection of Burlington County Route 541 and Fostertown Road. It was named for William Foster, who settled there in 1735.

77. GWP, General Correspondence, Israel Shreve to William Maxwell, June 1, 1778.

78. Stephen Moylan (1737-1811), born in Ireland and educated in Paris, was the muster master general and commanded the 4th Continental Dragoons until the war's end.

79. GWP, General Correspondence, Stephen Moylan to George Washington, May 13, 1778.

80. GWP, General Correspondence, George Washington to Alexander Clough, June 1, 1778.

81. Fitzpatrick, *Writings of George Washington*, vol. 12: 82-83.

82. CP 35:46, Joseph Galloway, Reason Against Abandoning Philadelphia and the Province of Pennsylvania, June 17, 1778.

83. Robert Morris, ed., *Memoirs of James Morris of South Farms in Litchfield* (New Haven, CT: Yale University Press, 1933), 26-27. American prisoners were taken on ships.

84. Showman, *The Papers of General Nathanael Greene*, vol. 4: 98-99, Silas Deane at Philadelphia to Nathanael Greene, May 29, 1779.

85. "Proprietary Tax List 1769," Northern Liberties, Philadelphia, Philadelphia County Archives, http://www.archive.org/stream/pennsylvaniaarc16penngoog/ pennsylvaniaarc16penngoog_djvu.txt, 131. A tax list of 1769 has Frederick Verner living in the west part of Northern Liberties, which is the part of

Liberties east of the Schuylkill River, and indicates his profession as a skinner. Hazard, *Pennsylvania Colonial Records*, vol. 11: 21, November 29, 1776. On November 29, 1776, the Council of Safety ordered a Mr. Nesbitt to pay Verner ten pounds for riding express to Cumberland, Lancaster, and York counties to countermand marching the militia.

86. War Office Papers, National Archives (Public Record Office), Kew, Richmond, Surrey, England. David Library of the American Revolution, Washington Crossing, PA, microfilm, class 71, vol. 85: 281–283, General Court Martial of James Garraty, private in the 46th Regiment of Foot, February 12-13, 1778, at Philadelphia.

87. JCC, vol. 11: 797, and PCC, no. 162, folio 142, Benedict Arnold to Congress.

88. JCC, vol. 11: 798.

89. Hazard, *Pennsylvania Colonial Records*, vol. 11, 561, August 22, 1778.

90. JCC, vol. 11: 848, August 28, 1778. See PA Archives, vol. 6: 713. The court-martial was July 29,1778, in Philadelphia.

91. Schraf, *History of Philadelphia*, vol. 3: 1827-1831. The new Philadelphia jail on Sixth Street was a two-story stone building begun in 1774. A basement containing the dungeons raised the first floor. On the southern edge of the lot, a workhouse was constructed on Prune (now known as Locust) Street. A twenty-foot-high wall enclosed the yard, where a brick building, three stories high and raised on arches, contained the sixteen solitary cells, each six feet by eight, and nine feet high. They were very dark, as the only light admitted came from above, through a peculiar form of blind. After the British arrived, the jail became their provost prison. People who were held at the jail and executed included James Molesworth, hanged as a spy, March 31, 1777; Abraham Carlisle and John Roberts, high treason, November 4, 1778; John Wilson, high treason and enlisting with the British, April 1780; and John Moody, hanged as a spy, November 13, 1781.

92. JCC, vol. 11: 1198, December 7, 1778, petition of Frederick Verner, December 7, 1778.

93. Hazard, *Pennsylvania Colonial Records*, vol. 11: 719-720.

94. PA Archives, vol. 8: 246, President [Joseph] Reed to John Jay, President of Congress, March 13, 1779.

95. Hazard, *Pennsylvania Colonial Records*, vol. 11: 719-720.

96. JCC, vol. 11: 315, March 15, 1779.

97. Hazard, *Pennsylvania Colonial Records*, vol. 11: 721, *Minutes of the Supreme Executive Council of Pennsylvania*, March 16, 1779.

98. Ibid., 752, *Minutes of the Supreme Executive Council of Pennsylvania*, April 16, 1779. Heitman, *Historical Register of Officers of the Continental Army*, 418 and 535.

99. HMC, *Report on American Manuscripts in the Royal Institution of Great Britain*, vol. 2 (1906): 121.

100. Hazard, *Pennsylvania Colonial Records*, *Minutes of the Supreme Executive Council of Pennsylvania*, vol. 12: 412, Friday July 7, 1780.

101. MacMaster, *Conscience in Crisis,* 462 and 465.

102. Schraf, *History of Philadelphia,* vol. 1: 387, 394, and 886.

103. Sabine, *Historical Memoirs of William Smith,* 10.

104. Reed, *Life and Correspondence of Joseph Reed,* 381-387.

105. GWP, Varick Transcripts, Letterbook 3: 152-154, George Washington, General Orders, April 13, 1778; and Richard Kerwin MacMaster, Samuel L. Horst, and Robert E. Ulle, *Conscience in Crisis: Mennonites and Other Peace Churches in America, 1739-1789: Interpretation and Documents* (Scottdale, PA: Herald Press, 1979), 474.

106. GWP, Varick Transcripts, Letterbook 3: 137-139, George Washington, General Orders, April 3, 1778. Note that Lorenzo Sabine, in *Biographical Sketches of Loyalists of the American Revolution, with an Historical Essay* (Boston: Little, Brown, 1864), vol. 2: 104, spelled "Morgan" as "Morganan."

107. MacMaster, *Conscience in Crisis,* 471, quoted from *Bucks County Bulletin,* 5 (1875), 268-269.

108. GWP, General Correspondence, Alexander Clough to Allen McLane, Orders, May 1778.

109. Sabine, *Biographical Sketches,* vol. 2: 112.

110. MacMaster, *Conscience in Crisis,* 472-474.

CHAPTER SEVEN

1. JCC, vol. 12: 1200, December 7, 1778.

2. JCC, vol. 11: 765, August 8, 1778.

3. JCC, vol. 12: 1086, October 31, 1778. John Penn was a nephew of Edmund Pendleton's and cousin of Nathaniel Pendleton's. Both were members of the Continental Congress. Born near Port Royal, Caroline County, Virginia, on May 17, 1741, he moved to North Carolina in 1774.

4. Samuel Chase was born in Princess Anne, Somerset County, Maryland, on April 17, 1741.

5. CP 231:28, Henry Stevenson Memorial to General Henry Clinton, undated.

6. CP 67:46 Edward Fox to Henry Stevenson, September 11, 1779.

7. Ibid.

8. CP 68:7, John André to Henry Stevenson, September 15, 1779.

9. CP 68:21, Edward Fox to Henry Stevenson, September 16, 1779.

10. CP 68:30, John André's Memorandum, after September 18, 1779.

11. GWP, Varick Transcripts, Letterbook 4: 389-392, Fitzpatrick, *Writings of George Washington,* vol. 16: 333-334, George Washington at West Point to Continental Congress, September 25, 1779.

12. JCC, vol. 17: 448, May 23, 1780.

13. JCC, vol. 23: 645, October 11, 1782, and vol. 24: 329, May 5, 1783.

14. CP 166:17, Edward Fox at Philadelphia to Dorsey, Wheeler & Company, Merchants at Baltimore, July 24, 1781. The British intercepted this letter in Baltimore. In it, Fox mentioned that he had sent a box of lemons to Chase in care of the company. It may have been intentionally allowed to fall into British

hands in an attempt to get the British to divulge one or more of their spies.

15. *Pennsylvania Packet or General Advertiser*, October 18, 1781, 4.

16. American War of Independence at Sea, http://www.awiatsea.com/Officers/Officers%20N.html.

CHAPTER EIGHT

1. Worthington Chauncey Ford, *British Officers Serving in the American Revolution, 1774-1783* (Brooklyn: Historical Printing Club, 1897), 62.

2. Bakeless, *Turncoats, Traitors, and Heroes*, 252-265.

3. Samuel Shoemaker was born in 1725. Rebecca was the daughter of Edward Warner of Philadelphia and Anna Coleman (daughter of William Coleman and sister of Judge William Coleman). Rebecca Warner married Francis Rawle on December 21, 1756, and had three children. Rawle died on June 7, 1761. Both of them were Quakers.

4. Shoemaker received a warrant for one hundred pounds for services rendered to the British government. Mackenzie Papers, Frederick Mackenzie Memo, March 29, 1783. Shoemaker left New York on November 18, 1783. While in London, he was introduced to King George III by painter Benjamin West.

5. Some of Rebecca Shoemaker's letters to her husband were carried through Rahway, New Jersey. Thomas Long, the only known British spy from Rahway, may have been the courier.

6. *Minutes of the Supreme Executive Council of Pennsylvania*, vol. 11: 770, denial of a pass, May 7, 1779.

7. Ibid., vol. 12: 270-271.

8. Ibid., 351-352.

9. Ann Rawle, Typescript Diary, Historical Society of Pennsylvania, Philadelphia, 403 (February, 28, 1781) and 428 (August 4, 1781). Charles Eddy and his wife carried some of the letters.

10. *Minutes of the Supreme Executive Council of Pennsylvania*, vol. 12: 351-352.

11. Nottingham Township in the eighteenth century was in Burlington County; it is now Hamilton Township in Mercer County.

12. Audit Office Papers of Great Britain, National Archives (Public Record Office), Kew, Richmond, Surrey, England, AO 13/111/117 (right), Deposition of Joseph Galloway, January 22, 1790. Great Britain, War Office: Printed *Army Annual Lists*: 1754-1784 on microfilm, London, National Archives, 1776. Galloway incorrectly remembered Trewren's name as Trurin.

13. Audit Office Papers of Great Britain, AO 13/111/117 (right), Deposition of Cortland Skinner at London, December 29, 1789.

14. Audit Office Papers of Great Britain, AO 13/111/110(right), Memorial of George Playter.

15. Audit Office Papers of Great Britain, AO 13/111/118, Deposition of Robert Alexander at London January 9, 1790.

16. CP 122:29, George Playter and Christopher Sower's plan, September 9, 1780.

17. CP 128:36, D. W.'s (Christopher Sower) intelligence report, November 5, 1780.

18. CP 133:19, George Playter's report, December 11, 1780.

19. CP 231:24, John Stapleton at Headquarters to Oliver De Lancey, January 5, 1781.

20. CP 230:28, George Playter to Oliver De Lancey, circa 1780.

21. CP 140:14, John Stapleton at headquarters to Oliver De Lancey.

22. William Thompson was born in Newtownbarry, Wexford, Leinster, Ireland. He was captain of horse in America during the French War (1759-1760). He is buried in the Carlisle Public Graveyard, also known as the Old Graveyard, Carlisle, Pennsylvania.

23. Carl Van Doren, *Mutiny in January* (New York: Viking, 1943), 177-178.

24. CP 175:18, Letter from W (Dr. Welding alias George Playter), September 21, 1781.

25. Audit Office Papers of Great Britain, AO 13/111/117 (right), Deposition of Cortland Skinner at London, December 29, 1789.

26. CP 180:37, Dr. Wilding's report, October 26, 1781.

27. CP 180:35, General Knyphausen to Sir Henry Clinton, October 26, 1781.

28. HMC, *Report on American Manuscripts in the Royal Institution of Great Britain*, vol. 4: 404 (vol. 32, no. 72), Sir Guy Carleton at New York to Governor John Parr, October 10, 1783. His property and personal effects were confiscated by the Americans and sold. His wife and children were dispossessed.

29. Pemberton Family Papers, Historical Society of Pennsylvania, Philadelphia, box 3, miscellaneous items.

30. Audit Office Papers of Great Britain, AO 13/111/117 (right), Deposition of Cortland Skinner at London, December 29, 1789.

31. CP 141:38, McFarlane's report, January 20, 1781, states that Mason "went to the college where Williams was."

32. The four roads would have merged at Green Street and South Pennsylvania Avenue in Morrisville, Pennsylvania.

33. Colvin's Ferry is now Morrisville, Pennsylvania.

34. GWP, General Correspondence, Philemon Dickinson to George Washington, January 12, 1781.

35. According to JCC, vol. 10, January 24, 1781: 82, the execution was at noon. Depending on the source consulted, the hanging took place either at 9 a.m. or noon. It was scheduled for 9 a.m., but with the delays, noon was more likely the actual time of execution.

36. CP 140:21, Andrew Gautier's report, January 12, 1781.

37. CP 90:12, Daniel Coxe at New York to John André, p. 3, March 28, 1780.

38. CP 90:12, New York, Daniel Coxe to John André, March 28, 1780.

39. Samuel Wallis married Lydia Hollingsworth of Philadelphia on March 1, 1770, and they moved to his Muncy property.

40. John F. Meginness, ed., *History of Lycoming County Pennsylvania* (Chicago: Brown, Runk, 1892), 66-80.

41. Squan is the area at the Manasquan River being either Brielle or Point Pleasant, New Jersey.

42. CP 124:28, Samuel Wallis to Daniel Coxe, September 24 and October 19, 1780. Wallis indicated that his mail had been previously sent through Squan to New York.

43. CP 129:4a, SW [Samuel Wallis] at Philadelphia to DC [Daniel Coxe], November 8, 1780. Wallis signed the letter "SW"; the letter is annotated by Coxe on the back as being from "Mr. Wallace."

44. CP 147:13, Sir Henry Clinton to Lord George Germain, February 27, 1781; also see CP 147:16, SW [Samuel Wallis] at Philadelphia to DC [Daniel Coxe], January 25, 1781, and CP 147:17.

45. CP 153:24, Philadelphia Gentlemen's report transcribed in George Beckwith's handwriting, March 24 to April 25, 1781.

46. CP 153:24, Philadelphia Gentlemen's report in George Beckwith's handwriting, March 24 to April 25, 1781.

47. CP 155:33, George Beckwith to Samuel Wallis in Philadelphia, May 15, 1781, and CP 156:14, Letter from Philadelphia (Wallis) to George Beckwith, May 22, 1781. Wallis's letter reached New York in four days.

48. CP 160:1, Sir Henry Clinton to Admiral Arbuthnot, June 20, 1781. The admiral's name appears in documents as Mariot, Mariott, and Marriott, and as Arbuthnot, Arbutnot and Arbutnott.

49. CP 161:28, Samuel Wallis to Daniel Coxe, June 27, 1781.

50. CP 161:27, Daniel Coxe to Oliver De Lancey, July 2, 1781.

51. CP 161:28, Samuel Wallis to Daniel Coxe, notation on the letter, June 27, 1781.

52. Valley Forge Legacy, "The Muster Roll Project," http://valleyforgemuster-roll.org.

53. *Minutes of the Supreme Executive Council of Pennsylvania*, vol. 12: 258, February 22, 1780.

54. PA Archives, 6th series, vol. 13: 64-65, Articles of an Agreement. GWP, Varick Transcripts, Letterbook 4: 16-17, George Washington at Prekaness to Joseph Reed, November 4, 1780. Shark River is the northern boundary of Belmar, Monmouth County, New Jersey. He also used the Manasquan River. Andrew Fürstner was a brother-in-law to James and John Rankin of York County, Pennsylvania. Rankin's Ferry was at the foot of Conewago Falls on the Lancaster County side of the Susquehanna River. James Rankin, a Quaker of Newberry Township, bought ten acres on December 28, 1770, for construction of a landing and ferry house. He was found to be a loyalist, and his property was confiscated.

55. GWP, General Correspondence, American Intelligence to John Hendricks, October 24, 1780.

56. Prince, in *Papers of William Livingston*, vol. 4, reports the "B." in B. Edgar Joel's name stood for Beasley, while Fitzpatrick, in *Writings of George Washington*, gives the name as Benjamin.

57. GWP, Varick Transcripts, Letterbook 5: 205-206, George Washington to Continental Congress War Board, June 14, 1780.

58. GWP, General Correspondence, Benjamin Edgar Joel at the Philadelphia Barracks to George Washington, July 21, 1780.

59. GWP, General Correspondence, Benjamin Edgar Joel at the Philadelphia Barracks to George Washington, August 8, 1780. The reference to Major Lee is probably to Major Henry "Light-Horse Harry" Lee of the 1st Continental Dragoons, but there was also a Major John Lee of the Virginia State Regiment at this time. Heitman, *Historical Register of Officers of the Continental Army*, 345.

60. GWP, General Correspondence, George Washington to Benjamin Edgar Joel, August 14, 1780.

61. Prince, *Papers of William Livingston*, vol. 4: 69: William Livingston to the Board of War, September 29, 1780.

62. Ibid., 55, B. Edgar Joel to William Livingston, [September 1780], two letters.

63. GWP, General Correspondence, Continental Congress War Board to George Washington, October 18, 1780.

64. GWP, Varick Transcripts, Letterbook 5: 347, George Washington to Continental Congress War Board, October 25, 1780.

65. Prince, *Papers of William Livingston*, vol. 4: 89-90, Joseph Reed to William Livingston, November 13, 1780.

66. Ibid., 90-91, William Livingston to Joseph Reed, November 15, 1780.

67. GWP, Financial Papers, Joseph Stansbury to George Washington, March 28, 1776, Revolutionary War Accounts, Vouchers, and Receipted Accounts 2.

68. Hazard, *Pennsylvania Archives First Series*, vol. 8: 624-625, President Joseph Reed to Governor William Livingston, 1780.

69. *Pennsylvania Evening Post*, 1775-1781, November 25, 1780, p2c2-3. Prince, *Papers of William Livingston*, vol. 4: 103, William Livingston to Joseph Reed, December 5, 1780.

70. Coldham, *American Loyalist Claims*, 496, and Coldham, *American Migrations*, 602-603.

71. Sabine, *Biographical Sketches*, vol. 2: 153, Paul, __.

72. Wilbur Henry Siebert, *The legacy of the American Revolution to the British West Indies and Bahamas: A Chapter out of the History of American Loyalists* (Columbus: Ohio State University, 1913), 70.

73. *Colonial Records of Pennsylvania, Minutes of the Supreme Executive Council*, vol. 12: 221: January 5, 1780. The doctors were named Chevitt and Phile.

74. Coldham, *American Migrations*, 723. In 1780, his house at Hampstead Hill was burned.

75. James Robertson was commissioned a major general on August 29, 1777, and appointed civil governor of New York on May 11, 1779. HMC, *Report on American Manuscripts in the Royal Institution of Great Britain*, vol. 2 [1906]: 306-307, John Pafford to Brigadier General Birch, July 1781.

CHAPTER NINE

1. Dr. Henry Norris inherited property in Elizabeth Town, New Jersey.

2. Carl Van Doren, *Secret History of the American Revolution* (New York: Viking, 1941), 133, quoted from transcripts of American Loyalist Claims at the New York Public Library.

3. Coldham, *American Migrations*, 477.

4. GWP, Varick Transcripts, Letterbook 3: 119-121, George Washington, General Orders, March 26, 1778. Valley Forge Legacy, "The Muster Roll Project," http://valleyforgemusterroll.org. The only Colonel Swift at Valley Forge was Colonel Heman Swift of the 7th Connecticut Regiment, who was from Cornwall, Connecticut.

5. Coldham, *American Migrations*, 461.

6. In 1777, Captain Martin Weaver of the Northumberland County militia was in the 4th Battalion under the command of Colonel Robert Elder, 6th Company, which was raised in Upper Paxtang Township, Pennsylvania. He was still with the county militia in 1781.

7. MacMaster, *Conscience in Crisis*, 462 and 465.

8. Trinity Lutheran Church is located where the Sower house stood at 5300 Germantown Avenue, Philadelphia.

9. Knauss, *Christopher Saur*, 12, quoted from transcripts of American Loyalist Claims at the New York Public Library, vol. 49: 463.

10. Van Doren, *Secret History*, 130-131, from CP 119:49, Sower Abstract and CP 54:12, André to Clinton, March 20, 1779.

11. CP 141: 3, Andrew George Fürstner's report, January 15-25, 1781.

12. MacMaster, *Conscience in Crisis*: 461-462. C. H. Hutchinson, *The Chronicles of Middletown [Present Dauphin Co.]: Containing a Compilation of Facts, Biographical Sketches, Reminiscences, Anecdotes, Etc.* . . . (self-published, 1906), 130. William Willis and James Rankin were Quakers. Daniel Shelley died June 21, 1802. He had eighteen children and outlived four wives.

13. GWP, Varick Transcripts, Letterbook 2: 170-173, George Washington, General Orders, June 7, 1777.

14. GWP, Varick Transcripts, Letterbook 2: 195-197, George Washington, General Orders, June 22, 1777.

15. CP 61:28, John André to William Rankin, after June 20, 1779.

16. CP 67:6, Andrew Fürstner to Christopher Sower, August 1779.

17. Van Doren, *Secret History*, 220-221, from CP 119:49, Sower Abstract.

18. GWP, Varick Transcripts, Letterbook 4: 16-17, George Washington to Joseph Reed, November 4, 1780.

19. MacMaster, *Conscience in Crisis*, 467.

20. Ibid., 248, document 129, Committee of York County to Committee of Safety of the Province of Pennsylvania, September 14, 1775.

21. Van Doren, *Secret History*, 220-221, from CP 119:49, Sower Abstract, August 30, 1780.

22. Ibid.

23. Coldham, *American Migrations*, 481-482.

24. CP 161:17, George Beckwith to Oliver De Lancey, July 1, 1781.

25. CP 160:31, Mr. _____ of Philadelphia to Captain George Beckwith.

26. Van Doren, *Secret History*, 412.

27. CP 166:10 Mr. _____ of Philadelphia to Beckwith, July 24, 1781; and Gilder Lehrman Manuscripts, New York Historical Society, GLC-05223, A Gentleman in Philadelphia to Captain Beckwith, July 24, 1781.

28. CP 159:30, Dr. Henry Norris, June 17, 1781.

29. CP 170:3, George Beckwith to Oliver De Lancey, August 10, 1781.

30. CP 186:23, Dr. Norris's report, December 11, 1781.

31. Knauss, *Christopher Saur*, 15-16, quoted from Audit Office Papers of Great Britain, class 13, bundle 102.

32. CP 186:23, Dr. Norris's report, December 11, 1781.

33. Coldham, *American Migrations*, 481-482.

34. CP 120:43, Christopher Sower to Major Oliver De Lancey, September 1, 1780.

35. MacMaster, *Conscience in Crisis*, 414-415, document 242 from the Pennsylvania Supreme Executive Council Records. PA Archives, 1st series, vol. 5: 495-496 and 508-509.

36. James Thacher, *A Military Journal during the American Revolutionary War, from 1775 to 1783* (Boston: Richardson and Lord, 1823), 228-231, April 19-29, 1780; and Thomas Meehan, "Newark," *The Catholic Encyclopedia*, vol. 10 (New York: Robert Appleton, 1911), http://www.newadvent.org/cathen/10779c.htm. While he was ill, Miralles was attended by Washington's personal physician as well as Washington's wife, Martha, in the Ford home.

37. GWP, Varick Transcripts, Letterbook 4: 397-400, George Washington to Joseph Reed, April 8, 1779.

38. GWP, Varick Transcripts, Letterbook 1: 365-369, George Washington to Marquis de Lafayette, October 20, 1779.

39. GWP, Varick Transcripts, Letterbook 8: 141-142, George Washington to William Patterson, March 1, 1779.

40. Revolutionary War Military Abstract Card File (Pennsylvania State Archives, Harrisburg, PA), Gres Getsham and Getshom Hicks. Getshom Hicks is listed in the records as having served from January 1, 1777, to August 1, 1780, from January 1, 1781, to January 1, 1782, and until January 1, 1783.

41. GWP, Varick Transcripts, Letterbook 8: 140-141, George Washington to Colonel Zebulon Butler, George Washington to Major Barnet Eichelberger, George Washington to Commanding Office at Fort Willis, March 1, 1779. Fort Willis was located at West Point Military Reservation. It was built of stone.

42. GWP, Varick Transcripts, Letterbook 8: 141-142, George Washington to Colonel William Patterson, March 1, 1779.

43. GWP, General Correspondence, William Patterson at Sunbury, Pennsylvania, to Nathanael Greene by way of Colonel Cox at Estherton, Pennsylvania (present Dauphin Co.), March 28, 1779. Heitman, *Historical Register of Officers of the Continental Army*, 136.

44. GWP, Varick Transcripts, Letterbook 8: 264, George Washington at Middle Brook to Colonel William Patterson, April 11, 1779.

45. GWP, General Correspondence, William Patterson at Philadelphia to George Washington, May 29, 1779.

46. Showman, *The Papers of General Nathanael Greene*, vol. 4: 100, William Patterson at Philadelphia to Nathanael Greene, May 29, 1779.

47. GWP, General Correspondence, George Washington to William Patterson, June 22, 1779.

48. GWP, General Correspondence, John Cox and William Patterson to George Washington, May 1779, Indian Affairs; Questions on Country of the Six Nations.

49. Van Doren, *Secret History*, 217.

50. Pennsylvania State Historical and Museum Commission, "Revolutionary War Militia Battalions and Companies," Northumberland County, http://www.portal.state.pa.us/portal/server.pt/community/revolutionary_war_mili tia_overview/4125.

51. CP: 63:3, Joseph Stansbury to John André, July 12, 1779.

52. Van Doren, *Secret History*, 219-220.

53. Ibid., 320 and 385.

54. *Lineage Book*, The National Society of the Daughters of the American Revolution (Washington, DC, 1895-1921), vol. 35: 328, and vol. 41: 224; William S. Stryker, *The New Jersey Volunteers (Loyalists) in the Revolutionary War* (Trenton, NJ: Naar, Day, and Naar, 1887), 56 and 345; and Heitman, *Historical Register of Officers of the Continental Army*, 352. Eleazer Lindsley (December 7, 1737–June 1, 1794) was born in Morristown, New Jersey, and was a member of the New Jersey Assembly in 1777. He served as a lieutenant colonel of the Morris County, New Jersey, militia, was an aide to General Lafayette, and was with General Sullivan in his expedition to the northwest, where he settled after the war. He died in Steuben County, New York.

55. Robert Land was born in 1736.

56. GWP, General Correspondence, Continental Army General Court Martial Proceedings at Minisink, New York, March 17-19, 1779. Also available at The On-Line Institute for Advanced Loyalist Studies, http://www.royalprovincial.com/military/courts/cmland.htm.

57. *Pennsylvania Gazette*, April 21, 1779.

58. GWP, General Correspondence, Continental Army General Court Martial Proceedings at Minisink, New York, March 17-19, 1779. Also available at The On-Line Institute for Advanced Loyalist Studies, http://www.royalprovincial.com /military/courts/cmland.htm.

59. Ibid.

60. Ibid.

61. Heitman, *Historical Register of Officers of the Continental Army*, 99. The Lieutenant Caleb Bennett who testified was from the Delaware Regiment.

62. GWP, General Correspondence, Continental Army General Court Martial

Proceedings at Minisink, New York, March 17-19, 1779. Also available at The On-Line Institute for Advanced Loyalist Studies, http://www.royalprovincial.com/military/courts/cmland.htm.
Additional Manuscripts, British Library, London, no. 21765, folio 64-65 at http://www.royalprovincial.com/military/musters/brangers/brcald1.htm.

63. GWP, General Correspondence, Continental Army General Court Martial Proceedings at Minisink, New York, March 17-19, 1779.

64. GWP, Varick Transcripts, Letterbook 8: 264, George Washington to William Patterson, April 11, 1779.

65. GWP, Varick Transcripts, Letterbook 8: 260, George Washington at Middle Brook, New Jersey, to Colonel Oliver Spencer, April 9, 1779.

66. PA Archives, vol. 8: 259, Samuel Rea to President Read, 1780.

67. Ralph Morden was born in Yorkshire, England, in 1742, and resided in Mt. Bethel Township, Northampton County, Pennsylvania. In 1765, he married Anne Durham, a Quaker from New Jersey, and adopted her religion.

68. PA Archives, vol. 8: 259, Samuel Rea to President Read, 1780.

69. The trial was at a court of oyer and terminer and general gaol delivery for Northampton County.

70. PA Archives, vol. 8: 597, C. J. McKean to Joseph Reed, 1780; and Hazard, *Pennsylvania Colonial Records*, vol. 12: 534-535, Supreme Executive Council, November 9, 1780. Gallows Hill in now South 5th Street in Easton.

71. Oscar Jewell Harvey and Ernest Gray Smith, *A History of Wilkes-Barre, Luzerne County, Pennsylvania: From Its First Beginnings to the Present Time* . . . . (Wilkes-Barre, PA: Readers Press, 1909), vol. 1: 189.

72. JCC, vol. 4: 225-226. The petition to Congress was read on March 20, 1776. It was sent to committee on March 22.

73. JCC, vol. 4: 273.

74. Sabine, *Biographical Sketches*, vol. 2: 273.

CHAPTER TEN

1. Benedict Arnold was born on January 14, 1741, in Norwich, Connecticut.

2. PCC, vol. 7: 132-133, February 19, 1777. William Alexander was more commonly known as Lord Stirling.

3. GWP, Varick Transcripts, Letterbook 2, 335-336, George Washington to Benedict Arnold, March 3, 1777.

4. GWP, Varick Transcripts, Letterbook 3, 6-7, George Washington to Benedict Arnold, April 3, 1777.

5. GWP, Varick Transcripts, Letterbook 3, 220-222, General Orders May 28, 1778.

6. GWP, General Correspondence, George Washington to Benedict Arnold, June 19, 1778.

7. JCC vol. 11: 571, June 4, 1778.

8. JCC vol. 12: 1071, October 28, 1778.

9. JCC vol. 13: 184, February 15, 1779.

10. JCC vol. 13: 324, March 17, 1779. The first, second, third, and fifth charges were grounds for a court-martial.

11. JCC vol. 13: 337, March 18, 1779 and original in PCC No. 162, folio 169.

12. Margaret "Peggy" Shippen was born on July 11, 1760, in Philadelphia.

13. GWP, General Correspondence, George Washington to Pennsylvania Council, April 20, 1779.

14. GWP, General Correspondence, Benedict Arnold to George Washington, May 5, 1779.

15. CP 241:6, Sir Henry Clinton's memorandum on Arnold, undated but after the war.

16. CP 241:5, Sir Henry Clinton note on Arnold, undated but suspected 1780.

17. CP 125:9, Sir Henry Clinton to Martha and Elizabeth Carter, October 4, 1780.

18. HMC, *Report on the American Manuscripts in the Royal Institution of Great Britain*, vol. 4: 266, (vol. 49, no. 112), Memorial of Joseph Stansbury to Sir Guy Carleton, August 6, 1783.

19. Carl Van Doren says he believes Arnold used the name Monk because it was the name of a Scottish general who in 1660 turned against Parliament to restore the monarchy and was handsomely rewarded. Arnold's analogy was that he would turn on Congress and be handsomely reward by the grateful monarch who would be restored over the American colonies.

20. CP 57:30, John André to Joseph Stansbury, May 10, 1779; and Van Doren, *Secret History*, 198-199.

21. Rattoon's tavern was at the end of the old road to Bordentown, now known as Main Street in South Amboy. The tavern is identified as the Railroad House Hotel (A. D. Vanpelt, Proprietor) on the Map of the County of Middlesex, New Jersey, by Smith Gallop & Co., published in 1861. The building was laid out in an east and west direction nearly parallel with the shoreline. The tavern had a dock about a half mile away across a salt marsh. The marsh provided ample coverage for anyone traversing from the bay to the tavern or vise versa who did not want to be seen. W. Woodward Clayton, ed., *History of Union and Middlesex Counties with Biographical Sketches of Many of Their Pioneers and Prominent Men* (Philadelphia, Everts and Peck, 1882), 824.

22. CP 157:7, Captain Beckwith's memo, May 31, 1781.

23. The armed vessel that was sometimes at Sandy Hook would have been referred to as being at the Hook. The vessel referred to in Beckwith's document was off of the southeast end of Staten Island at Princess Bay.

24. CP 157:7, Captain Beckwith's memo, May 31, 1781.

25. CP 60:47, Jonathan Odell to John André, June 13, 1779.

26. Ibid. John Rattoon brought Joseph Stansbury's letters of June 4 and 9, 1779.

27. CP 59:27A, John André to Margaret Chew, May (?), 1779.

28. CP 59:30, Benedict Arnold through Joseph Stansbury to John André, pre-May 23, 1779.

29. Heitman, *Historical Register of Officers of the Continental Army*, 72.

30. CP 59:7, Joseph Stansbury to Jonathan Odell, May 26, 1779.

31. CP 63:19, Jonathan Odell to John André, July 18, 1779, enclosing CP 63:3, Jonathan Stevens (Joseph Stansbury) to John Anderson (John André), July 11, 1779.

32. CP 59:27, Jonathan Odell to John André, May 31, 1779.

33. CP 60:48, Jonathan Odell to Joseph Stansbury, June 9, 1779, copy provided to John André.

34. CP 59:27, Jonathan Odell to John André, May 31, 1779.

35. CP 234:2, Jonathan Odell notes that the cipher was for Mr. L., who is not identified. However, in CP 60:48, Jonathan Odell to Joseph Stansbury, June 9, 1779, Odell says "Lothario is impatient," referring to John André.

36. CP: 62:35, John André to Benedict Arnold, middle of June 1779.

37. CP 63:3, Jonathan Stevens (Joseph Stansbury) to John Anderson (John André), July 11, 1779.

38. CP 63:19, Jonathan Odell to John André, July 18, 1779, enclosing CP 63:3, Jonathan Stevens (Joseph Stansbury) to John Anderson (John André), July 11, 1779.

39. CP 63:26, Jonathan Odell to John André, July 21, 1779.

40. CP 81:24, Jonathan Odell to John André, December 21, 1779; see endorsement of December 24, 1779, at the end of this letter.

41. CP 60:40, Joseph Stansbury to Jonathan Odell, December 3, 1779.

42. Joseph Plumb Martin, *Private Yankee Doodle* (Boston: Little Brown, 1962), 149-150.

43. American General Benjamin Lincoln surrendered Charleston, South Carolina, to General Henry Clinton on May 12, 1780. CP 111:12, J. [Jonathan] O. [Odell] to M[ajo]r A[ndré], July 29, 1780.

44. CP 102:37, Knyphausen's Notes, Draft, Answer, and Memo, May 1780.

45. CP 104:26, Benedict Arnold to the executor of John Anderson (John André), who was George Beckwith, June 7, 1780.

46. CP 104:27, Joseph Stansbury to George Beckwith, George Washington, and Marquis de Lafayette, [June 1780].

47. A translation of the proclamation was forwarded by General Clinton to Lord George Germain in his dispatch of August 31, 1780. A copy of it is in the Records of the British Colonial Office, class 5, microfilm 53 reels. Library of Congress (Washington, DC), C. O. 5, vol. 100, folio 243. GWP, Varick Transcripts, Letterbook 11, George Washington to Marquis de Lafayette, May 19, 1780; and GWP, General Correspondence, George Washington at Morristown to Benedict Arnold in Philadelphia, June 4, 1780.

48. CP 110:23, Joseph Stansbury to George Beckwith or John André, July 7, 1780.

49. CP 111:12, J. Moore to John Anderson [John André] merchant to the care of James Osborn [Jonathan Odell] and to be left at Mr. [Jonathan] Odell's, July 11, 1780. Odell lived on Wall Street.

50. GWP, General Correspondence, Gustavus to John Anderson [John André]

merchant to the care of James Osborn [Jonathan Odell] and to be left at Reverend [Jonathan] Odell's, August 30, 1780.

51. CP 111:12, J. [Jonathan] O. [Odell] to M[ajo]r A[ndré], July 29, 1780.

52. CP 111:12, J. Moore to John Anderson [John André] merchant to the care of James Osborn [Jonathan Odell] and to be left at Mr. [Jonathan] Odell's, July 12, 1780, filed in same folder with item of July 11, 1780.

53. Gold Star Box, Moore [Benedict Arnold] to Captain John Anderson [John André] to be left at Mr. Odell's, Baltimore, July 15, 1780.

54. CP 113:11, James Osborne [Reverend Jonathan Odell] to Mr. Stevens [Joseph Stansbury], July 24, 1780.

55. CP 113:11, [John André to Benedict Arnold] accompanied with James Osborne [Reverend Jonathan Odell] to Mr. Stevens [Joseph Stansbury].

56. CP 111:12, George Beckwith, ADC at Head Quarters Morris House, July 30 [1780], twelve at night and endorsed [in John André's handwriting] Captain Beckwith.

57. CP 111:12, J. [Jonathan] O. [Odell] to M[ajo]r A[ndré], July 29, 1780.

58. CP 118:31, Mr. Stevens [Joseph Stansbury] to Jasper Overhill [Jonathan Odell], August 14, 1780, received in New York City on August 23, 1780, via John Rattoon.

59. CP 111:12, George Beckwith, ADC Morris House to Major André, August 27, 1780.

60. CP 122:17, Jonathan Odell to John André, September 7, 1780, enclosing Thomas Charlton [Joseph Stansbury] to Jasper Overhill [Jonathan Odell], August 25, 1780.

61. CP 123:19, Benedict Arnold to ____ [John André], September 15, 1780, transcribed by Jonathan Odell.

62. Van Doren, *Secret History*, 340.

63. GWP, General Correspondence, Continental Army, September 29, 1780, Proceedings against John André as a Spy, by Continental Army Board of General Officers.

64. GWP, Varick Transcripts, Letterbook 5: 180-181, George Washington, October 1, 1780, General Orders.

CHAPTER ELEVEN

1. Max Savelle, *George Morgan Colony Builder* (New York: Columbia University Press, 1932), 132.

2. George Morgan was born in Philadelphia on February 14, 1743, to Evan and Joanna (Biles) Morgan. He was the brother of Dr. John Morgan, who in 1775 was physician in chief of the Continental Army. George was apprenticed to Baynton and Wharton trading house in 1756. He married Mary Baynton on October 21, 1764, and became a partner in Baynton and Wharton the same year. He was a colonel, deputy commissary general for purchases, and Indian agent at Fort Pitt from 1776 to 1779. He left Pittsburgh and settled at Princeton, where he built a stone farm house on the crest of a hill. The Continental

Congress met there in 1783, before moving to Nassau Hall. The house was torn down in 1849. http://etcweb.princeton.edu/CampusWWW/Companion/prospect.html. After 1796, Morgan became a western Pennsylvania farmer. He called his farm Morganza, and it later became the Western State School and Hospital, Cecil Township, Washington County, Pennsylvania. Morgan died at Morganza on March 10, 1810.

3. Savelle, *George Morgan Colony Builder*: 136.

4. Nelson, Larry L. *A Man of Distinction among Them: Alexander McKee and the Ohio Country Frontier, 1754–1799*. (Kent, OH: Kent State University Press, 1999), 96-97. In 1777, Paul Long would be used as a courier to the Delaware Indians.

5. Dreer, Ferdinand J., Collection. Papers. Historical Society of Pennsylvania, (Philadelphia), George Morgan to Mr. J. Vraiment, June 10, 1776.

6. Termites were a major problem in wooden forts and were most likely the cause of the blockhouse's demise. The Cedars is on the north shore of the Saint Lawrence River, about twenty-eight miles from the center of modern Montreal.

7. Michigan Collection, William L. Clements Library, University of Michigan, Ann Arbor, George Morgan Intelligence from Detroit, December 12, 1776. A fascine is a long bundle of sticks bound together, used in building earthworks and batteries, and in strengthening ramparts.

8. Papers of Thomas Jefferson (Princeton, NJ: Princeton University Press, 1950 to present), series 1, General Correspondence, David Zeisberger, from Cuchackunk to _____, September 23, 1777.

9. Heckewelder was born in Bedford, England, in 1743, and was brought to British North American in 1754.

10. Diedrich Collection, manuscripts, William L. Clements Library, University of Michigan, Ann Arbor. Letter from John Heckewelder to Samuel Sitgreaves at Bethlehem, Pennsylvania, January 21, 1799. Heckewelder admitted to being an American spy during the revolution.

11. CP 229:36, McLaurens, Sir Henry Clinton's note, between 1776 and 1779.

12. Major Arent Schuyler De Peyster had been in command of Fort Michilimackinac and its dependencies from 1774 to 1779. It was a French wooden fort built in 1715 and turned over to the British in 1761. It was at the northern end of the lower peninsula of the present-day state of Michigan at the Straits of Mackinac, which connect Lake Huron and Lake Michigan.

13. Peckham, *Toll of Independence*, 65, October 4, 1779. Rogers had been able to get supplies from the Spanish in New Orleans through Oliver Pollock, Virginia's agent at New Orleans.

14. CP 91:39, Indian alliance–Arent Schuyler De Peyster, April 5, 1780.

15. Matthew Elliott was born around 1739, in County Donegal, Ireland, emigrated to Pennsylvania in 1761, settled in Pittsburgh, and died May 7, 1814, at what is today Burlington, Ontario, Canada.

16. Reginald Horsman, *Matthew Elliott, British Indian Agent* (Detroit: Wayne State University Press, 1964), 16-18.

17. Consul Willshire Butterfield, *History of the Girtys* (Cincinnati: Robert Clarke, 1890), 44-45.

18. For comments on McKee's behavior concerning his escape, see the letter of March 30, 1778, from Jasper Ewing at Fort Pitt to Jasper Yeates, Esq., at Lancaster, in the Ferdinand J. Dreer Collection, Historical Society of Pennsylvania, Philadelphia. Dale Van Every, *A Company of Heroes: The American Frontier, 1775-1783* (New York: Morrow, 1962), 175.

19. Butterfield, *History of the Girtys*, 61-62.

20. Ibid., 90.

21. Sir Frederick Haldimand Papers on microfilm, David Library of the American Revolution, Washington Crossing, PA, B 122, p 144, Henry Hamilton's Report, List of officers: Indian Department District of Detroit, Sept. 5, 1778. Enclosed in Lieutenant Governor Hamilton's letter without date but supposed to be the beginning of September and received the twenty-seventh at Sorel, marked Detroit No. 13. When the British finally surrendered Fort Detroit on July 11, 1796, McKee moved to the River Thames in what would become southwestern Ontario, Canada, and died there of lockjaw on January 13, 1799.

22. *Collections of the Illinois State Historical Library, George Rogers Clark Papers, 1771-1781.* (Springfield: Trustees of the Illinois State Historical Library, 1912), 101-102, David Lyster at Detroit to George Moorehead, February 4, 1779, Draper MSS, 49J20 and 108-109, Captain R. B. Lernoult at Detroit to Lieutenant Governor Henry Hamilton, February 9, 1779, Draper MSS 49J26.

23. Ibid., 104-109, Alexander Macob at Detroit to Lieutenant Governor Henry Hamilton, February 4, 1779, Draper MSS 49J22.

24. Louise Phelps Kellogg, ed., *Frontier Advance on the Upper Ohio, 1778-1779*, Collections vol. 23, Drapier Series, vol. 4 (Madison: Wisconsin State Historical Society, 1916), 199.

25. Butterfield, *History of the Girtys*, 213-214.

26. Kellogg, *Frontier Advance*, 385-386.

27. Ibid., 246.

28. Ibid., 382-383, Coochocking, Alexander McCormick to Daniel Brodhead, June 29, 1779.

29. Ibid., 218.

30. Ibid., 385-386, John Heckewelder at Coshocton, to Colonel Daniel Brodhead, summary of letter of July 8, 1779.

31. Miscellaneous Collection, Historical Society of Pennsylvania, Philadelphia, Rusticus (Daniel Brodhead) to Walter Jenifer Stone, December 30, 1782. Kellogg, *Frontier Advance*, 384, Colonel Daniel Brodhead at Pittsburgh, to Colonel Stephen Bayard, July 1, 1779. Daniel Brodhead used the code name Rusticus to hide his identity.

32. Kellogg, *Frontier Advance*, 384, Colonel George Woods of the Bedford County militia at Bedford, Pennsylvania, to Thomas Uric of East Pennsboro Township, Cumberland County, Pennsylvania, July 4, 1779.

33. GWP, General Correspondence, Daniel Brodhead at Fort Pitt to George Washington, March 27, 1781.

34. GWP, General Correspondence, Myndert Fisher but signed Thomas Girty to Simon Girty, January 21, 1781.

35. Louise Phelps Kellogg, ed., *Frontier Retreat on the Upper Ohio, 1779-1781,* Collections vol. 24, Drapier Series, vol. 5 (Madison: Wisconsin State Historical Society, 1917), 491, trial of Myndart Fisher, presided by Colonel S. Bayard, commanding the 8th Pennsylvania Regiment, July 26, 1781. The letter that was sent read, "Gentlemen, If Mr. Graverod would succeed with the help of you, the errant he is going upon, would be of Infinite service both to me your brother, and himself, and friends here present, that is only waiting for his return, and the honorable commanders answers from Detroit, which I suppose, there will be no less than one hundred that will accompany him to said place, if the Commander will pleas to give him the least Encouragement possibly he can. Thomas Girty."

36. GWP, General Correspondence, John Dodge to George Washington, July 1781.

37. GWP, Varick Transcripts, Letterbook 14: 288-289, George Washington to William Irvine, November 1, 1781.

38. Percy B. Caley, "Life and Adventures of Lieutenant, Colonel John Connolly: The Story of a Tory: Chapter V: Plans to Invade Ohio Country: His Capture," *Western Pennsylvania History,* vol. 11, no. 3 (July 1928), (Pittsburgh: Historical Society of Western Pennsylvania), 144-156, William Cowley's deposition before Abraham Fuller, Justice of the Peace, October 12, 1775.

39. GWP, Letterbook 7: 110-115, George Washington to Continental Congress, October 12, 1775.

40. Allan Cameron was a native of Scotland who had emigrated with the intention of purchasing land in the backcountry of Virginia. Dr. John Smith was a native of Scotland who lived about two miles south of Cedar Point, Charles County, Maryland. He had to leave for political reasons. After failing in an attempt to get to the Mississippi River, he went to Norfolk in 1775.

41. John Ferdinand Smyth, "Narrative or Journal of Captain John Ferdinand Dalziel Smyth, of the Queen's Rangers," *Pennsylvania Magazine of History and Biography,* vol. 39: 152.

42. Ibid., 156.

43. Ibid., 157.

44. GWP, Letterbook 7: 164-166, George Washington to Continental Congress, December 25, 1775. The tree of a saddle is the frame under the seat.

45. GWP, Letterbook 7: 210-215, George Washington to Continental Congress, January 30, 1776.

46. *Pennsylvania Magazine of History and Biography,* vol. 12: 310, Connolly Narrative.

47. Indian River is just south of Rehoboth Bay in Sussex County, Delaware. Simon Kollock was commissioned a captain in the Independent Loyalist Companies on May 1, 1777.

48. Force, *American Archives,* 4th series, vol. 4: 615-617. John Connolly to Susanna Connolly, December 16, 1775, and John Connolly to Alexander McKee, December 16, 1775; Hazard, *Pennsylvania Colonial Records,* vol. 10: 470-471; and Ferdinand Smyth Stuart, *The Case of Ferdinand Smyth Stuart with his*

Memorials to the King, the Lords of the Treasury, &c. (London: Cox, Son, and Baylis, 1807), 4-5 and 18-20.

49. *Pennsylvania Colonial Records*, vol. X: 470-471.

50. *Minutes of the Supreme Executive Council of Pennsylvania*, vol. 11, April 2, 1777.

51. Peters, Family. Papers. Historical Society of Pennsylvania, Philadelphia, John Connolly to Board of War, January 13, 1778.

52. Thomas Bradford Collection, *British Army Prisoners*, Historical Society of Pennsylvania, Philadelphia, vol. 2: 19, P. Scull, Secretary to the War Office, to Thomas Bradford, April 27, 1779, transmitting a letter from the Board of War, vol. 2: 20.

53. *British Army Prisoners*, vol. 1: 57, John Hay, York County, a pass to John Connolly, Major Prichard, W. Stockton, Captain Asher Dunham, Captain Robert Morris, and Lieutenant Francis Frazier to travel to Philadelphia.

54. Simon Gratz Papers, Historical Society of Pennsylvania, Philadelphia, case 2, box 32, James Ewing at Susquehanna to Dr. John Connolly in the State Prison at Philadelphia.

55. *British Army Prisoners*, vol. 1: 81, Jonathan Beatty, Elizabeth Town, New Jersey, to Thomas Bradford, November 29, 1778.

56. Ibid., vol. 2: 121, Ben Stoddert, Secretary to the War Office, instructions to take John Connolly's parole to stay at Germantown and his son to go with him, November 20, 1779; and *Society Collection*, Historical Society of Pennsylvania, Philadelphia, Parole of John Connolly, Philadelphia, November 21, 1779.

57. *British Army Prisoners*, vol. 3: 45, War Office extended John Connolly's jail limits, April 12, 1780.

58. Ibid., vol. 3: 75, Ben Stoddert, Secretary to the War Office, to Thomas Bradford, June 30, 1780, he can take possession of Connolly's parole document, and vol. 3: 78, Parole of John Connolly, Philadelphia, July 3, 1780.

59. Ibid., vol. 3: 84, John Connolly to Thomas Bradford, July 6, 1780.

60. CP 131:23, John Connolly at New York to Sir Henry Clinton, November 25, 1780. Presque Isle is a small peninsula on the southeastern shore of Lake Erie, opposite present-day Erie, Pennsylvania.

61. CP 152:48, John Connolly at Flatbush to Sir Henry Clinton, April 20, 1781. CP 149:29, John Connolly at Flatbush to Sir Henry Clinton, March 15, 1781, John Connolly was living at 40 Upper Marybone Street.

62. CP 158:12, Sir Henry Clinton to Lord Cornwallis, June 9, 1781. CP 161:26, Beckwith to Oliver De Lancey, July 2, 1781. After Connolly left New York, Beckwith was sending his mail to him through Oliver De Lancey.

63. *Society Collection*, John Connolly to Thomas Bradford, December 27, 1781, Case 19-31.

64. Ibid., Case 19-31, Lieutenant Colonel John Connolly to Lord Sydney, March 11, 1784.

65. Duane, *Extracts from the Diary of Christopher Marshall*, 126, September 11, 1777.

66. Kellogg, *Frontier Retreat*, Colonel Daniel Brodhead at Fort Pitt to the Delaware chiefs, November 19, 1780. Coochocking was another spelling for

Coshocton, which was also spelled Coochoquin, Cooshawing, and Cooshockung. It was both a fort and an Indian village.

67. PCC: r92, i78, v4: 141-143, Heckewelder at Salem, Ohio, to Colonel Brodhead, February 26, 1781. Killbuck, also known as John Killbuck Jr., was the chief Gelelemend (1737–1811).

68. Kellogg, *Frontier Advance*, 343-344, Colonel George Morgan to John Jay, May 28, 1779.

CHAPTER TWELVE

1. Charles William Frédéric Dumas was born in Kloster Heilbron, Ansbach, Bavaria in 1721.

2. According to www.rootsweb.com, Cornelius Stevenson may have been born in Flushing, New York, on April 4, 1738. Robert had been on the island since 1755 and had a slave. Some documents list their last name as Stevens, but it is Stevenson.

3. Benjamin Franklin, *Papers of Benjamin Franklin Series* (New Haven, CT: Yale University Press, 1959–present), vol. 23: 61, (Samuel Wharton) at London to Benjamin Franklin at Paris, December 21, 1776.

4. Ibid., 150, (Samuel Wharton at London to Dr. Edward Bancroft) with a post script to Benjamin Franklin, January 10, 1777.

5. Ibid., 202, (Samuel Wharton at London to Benjamin Franklin), January 17, 1777. Peter Evans's house was opposite Holt's the Sadler.

6. Ibid., vol. 25: 202, W. S. (Samuel Wharton at London) to Monsr. François Chez [and] Monsr. De Chaumont, á Passy, prés de Paris, November 21, 1777.

7. Esmond Wright, *Franklin of Philadelphia* (Cambridge, MA: Belknap Press of Harvard University Press, 1986), 287.

8. PBF, vol. 23: 162, Juliana Ritchie to Benjamin Franklin, January 12, 1777.

9. PBF, vol. 23: 211, Benjamin Franklin to Juliana Ritchie, January 19, 1777. Juliana Ritchie had moved to London and become friends with Elizabeth Graeme, a former love interest of William Franklin's. For financial reasons she emigrated to Cambray (now Cambrai), France, where she lived in a convent.

10. Herman Melville, *Israel Potter: His Fifty Years of Exile,* ed. Hennig Cohen (New York: Fordham University Press, 1991), 375-376. This is a work of fiction with explanatory notes to Israel Potter's memoir. The local Brentford tax church book indicates the name as John Edward Bridges instead of James Bridges. In the novel, Israel Potter identifies Squire Woodcock as a gentleman of Brentford. The local records provide the name of Charles Woodcocke. John Horne, also known as Horne Tooke, was tried on July 4, 1777, for libeling the king's government and the employment of his troops on June 8 and July 14, 1775. He was found guilty. See John (Tooke) Horne, *The Trial (at Large) of John Horne, esq. upon Information Filed Ex Officio, by His Majesty's Attorney General, for a Libel. Before the Right Hon. William, Earl of Mansfield . . . . Published by the Defendant, from Mr. Gurney's Short-Hand Notes ...* (London, G. Hearsly, 1777); and John (Tooke) Horne, *The Trial of John Horne, Esq.; upon an Information Filed Ex Officio by His*

Majesty's Attorney General, for a Libel . . . (London: S. Blandon, 1777). Horne would be arrested again on May 16, 1794, as a traitor, interrogated by the Privy Council, and put in the Tower of London. Public Record Office PC1/21/A35(a) and PC1/22/A36(a), quoted from Elizabeth Mary Sparrow, *Secret Service: British Agents in France, 1792-1815* (Woodbridge, Suffolk, England: Boydell Press, 1999), 27. The Brintford that appears in Henry Trumbull, *Life and Remarkable Adventures of Israel R. Potter* (Providence, RI: J. Howard, 1824), is Brentford, where Horne was a minister. It is on the north bank of the Thames River about ten miles west of London and twenty-five miles east of White Waltham.

11. Benjamin Franklin Papers, American Philosophical Society, Philadelphia, CWK and JH (John Horne) to Benjamin Franklin at Paris, February 14, 1777. A copy appears in *Papers of Benjamin Franklin* Series, vol. 23: 332-334.

12. Trumbull, *Life and Remarkable Adventures of Israel R. Potter*, 46-52.

13. Claude Anne Lopez, *My Life with Benjamin Franklin* (New Haven, CT: Yale University Press, 2000), 64.

14. PBF, vol. 24: 470, An American whom you have seen at Paris, from London to _____ (Benjamin Franklin), August 26, 1777.

15. Ibid., vol. 26: 518, Peter Allaire at Calais to Dr. Benjamin Franklin at Passy, May 22, 1778.

16. PBF at http://franklinpapers.org/franklin/, Peter Allaire to William Temple Franklin, January 26, 1780.

17. PBF, vol. 31: 428, Peter Allaire to Benjamin Franklin, January 31, 1780.

18. PBF at http://franklinpapers.org/franklin/, Peter Allaire still at the Hotel Saxe to William Temple Franklin, February 14, 1780.

19. Ibid., William Temple Franklin to Peter Allaire, February 14, 1780.

20. Wright, *Franklin of Philadelphia*, 289-290.

21. Sir John Fortescue, ed., *The Correspondence of King George the Third, from 1760 to December 1783* (London: Macmillan, 1928), vol. 6: 339. Peter Allaire was brought from Flanders to England by a M. Fox. Allaire had the idea of setting up a plan for gathering intelligence.

22. Frank T. Reuter, "Petty Spy or Effective Diplomat: The Role of George Beckwith," *Journal of the Early Republic* (Philadelphia: University of Pennsylvania Press, 1981 to present), vol. 10, no. 4 (winter 1990), 478.

23. Patience Lovell Wright's home at 100 Farnsworth Avenue, Bordentown, New Jersey, still stands.

24. Patience Lovell Wright sculpted Lord Chatham, Benjamin Franklin, Admiral Richard Howe, Lord Lyttleton, and Thomas Penn.

25. Joan N. Burstyn, *Past and Promise: Lives of New Jersey Women* (Metuchen, NJ: Scarecrow Press, 1990), 41-43.

26. Charles Coleman Sellers, *Patience Wright: American Artist and Spy in George III's London* (Middletown, CT: Wesleyan University Press, 1976), 69-73.

27. Burstyn, *Past and Promise*, 41-43.

28. PBF online at http://franklinpapers.org/franklin/, David Salisbury Franks at Brest to William Temple Franklin, December 10, 1781 (unpublished).

29. PBF, vol. 36: 285-286, David Salisbury Franks at Brest to ___, December 23, 1781.

CHAPTER THIRTEEN

1. CP 69:24, Sir Henry Clinton to Lord George Germain, marked secret, September 27, 1779. Lord George Germain was known as Lord George Sackville until 1770. He was a general who was court-martialed for his conduct at the Battle of Minden in August 1759, and was considered unfit to command in any military capacity. He was the secretary of state for the American Department from November 10, 1775, to February 1782, and director of the war in the western Atlantic. He was blamed for the loss of the America colonies.
2. *Biographical Directory of the United States Congress, 1774-Present*, http://bioguide.congress.gov/biosearch/biosearch.asp.
3. Transcription, Audit Office Treasury of Great Britain, New York Public Library, class 1, vol. 642, folio 239, March 14, 1785.
4. Aquidneck Island is also known as the island of Rhode Island where the city of Newport is located.
5. CP 126:11, Stephen Holland to Oliver De Lancey, October 14, 1780.
6. Frank C. Mevers, *The Papers of Josiah Bartlett* (Hanover, NH: University Press of New England, 1979), 163n2. Goreham was also spelled Gorham. In 1760, the unit was taken into the regular British army and renamed the North American Rangers. After the war, Stephen Holland, who had been described as being of slender build, returned to Ireland, where he was living in 1797. The British government compensated him for the large land holdings confiscated by New Hampshire.
7. State of New Hampshire, *Provincial and State Papers* (Concord, NH: Edward D. Pearson, Printer, 1895), vol. 25, Town Charters, part 2: 269-271, Grant to Stephen Holland, 1770.
8. Kenneth Scott, "Major General John Sullivan, and Captain Stephen Holland," *New England Quarterly* (Boston: Colonial Society of Massachusetts, Northeastern University, 1928 to present), vol. 18, no. 3 (September 1945): 304.
9. Nathaniel Bouton, ed., *Documents and Records Relating to the State of New Hampshire: During the Period of the American Revolution from 1776 to 1783* (Concord, NH: E. A. Jenks, State Printer, 1874), vol. 8: 507.
10. Ibid., 546. Brigadier General Oliver Prescott was a physician who was born April 27, 1731, graduated from Harvard, and opened his practice in Groton, Massachusetts.
11. Audit Office Treasury of Great Britain, class 1, vol. 642, folio 248, Major General Archibald Campbell at London, England, September 10, 1785.
12. Samuel Folsom was a brother of General Nathaniel Folsom. He kept a tavern and lived at the easterly corner of Court Square and Water Street in Exeter.
13. Bouton, *Documents and Records Relating to the State of New Hampshire*, 582.
14. Ibid., 703, Stephen Holland to [New Hampshire Committee of Safety], October 4, 1777.

15. Ibid., 732-733, letter from the selectmen and Committee of Londonderry relative to Captain Holland, no date [November 1777].

16. Coldham, *American Migrations*, 125.

17. Audit Office Treasury of Great Britain, class 1, vol. 642, folio 249, Major General Archibald Campbell at London, England, September 10, 1785, copy of his letter to Sir Henry Clinton of May 10, 1778.

18. Ibid., folio 244, General Sir Henry Clinton to Captain Stephen Holland, March 12, 1778, and folio 241-242, Stephen Holland to Lieutenant General Sir William Fawcett and Major General Roy, December 28, 1786.

19. Mevers, *Papers of Josiah Bartlett*, 163, and Audit Office Treasury of Great Britain, class 1, vol. 642, folio 241-242, Stephen Holland to Lieutenant General Sir William Fawcett and Major General Roy, December 28, 1786.

20. Eric Spierer, *Those "Inimical to the American Cause": Loyalists in New Hampshire during the American Revolution* (Middletown, CT: Wesleyan University, 2010), 91-92, Petitions 1778-1779, Selectmen of Londonderry to Committee of Safety, April 11, 1778, http://wesscholar.wesleyan.edu/cgi/viewcontent.cgi?article=1484&context=etd_hon_theses.

21. Ibid., 107, Petitions July 1776-1777, William Vance to the Committee of Safety, September 6, 1777, and New Hampshire Claims 1864-1865, William Vance.

22. CP 171:39, Stephen Holland at New York to Oliver De Lancey, August 23, 1781.

23. CP 174:9, William Vance's report, September 8, 1781.

24. CP 174:20, Unidentified report, September 13-16, 1781, mentions reports of Saturday, September 8, and Tuesday, September 11. The only spy report found in General Henry Clinton's papers dated September 8, 1781, is William Vance's report.

25. CP 174:9, William Vance's report, September 8, 1781.

26. CP 176:37, William Vance at New York to Oliver De Lancey, September 26, 1781.

27. CP 184:14, Captain Holland, November 27, 1781.

28. Coldham, *American Migrations*, 130. CP 187:17, Stephen Holland to Oliver De Lancey, December 18, 1781. JCC, vol. 22: 218. John Stinson (sometimes spelled Stimson) claimed to have gone on twenty-eight assignments as a spy.

29. *Biographical Directory of the United States Congress, 1774-Present*, http://bioguide.congress.gov/biosearch/biosearch.asp.

30. Van Doren, *Secret History*, 400.

31. Scott, "Major General John Sullivan, and Captain Stephen Holland," 308-309. Maine was part of Massachusetts in the eighteenth century.

32. Ibid., 309.

33. Thomas Coffin Amory, *Daniel Sullivan's Visits, May and June 1781 to General John Sullivan in Philadelphia to Explain Declarations in Sir Henry Clinton's Secret Journal* (Cambridge, MA: J. Wilson and Son, University Press, 1884), 7.

34. Amory, in *Daniel Sullivan's Visits*, believed that the report was written because no response was received from Sullivan. Captain Sullivan left Philadelphia on May 7, but we do not know when he reached New York. Also, a deposition would have been taken and sent to headquarters as standard policy of returning agents.

35. CP 155:37, De Lancey, Sullivan, and Holland's report, May 17, 1781. A copy of the report was published in the *Magazine of American History* (January 1884), vol. 11: 156-157. Complete copies of the two drafts of the letter and the report are published in Scott, "Major General John Sullivan, and Captain Stephen Holland," 310-314.

36. Dr. Thomas Addis Emmett, contributor, "Sir Henry Clinton's Original Secret Record of Private Daily Intelligence," *Magazine of American History with Notes and Queries* (New York: Historical Publications, vol. 11, January-June, 1884), 538; Amory, *Daniel Sullivan's Visits*, 21; and Emmett Collection, papers and microfilm, New York Public Library, Daniel Sullivan's deposition, July 4, 1781.

37. Van Doren, *Secret History*, 402.

38. Scott, "Major General John Sullivan, and Captain Stephen Holland," 315-318.

39. The letter is printed in *American Historical Review*, vol. 11: 538-539, and Scott, "Major General John Sullivan, and Captain Stephen Holland," 319, Stephen Holland to John Sullivan.

40. CP 158:11, Capt[ain] H__d [Stephen Holland] to Gl S__n [General John Sullivan], June 9, 1781. Vergennes's letter is in *American Historical Review*, vol. 11: 160, Vergennes to Luzerne, July 27, 1781.

41. Van Doren, *Secret History*, 403-404.

42. Scott, "Major General John Sullivan, and Captain Stephen Holland," 320-321, John Sullivan to John Langdon, September 10, 1782.

43. Bouton, *Documents and Records Relating to the State of New Hampshire*, 949, proceedings of the General Assembly, September 12, 1782.

44. Isaac W. Hammond, ed., *State of New Hampshire, Miscellaneous Provincial and State Papers, 1725-1800*, vol. 18 (Manchester, NH: John B. Clarke, 1890), 723, John Sullivan to John Langdon, November 15, 1782.

45. Bouton, *Documents and Records Relating to the State of New Hampshire*, 953, proceedings of the General Assembly, November 15, 1782.

46. Ibid., 960.

47. Scott, "Major General John Sullivan, and Captain Stephen Holland," 322-323.

48. GWP, General Correspondence, John Sullivan to George Washington, December 30, 1782.

49. GWP, Varick Transcripts, Letterbook 16: 69, George Washington to John Sullivan, January 15, 1783.

50. John W. Jordan, ed., *Colonial and Revolutionary Families of Pennsylvania*, vol. 1, reprinted from 1911 (Baltimore: Genealogical Publishing, 1978), 288-289. Israel Pemberton Jr. was born May 10, 1715, and died April 22, 1779, in Philadelphia.

51. CP 177:23, William Rankin's report, September 1781.

52. CP 33:33, Cortland Skinner at New York to General William Howe, p. 4, April 13, 1778.

53. Thacher, *A Military Journal*, 315.

54. Joseph Lapsley Wilson, *Book of the First Troop, Philadelphia City Cavalry, 1774-1914* (Philadelphia: Hallowell, 1915), 12, War Office to Lieutenant Commandant James Budden, November 7, 1781.

55. *Boston Gazette or Country Journal* (Boston, 1755-1793), December 3, 1781, and *Independent Chronicle and the Universal Advertiser* (Boston, 1776-1801), December 6, 1781. See also letter of Lafayette of November 14 in the *Maryland Journal, and Baltimore Advertiser* (Baltimore, 1773-1794), November 20, 1781. All reported in J. Bennett Nolan, *Lafayette in America Day by Day* (Baltimore: Johns Hopkins Press, 1934), 207-208.

56. CP 182:10, Unknown person in Philadelphia to Beckwith, November 8-15, 1781, received on December 13, 1781.

57. William Digby Lawler was a native of Ireland and a quartermaster in the 17th Light Dragoons. On August 25, 1780, he became the adjutant in the Queen's Rangers, cornet about October 25, 1780, and on December 1, 1780, a lieutenant.

58. CP 183:17, Lieutenant L____r's report [William Digby Lawler] of the Queen's Rangers. Lawrence Marr was from Northampton County, Pennsylvania.

59. CP 189:25, Proposal to get [John] Moody released by Major [Daniel Isaac] Browne and Joseph Hayden, 1781.

60. *Pennsylvania Gazette*, Philadelphia, 1728-1815, November 14, 1781.

61. *Pennsylvania Packet or General Advertiser*, Philadelphia, 1776-1781, November 15, 1781, p. 3, col. 2.

62. *Boston Gazette or Country Journal*, 1755-1793, December 3, 1781, and *Independent Chronicle and the Universal Advertiser,* Boston, 1776-1801, December 6, 1781.

63. GWP, Varick Transcripts, General Correspondence, Letterbook 4: 274-275, and Fitzpatrick, *Writings of Washington*, vol. 23: 445, George Washington at Philadelphia to William Livingston, January 12, 1782. Captain Jonathan Lawrence Jr. of the Orange County, New York, state troops captured James Moody at Liberty Pole (now Englewood), New Jersey, on July 21, 1780, while the Bull's Ferry blockhouse was being attacked by Brigadier General Anthony Wayne with ninety New Jersey militiamen, the 1st and 2nd Pennsylvania brigades, and Colonel Stephen Moylan's regiment of dragoons.

CONCLUSION

1. Diedrich Collection, manuscripts, William L. Clements Library, University of Michigan, Ann Arbor. Letter from John Heckewelder to Samuel Sitgreaves at Bethlehem, Pennsylvania, January 21, 1799. Heckewelder admitted to being an American spy during the revolution.

2. CP 35:7, Account of moneys paid for Secret Service for the period January 13, 1778, to May 22, 1778.

3. John Blair Linn and William H. Egle, eds., *Pennsylvania in the War of the Revolution, Battalions and Line, 1775-1783* (Harrisburg, PA: L. S. Hart, State Printer, 1880), vol. 1: 400.

4. GWP, General Correspondence, American Intelligence Report to George Washington, December 4, 1777, from "W. D."

BIBLIOGRAPHY

MANUSCRIPT COLLECTIONS

Adams Family. Papers. Massachusetts Historical Society, Boston.

Additional Manuscripts. Papers. British Library, London, England.

American Loyalist Claims. Transcripts. New York Public Library.

Archives Diplomatiques for the Foreign Secretary. Mémoires et Documents, La Courneuvem, France.

Archives du Ministere des Affaires Etrangeres, England supplement. Manuscripts. La Courneuvem, France.

Audit Office Papers of Great Britain. British National Archives (Public Record Office). Kew, Richmond, Surrey, England.

Audit Office Treasury of Great Britain. Transcription. New York Public Library.

British Army Prisoners in Thomas Bradford Collection. Papers. Historical Society of Pennsylvania, Philadelphia.

Chalmers, George. Microfilm. New York Public Library.

Clinton, Henry. Maps. William L. Clements Library, University of Michigan, Ann Arbor.

Clinton, Henry. Papers. William L. Clements Library, University of Michigan, Ann Arbor.

Delaval, Sir John Hussey. Papers. Northumberland Archives, Ashington, Northumberland, England.

Diedrich Collection. Manuscripts. William L. Clements Library, University of Michigan, Ann Arbor.

Dreer, Ferdinand J., Collection. Papers. Historical Society of Pennsylvania, Philadelphia.

Emmett Collection. Papers and Microfilm. New York Public Library.

Feinstone Collection. Papers and Microfilm. David Library of the American Revolution, Washington Crossing, PA.

Franklin, Benjamin. Papers. American Philosophical Society, Philadelphia.

Germain, George. Papers. William L. Clements Library, University of Michigan, Ann Arbor.

Gilder Lehrman Collection. Manuscripts. New York Historical Society.

Simon Gratz Collection. Papers. Historical Society of Pennsylvania, Philadelphia.

Greene, Nathanael. Papers. William L. Clements Library, University of Michigan, Ann Arbor.

Haldimand, Sir Frederick. Papers and Microfilm. David Library of the American Revolution, Washington Crossing, PA.

Jay, John. Papers on the Internet. Columbia University Libraries, New York.

Michigan Collection. Papers. William L. Clements Library, University of Michigan, Ann Arbor.

Miscellaneous Collection. Papers. Historical Society of Pennsylvania, Philadelphia.

Morris, Robert. Letters. Rosenbach Museum and Library, Philadelphia.

North Liberties, Philadelphia. Tax Lists. Philadelphia County Archives, Philadelphia. http://www.archive.org/stream/pennsylvaniaarc16penngoog/pennsylvaniaarc16penngoog_djvu.txt.

Parker Family. Papers 1760-1795. Liverpool Public Library, Liverpool, England.

Pemberton Family. Papers. Historical Society of Pennsylvania, Philadelphia.

Peters Family. Papers. Historical Society of Pennsylvania, Philadelphia.

Philadelphia Monthly Meeting Minute Book for 1782-1789. Manuscript. Haverford College, Haverford, PA.

Rawle, Ann. Typescript Diary. Historical Society of Pennsylvania, Philadelphia.

Records of the British Colonial Office, Class 5. Microfilm. Library of Congress, Washington, DC.

Revolutionary War Military Abstract Card File. Pennsylvania State Archives, Harrisburg, PA.

Revolutionary War Militia Battalions and Companies. Pennsylvania State Historical and Museum Commission, Harrisburg, PA. http://www.portal.state.pa.us/portal/server.pt/community/revolutionary_war_militia_overview/4125.

Revolutionary War Pension and Bounty Land Warrant Application Files. United States National Archives.

Revolutionary War Pension Applications. Microfilm. United States National Archives.

Revolutionary War Warrant Books. Manuscript. Library of Congress, Washington, DC.

Society Collection. Papers. Historical Society of Pennsylvania, Philadelphia.

War Office Papers. British National Archives (Public Record Office). Kew, Richmond, Surrey, England.

Washington, George. Letters. Rosenbach Museum and Library, Philadelphia.

Washington, George. Papers. Library of Congress, Washington, DC.

PUBLISHED MATERIALS

Alotta, Robert I. *Another Part of the Field: Philadelphia's American Revolution.* Shippensburg, PA: White Mane Publishing, 1991.

American Historical Review. Washington, DC: American Historical Association, October 1895 to present.

American Quarterly Review, Vol. 1 No. 1 (March 1827). Philadelphia: Robert Walsh.

American War of Independence at Sea, http://www.awiatsea.com/Officers/Officers%20N.html.

American Whig Society. *Addresses and Proceedings at the Celebration of the One Hundredth Anniversary of the Founding of the American Whig Society of the College of New Jersey*. Princeton, NJ: Steele and Smith, 1871.

Amory, Thomas Coffin. *Daniel Sullivan's Visits, May and June 1781 to General John Sullivan in Philadelphia to Explain Declarations in Sir Henry Clinton's Secret Journal*. Cambridge, MA: J. Wilson and Son, University Press, 1884.

Archives of Maryland Online, Vols. 215+. Baltimore and Annapolis, 1883–present, http://www.aomol.net/html/volumes.html.

Archives of the State of New Jersey. Series 2, Vol. 1, *Documents Relating to the Revolutionary History of the State of New Jersey: Extracts from American Newspapers, 1776–1777*. Trenton, NJ: J. L. Murphy, 1901.

Atlantic Monthly. Boston: Atlantic Monthly Group.

Bakeless, John Edwin. *Turncoats, Traitors and Heroes*. Philadelphia: J. B. Lippincott, 1959.

Balch, Thomas Willing, trans. *The French in America during the War of Independence 1777–1783*. Philadelphia: Porter and Coates, 1891.

Ballagh, James Curtis. *The Letters of Richard Henry Lee, Vol. 1, 1762–1778*. New York: Macmillan, 1911.

Bancroft, George. *History of the United States from the Discovery of the American Continent*. Boston: Little, Brown, 1856–1874.

Barkly, Gilbert. A Reply to John Hay's Answer to Gilbert Barkly's Representation to the Publick. Quebec: Brown and Gilmore, 1764.

____. *A Representation to the Public of Affairs between Gilbert Barkly of Philadelphia and John Hay of Quebec*. Quebec: Brown and Gilmore, 1764.

Barratt, Norris Stanley. *Outline of the History of Old St. Paul's Church, Philadelphia*. Lancaster, PA: Colonial Society of Pennsylvania, New Era Printing, 1917.

Barratt, Norris Stanley, and Julius Friedrich Sachse. *Freemasonry in Pennsylvania, 1727–1907, as Shown by the Records of Lodge No. 2, F. and A. M. of Philadelphia from the Year A.L. 5757, A.D. 1757*. Lancaster, PA: New Era Printing, 1909.

Bigelow, John, ed. *The Complete Works of Benjamin Franklin*, Vol. 5 (1772–1775), New York: G. P. Putnam's Sons, 1887.

Biographical Directory of the United States Congress, 1774–Present. http://bioguide.congress.gov/biosearch/biosearch.asp.

Boston Gazette or Country Journal, Boston, 1755–1793.

Boudinot, Elias. *Journal of Events in the Revolution*. Edited by Frederick Bourquin. Philadelphia: H. J. Bicking Printer, 1894.

Bouton, Nathaniel, ed. *Documents and Records Relating to the State of New Hampshire: During the Period of the American Revolution from 1776 to 1783*, Vol. 8. Concord, NH: E. A. Jenks, State Printer, 1874.

Bulletin of the Historical Society of Pennsylvania. Philadelphia: The Society, 1845–1848.

Burstyn, Joan N. *Past and Promise: Lives of New Jersey Women*. Metuchen, NJ: Scarecrow Press, 1990.

Butterfield, Consul Willshire. *History of the Girtys*. Cincinnati: Robert Clarke, 1890.

Caley, Percy B. "Life and Adventures of Lieutenant, Colonel John Connolly: The Story of a Tory: Chapter V: Plans to Invade Ohio Country : His Capture," *Western Pennsylvania History*, Vol. 11, No. 3 (July 1928). Pittsburgh: Historical Society of Western Pennsylvania.

Casey, William J. *Where and How the War Was Fought*. New York: William Morrow, 1976.

Clayton, W. Woodward, ed. *History of Union and Middlesex Counties with Biographical Sketches of Many of their Pioneers and Prominent Men*. Philadelphia: Everts and Peck, 1882.

Coldham, Peter Wilson. *American Loyalist Claims,* Vol. 1, abstracted from the Public Records Office, Series 13, Bundles 1–35 and 37. Washington, DC: National Genealogical Society, 1980.

____. *American Migrations 1765–1799*. Baltimore: Genealogical Publishing, 2000.

Collections of the Illinois State Historical Library, George Rogers Clark Papers, 1771–1781. Springfield: Trustees of the Illinois State Historical Library, 1912.

Collections of the New York Historical Society. New York: New York Historical Society, 1811–.

Colonial Records of Pennsylvania, Minutes of the Supreme Executive Council, Vol. 12. Harrisburg, PA: Theo Fenn, 1853.

Cope, Gilbert, and John Smith Futhey. *History of Chester County, Pennsylvania with Genealogical and Biographical Sketches*, Vol. 1. Original 1881, and reprint, Westminster, MD: Heritage Press, 1995.

Crier, Vol. 55. Philadelphia: Germantown Historical Society, 2005.

Daly, T. A. *The Wissahickon*. Philadelphia: The Garden Club of Philadelphia, 1922.

Delaware County Planning Department. *Report of the Findings of the Delaware County Historic Resources Survey for Newton Township, June 1984*.

Doniol, Henri. Historie de la participation de la France à l'établissement des États–Unis d'Amérique. Paris: Imprimerie Nationale (1886–1892), Vol. 1.

Dorland, W. A. Newman. "Second Troop Philadelphia City Cavalry," *Pennsylvania Magazine of History and Biography*. Philadelphia: Pennsylvania Historical Society, Vol. 45, No. 4 (1921).

Dorwart, Jeffrey M. *Fort Mifflin of Philadelphia: An Illustrated History*. Philadelphia: University of Pennsylvania Press, 1998.

Drake, Francis Samuel. *Tea Leaves: Being a Collection of Letters, and Documents Relating to the Shipment of Tea to the American Colonies in the Year 1773, by the East India Tea Company; Now First Printed from the Original Manuscript, With an Introduction, Notes, and Biographical Notices of the Boston Tea Party*. Boston: A. O. Crane, 1884.

Drake, Samuel Adams. *Nooks and Corners of the New England Coast*. New York: Harper and Brothers, 1875.

Duane, William, ed. *Extracts from the Diary of Christopher Marshall, Kept in Philadelphia and Lancaster during the American Revolution, 1774–1781*. Albany, NY: Joel Munsell, 1877.

Egerton, Hugh E., ed. *The Royal Commission on the Losses and Services of American Loyalists, 1783–1785.* Oxford: H. Hart at the Oxford University Press, 1915; reprinted New York: Burt Franklin, 1971.

Emmett, Dr. Thomas Addis, contributor. "Sir Henry Clinton's Original Secret Record of Private Daily Intelligence," *Magazine of American History with Notes and Queries.* New York: Historical Publications, Vol. 11, January–June, 1884.

Engle, William Henry, ed. *Proprietary and Other Tax Lists of the County of Bucks for the Years 1779, 1781, 1782, 1783, 1784, 1785, and 1786.* Harrisburg, PA: W. S. Ray, State Printer of Pennsylvania, 1897.

Fisher, Elijah. *Elijah Fisher's Journal while in the War for Independence, 1775–1784.* Augusta, ME: Badger & Manley, 1880.

Fitzpatrick, John C., ed. *Writings of George Washington from the Original Manuscript Sources, 1745–1799.* Washington, DC: Government Printing Office, 39 Vols., 1931–1944.

Flexner, James Thomas. *George Washington in the American Revolution, 1775–1783.* Boston: Little, Brown, 1968.

Force, Peter. *American Archives.* Reprint of 1837–1853 editions. New York: Johnson Reprint, 1972.

Ford, Worthington Chauncey. *British Officers Serving in the American Revolution, 1774–1783.* Brooklyn: Historical Printing Club, 1897.

____. *Letters of William Lee,* Vols. 1–3. Brooklyn: Historical Printing Club, 1891.

____. *Writings of George Washington: 1775–1776,* Vol. 3. New York: G. P. Putnam's Sons, 1889.

____, et al., eds. *Journals of the Continental Congress, 1774–1789.* Washington, DC: Government Printing Office, 1904–1937.

Fortescue, Sir John, ed. *The Correspondence of King George the Third, from 1760 to December 1783.* London: Macmillan, 1928.

Franklin, Benjamin. *Papers of Benjamin Franklin Series.* New Haven, CT: Yale University Press, 1959–present.

____. *Papers of Benjamin Franklin Series* at http://franklinpapers.org/franklin/.

The (Philadelphia) Freeman's Journal, or, the North American Intelligencer, 1781.

Genealogies of Pennsylvania Families: From the Pennsylvania Genealogical Magazine, Vol. 1. Baltimore: Genealogical Publishing, 1982.

General Catalog of Princeton University 1746–1906. Princeton, NJ: Princeton University, 1908.

Great Britain, War Office. Printed Army Annual Lists: 1754–1784 on microfilm, London, National Archives.

Gruber, Ira D., ed. *John Peebles' American War: The Diary of a Scottish Grenadier, 1776–1782.* Mechanicsburg, PA: Stackpole, 1998.

Hammond, Isaac W., ed. *State of New Hampshire, Miscellaneous Provincial and State Papers, 1725–1800,* Vol. 18. Manchester, NH: John B. Clarke, 1890.

Harvey, Oscar Jewell, and Ernest Gray Smith. *A History of Wilkes-Barre, Luzerne County, Pennsylvania: From Its First Beginnings to the Present Time, Including Chapters of Newly-Discovered Early Wyoming Valley History, Together with Many Biographical*

Sketches and Much Genealogical Material, Vol. 1. Wilkes-Barre, PA: Readers Press, 1909.

Hay, John. *Answers to a Printed Libel Entitled a Representation to the Public of Affairs between Gilbert Barkly of Philadelphia and John Hay of Quebec.* Quebec: Brown and Gilmore, 1764.

Hazard, Samuel. *Hazard's Register of Pennsylvania Devoted to the Preservation of Facts and Documents and Every Other Kind of Useful Information Respecting the State of Pennsylvania.* 16 Vols. Philadelphia: William F. Geddes, 1828–1836.

____. *Pennsylvania Archives First Series.* 12 Vols. Harrisburg, PA: Joseph Severns, 1852–1856.

____. *Pennsylvania Colonial Records Series.* Harrisburg, PA: T. Fenn, 1838–1853.

Heitman, Francis B. *Historical Register of Officers of the Continental Army during the War of the Revolution, April, 1775, to December, 1783.* Washington, DC: Rare Book Shop Publishing, 1914.

Historical Magazine, and Notes and Queries Concerning the Antiquities, History, and Biography of America. Boston: C.B. Richardson, 1857–1875.

Historical Manuscript Commission. *Manuscripts of the Earl of Dartmouth, American Papers*, Vol. 2, 14th Report, Appendix, Part 10, 1895. Reprint, Boston: Gregg Press, 1972.

____. *Report on American Manuscripts in the Royal Institution of Great Britain*, Vol. 1. London: Mackie, 1904.

____. *Report on American Manuscripts in the Royal Institution of Great Britain*, 15th Report, Appendix, Part 6, Manuscripts of the Earl of Carlisle Preserved at Castle Howard. London: Eyre and Spottiswoode, 1897.

Historical Society of Pennsylvania. *Bulletin of the Historical Society of Pennsylvania*, Vol. 1, 1845–1847. Philadelphia: Merrihew and Thompson, 1848.

Horne, John (Tooke). *The Trial (at Large) of John Horne, Esq. upon Information Filed Ex Officio, by His Majesty's Attorney General, for a Libel. Before the Right Hon. William, Earl of Mansfield, in the Court of King's Bench, Guildhall, on Friday the Fourth of July 1777. Published by the Defendant, From Mr. Gurney's Short-Hand Notes . . . .* London: G. Hearsly, 1777.

____. *The Trial of John Horne, Esq; upon an Information Filed Ex Officio by His Majesty's Attorney General, for a Libel . . . .* London: S. Blandon, 1777.

Horsman, Reginald. *Matthew Elliott, British Indian Agent.* Detroit: Wayne State University Press, 1964.

Howe, Sir William. *The Narrative of Lieut. Gen. Sir William Howe* London: H. Baldwin, 1780.

Hutchinson, C. H. *The Chronicles of Middletown: Containing a Compilation of Facts, Biographical Sketches, Reminiscences, Anecdotes, etc., Connected with the History of One of the Oldest Towns in Pennsylvania.* Self-Published, 1906.

Independent Chronicle and the Universal Advertiser. Boston, 1776–1801.

Jackson, John W. *With the British Army in Philadelphia 1777–1778.* San Rafael, CA: Presidio Press, 1979.

Jefferson, Thomas. *The Papers of Thomas Jefferson Series.* Princeton, NJ: Princeton University Press, 1950–present.

Johnson, Amandus. *The Journal and Biography of Nicholas Collin 1746–1831.*
Philadelphia: New Jersey Society of Pennsylvania, 1936.

Jordan, John W., ed. *Colonial and Revolutionary Families of Pennsylvania*, Vol. 1.
Reprinted from 1911. Baltimore: Genealogical Publishing, 1978.

Journal of American History. Bloomington, IL: Organization of American
Historians, 2000.

Kapp, Friedrich. *The Life of John Kalb, Major-General in the Revolutionary Army.* New
York: H. Holt, 1884.

Kellogg, Louise Phelps, ed. *Frontier Advance on the Upper Ohio, 1778–1779.*
Collections Vol. 23, Drapier Series Vol. 4. Madison: Wisconsin State
Historical Society, 1916.

_____. *Frontier Retreat on the Upper Ohio, 1779–1781.* Collections Vol. 24, Drapier
Series Vol. 5. Madison: Wisconsin State Historical Society, 1917.

Knauss, James O. *Christopher Saur the Third.* Worcester, MA: American
Antiquarian Society, 1931.

Kuntzleman, Oliver Charles. "Joseph Galloway, Loyalist." EdD thesis, Temple
University, Philadelphia, 1941.

Labaree, Leonard W., ed. *The Papers of Benjamin Franklin.* New Haven, CT: Yale
University Press, 1959 to present.

Laurens, John. *Correspondence of Colonel John Laurens in the Years 1777–1778.* New
York: John B. Moreau, 1867. Reprint, New York: Arno Press, 1969.

Lederer, Richard M. Jr. *Colonial American English.* Essex, CT: Verbatim Books,
1985.

Levering, John. *Levering Family: History and Genealogy.* Albany, NY: Joel Munsell,
1887.

Lineage Book. Washington, DC: National Society of the Daughters of the
American Revolution, 1895–1921.

Linn, John Blair, and William H. Egle, eds. *Pennsylvania in the War of the
Revolution, Battalions and Line. 1775–1783.* Harrisburg, PA: L. S. Hart, State
Printer, 1880.

Lloyd's Evening Post and British Chronicle, London, 1776.

Lopez, Claude Anne. *My Life with Benjamin Franklin.* New Haven, CT: Yale
University Press, 2000.

MacMaster, Richard Kerwin, Samuel L. Horst, and Robert E. Ulle. *Conscience in
Crisis: Mennonites and Other Peace Churches in America, 1739–1789: Interpretation and
Documents.* Scottdale, PA: Herald Press, 1979.

The Magazine of History, extra No. 6 (bound Vol. 2 contains extra Nos. 5–8).
Reprint, New York: William Abbatt, 1909.

Martin, John Hill. *Martin's Bench and Bar of Philadelphia.* Philadelphia: Rees
Welch, 1883.

Martin, Joseph Plumb. *Private Yankee Doodle.* Boston: Little Brown, 1962.

Maryland Journal, and Baltimore Advertiser. Baltimore, 1773–1794.

Maurepas, Arnaud de, and Antoine Boulant. *Les ministres et les ministères du siècle
des Lumières (1715–1789): étude et dictionnaire.* Paris: Christian, 1996.

Maxwell, W. J., compiler. *General Alumni Catalog of the University of Pennsylvania.* Philadelphia: Alumni Association of the University, 1922.

McConaghy, Mary D., Michael Silberman, and Irina Kalashnikova. *Penn in the 18th Century.* http://www.archives.upenn.edu/histy/features/1700s/penn1700s.html. Philadelphia: University of Pennsylvania, 2004.

Meehan, Thomas. "Newark." *The Catholic Encyclopedia,* Vol. 10. New York: Robert Appleton, 1911. http://www.newadvent.org/cathen/10779c.htm.

Meginness, John F., ed. *History of Lycoming County Pennsylvania.* Chicago: Brown, Runk, 1892.

Melville, Herman. *Israel Potter: His Fifty Years of Exile.* Edited by Hennig Cohen. New York: Fordham University Press, 1991.

The Mennonite. Magazine of Mennonite Church USA. Hillsboro, KS: Mennonite Book Concern, 1885 to present.

Mevers, Frank C. *The Papers of Josiah Bartlett.* Hanover, NH: University Press of New England, 1979.

Minutes of the Council of Safety of the State of New Jersey. Jersey City: J. H. Lyon, 1872.

Minutes of the Supreme Executive Council of Pennsylvania from its Organization to the Termination of the Revolution, Vol. 11. Harrisburg, PA: Theo. Fenn, 1852.

Montgomery, Thomas Lynch. *Pennsylvania Archives Sixth Series.* 15 Vols. Harrisburg, PA: Harrisburg Publishing, 1906–1907.

Montresor, John. *The Journal of Captain John Montresor.* New York: New York Historical Society, 1881.

Morris, Robert, ed. *Memoirs of James Morris of South Farms in Litchfield.* New Haven, CT: Yale University Press, 1933.

Moscow, Henry. *The Street Book: An Encyclopedia of Manhattan's Street Names and Their Origins.* New York: Macmillan, 1990.

Moss, Roger W., and Tom Crane. *Historic Houses of Philadelphia: A Tour of the Region's Museum Homes.* Philadelphia: University of Pennsylvania Press, 1998.

"Narrative of Lieutenant Luke Matthewman of the Revolutionary Navy," *Magazine of American History with Notes and Queries,* Vol. 2, Part 1. New York: A. S. Barnes, 1878.

Naval Documents of the American Revolution. Series Vols. 1 to 11. Washington, DC: Government Printing Office, 1964 to present.

Neagles, James C. *Summer Soldiers: A Survey and Index of Revolutionary War Courts-Martial.* Salt Lake City, UT: Ancestry Inc., 1986.

Nelson, Larry L. *A Man of Distinction among Them: Alexander McKee and the Ohio Country Frontier, 1754–1799.* Kent, OH: Kent State University Press, 1999.

New England Quarterly. Boston: Colonial Society of Massachusetts, Northeastern University, 1928 to present.

New Hampshire, State of. *Provincial and State Papers,* Vol. 25, Town Charters, Part 2. Concord, NH: Edward D. Pearson, Printer, 1895.

New Jersey Archives Series, 1880–1950. Trenton: New Jersey Bureau of Archives and History.

New York Gazette and Weekly Mercury, 1768–1783. New York, and Sept. 21 to Nov. 2, 1776, at Newark, NJ.

Nolan, J. Bennett. *Lafayette in America Day by Day*. Baltimore: Johns Hopkins Press, 1934.

Oaks, Robert F. "Philadelphians in Exile: the Problem of Loyalty during the American Revolution," *Pennsylvania Magazine of History and Biography*, Vol. 96, No. 3 (July 1972).

O'Callaghan, E. B. *Documents Relative to the Colonial History of New York*, Vol. 8. Albany, NY: Weed, Parsons, 1857.

On-Line Institute for Advanced Loyalist Studies on the Internet. http://www.royal-provincial.com/.

Packard, Francis Randolph, ed. *Annals of Medical History*. New York: Paul B. Hoeber, 1918–1942.

Palmer, Dr. William P., ed. *Calendar of Virginia State Papers and Other Manuscripts*, Vols. 1–3. Richmond: 1875, 1881, and 1883. Reprint, New York: Kraus Reprint, 1968.

The Papers of George Washington, Revolutionary War Series (1775–1783), Vols. 1–19. Charlottesville, VA: University of Virginia, 1985 to present.

The Papers of George Washington, "Washington's Revolutionary War Itinerary and the Location of His Headquarters, 1775–1783." Charlottesville, VA: University of Virginia. http://gwpapers.virginia.edu/documents/revolution/itinerary/all.html.

Papers of the Continental Congress, 1774–1789. Published and on microfilm. Washington: National Archives and Records Service, General Services Administration, 1971.

Papers of Thomas Jefferson. Series. 36 Vols. Princeton, NJ: Princeton University Press, 1950 to present.

Parliament of Great Britain. *The Examination of Joseph Galloway, esq. Late Speaker of the House of Assembly of Pennsylvania before the House of Commons in a Committee on the American Papers with Explanatory Notes*. London: J. Wilkie, 1779.

Peckham, Howard Henry, ed. *The Toll of Independence: Engagements and Battle Casualties of the American Revolution*. Chicago: University of Chicago Press, 1974.

Pennsylvania Evening Post, 1775–1781. Philadelphia.

Pennsylvania Gazette, Philadelphia, 1728–1815.

Pennsylvania Genealogical Magazine. Philadelphia: Genealogical Society of Pennsylvania.

Pennsylvania Magazine of History and Biography. Philadelphia: Pennsylvania Historical Society.

Pennsylvania Packet or General Advertiser, Philadelphia, 1776–1781.

Pennsylvania, University of. *Biographical Catalogue of the Matriculates of the College Together with Lists of the Members of the College Faculty and the Trustees, Officers and Recipients Of Honorary Degrees, 1749–1893*. Philadelphia: Alumni Society, Avil Printing, 1894.

Pennypacker, Morton. *General Washington's Spies on Long Island and in New York*.

Garden City, NY: Long Island Historical Society by Country Life Press, 1939.

Perrault, Gilles. *Le Secret du Roi*, Vol. 3. Paris: Fayard 1996.

Plain Dealer, Bridgeton, NJ, 1776.

Prince, Carl E., ed. *The Papers of William Livingston,* 5 Vols. (1774–1988). Trenton, NJ: New Jersey Historical Commission, 1979.

Princeton University. *General Catalog of Princeton University 1746–1906.* Princeton, NJ: Princeton University, 1908.

Proceedings of the American Philosophical Society. Philadelphia: American Philosophical Society.

Proceedings of the Massachusetts Historical Society Series. Boston: Massachusetts Historical Society.

Proceedings of the New Jersey Historical Society, Vol. 7, Nos. 1 and 2. Newark, NJ: New Jersey Historical Society, 1922.

Reed, John F. *Valley Forge, Crucible of Victory.* Monmouth Beach, NJ: Philip Freneau, 1969.

Reed, William B. *Life and Correspondence of Joseph Reed: Military Secretary of Washington, at Cambridge, Adjutant-General of the Continental Army, Member of the Congress of the United States, and President of the Executive Council of the State of Pennsylvania/by His Grandson, William B. Reed.* 2 Vols. Philadelphia: Lindsay and Blakiston, 1847.

Reiss, Oscar. *Jews in Colonial America.* Jefferson, NC: McFarland, 2004.

Reuter, Frank T. "Petty Spy or Effective Diplomat: The Role of George Beckwith," *Journal of the Early Republic.* Philadelphia: University of Pennsylvania Press, 1981.

Rowe, Gail Stuart. *Embattled Bench: The Pennsylvania Supreme Court and the Forging of a Democratic Society, 1684–1809.* Newark, DE: University of Delaware Press, 1994.

Ruschenberger, W. S. W. *Obituary Notice of Dr. Robert Bridges* (read before the American Philosophical Society, February 15, 1884). Proceedings of the American Philosophical Society, Vol. 21, No. 115, Philadelphia: American Philosophical Society, 1884.

Sabine, Lorenzo. *Biographical Sketches of Loyalists of the American Revolution, with an Historical Essay.* Boston: Little, Brown, 1864.

Sabine, William H. W., ed. *Historical Memoirs of William Smith 1763–1778,* Vol. 2. New York: New York Times and Arno Press, 1969.

Savelle, Max. *George Morgan Colony Builder.* New York: Columbia University Press, 1932.

Schraf, John Thomas, and Thompson Westcott. *History of Philadelphia 1609–1884,* 3 Vols. Philadelphia: L. H. Everts, 1884.

Scott, Kenneth. "Major General John Sullivan, and Captain Stephen Holland." *New England Quarterly* (Boston: Colonial Society of Massachusetts, Northeastern University, 1928 to present), Vol. 18, No. 3 (September 1945).

Scoville, Joseph Alfred. The Old Merchants of New York, Vols. 1–5. New York: Carleton, 1885.

Sellers, Charles Coleman. *Patience Wright: American Artist and Spy in George III's London.* Middletown, CT: Wesleyan University Press, 1976.

Sheldon, Laura Charlotte. *France and the American Revolution 1763–1778.* Ithaca, NY: Andrus and Church, 1900.

Showman, Richard K., ed. *The Papers of General Nathanael Greene,* 13 Vols. Chapel Hill: University of North Carolina Press, 1976–2005.

Siebert, Wilbur Henry. *The Legacy of the American Revolution to the British West Indies and Bahamas: A Chapter out of the History of American Loyalists.* Columbus: Ohio State University, 1913.

Simcoe, John Graves. *A History of the Operations of a Partisan Corps Called the Queen's Rangers.* New York: Bartlett & Welford, 1844.

Smith, John Spear. *Memoir of the Baron de Kalb: Read at the Meeting of the Maryland Historical Society, 7th January, 1858.* Baltimore: John D. Toy, 1858.

Smith, Paul H., et al., eds. *Letters of Delegates to Congress, 1774–1789,* 25 Vols. Washington, DC: Library of Congress, 1976–2000.

Smyth, John Ferdinand. "Narrative or Journal of Captain John Ferdinand Dalziel Smyth, of the Queen's Rangers," *Pennsylvania Magazine of History and Biography,* Vol. 39.

Sparks, Jared. *Correspondence of the American Revolution: Being Letters of Eminent Men to George Washington, from the Time of His Taking Command of the Army to the End of his Presidency.* Boston: Little, Brown, 1853.

Sparrow, Elizabeth Mary. *Secret Service: British Agents in France, 1792–1815.* Woodbridge, England: Boydell Press, 1999.

Spierer, Eric. *Those "Inimical to the American Cause": Loyalists in New Hampshire during the American Revolution.* Middletown, CT. Wesleyan University, 2010. http://wesscholar.wesleyan.edu/cgi/viewcontent.cgi?article=1484&context=etd _hon_theses.

Stryker, William S. *The New Jersey Volunteers (Loyalists) in the Revolutionary War.* Trenton, NJ: Naar, Day and Naar, 1887.

Stuart, Ferdinand Smyth. *The Case of Ferdinand Smyth Stuart with His Memorials to the King, the Lords of the Treasury, &c.* London: Cox, Son, and Baylis, 1807.

Tallmadge, Benjamin. *Memoir of Colonel Benjamin Tallmadge.* New York: Thomas Holman, 1858. Reprint, New York: New York Times and Arno Press, 1968.

Thacher, James. *A Military Journal during the American Revolutionary War, from 1775 to 1783.* Boston: Richardson and Lord, 1823.

Tilghman, Oswald. *Memoir of Lieutenant Colonel Tench Tilghman: Secretary and Aid to Washington.* Albany, NY: J. Munsell, 1876.

Trumbull, Henry. *Life and Remarkable Adventures of Israel R. Potter.* Providence, RI: J. Howard, 1824.

Trussell, John B. B. Jr. *The Pennsylvania Line Regimental Organization and Operations, 1776–1783.* Harrisburg, PA: Pennsylvania Historical and Museum Commission, 1977.

Uhlendorf, Bernhard A., trans. and annotator. *Revolution in America: Confidential Letters and Journals 1776–1784 of the Adjutant General Major Bauermeister of the Hessian Forces.* New Brunswick, NJ: Rutgers University Press, 1957.

_____, trans. and ed. *The Siege of Charleston: Diaries of Captain Johann Ewald, Major General Johann Christop Von Huyn, and Captain Johann Hinricks*. Ann Arbor: University of Michigan Press, 1938.

Valley Forge Legacy, "The Muster Roll Project." http://valleyforgemusterroll.org.

Van Doren, Carl. *Benjamin Franklin*. New York: Viking, 1938.

_____. *Mutiny in January*. New York: Viking, 1943.

_____. *Secret History of the American Revolution*. New York: Viking, 1941.

Van Every, Dale. *A Company of Heroes: The American Frontier, 1775–1783*. New York: Morrow, 1962.

Virginia Gazette (John Dixon and William Hunter Jr. owners). Williamsburg, VA: 1775–1778.

Virginia Magazine of History and Biography. Richmond, VA: Virginia Historical Society, 1893 to present.

Watson, John F. *Annals of Philadelphia*, 3 Vols. Philadelphia: E. S. Stuart, 1877.

Watson, Winslow C., ed. *Men and Times of the Revolution, or, Memoirs of Elkanah Watson: Including Journals of Travels in Europe and America, from the Year 1777 to 1842: and His Correspondence with Public Men, and Reminisce*. New York: Dana, 1856.

Weaks, Mabel Clare. *Calendar of the Kentucky Papers of the Draper Collection of Manuscripts*, Vol. 2. Madison: Wisconsin Historical Society, 1925.

Weis, Frederick Lewis. *The Colonial Clergy of the Middle Colonies: New York, New Jersey, and Pennsylvania, 1628–1776*. Baltimore: Genealogical Publishing, 1978.

Westcott, Thompson. *The Historic Mansions and Buildings of Philadelphia: With Some Notice of Their Owners and Occupants*. Philadelphia: Porter and Coates, 1877.

Western Pennsylvania Historical Magazine, Vol. 11. Pittsburgh: Historical Society of Western Pennsylvania.

Wild, Ebenezer. "Journal of Ebenezer Wild (1776–1781)." *Proceedings of the Massachusetts Historical Society*, 2nd Series, Vol. 6 (1890–1891). Boston: Massachusetts Historical Society.

Wilson, James Grant, ed. *The Memorial History of the City of New York from its Founding to the Year 1892*, Vol. 2. New York: New York History Company, 1892.

Wilson, James Grant, John Fiske, and Stanley L. Klos, eds. *Appleton's Cyclopedia of American Biography*. New York: D. Appleton, 1887–1889.

Wilson, Joseph Lapsley. *Book of the First Troop, Philadelphia City Cavalry, 1774–1914*. Philadelphia: Hallowell, 1915.

Wright, Esmond. *Franklin of Philadelphia*. Cambridge, MA: Belknap Press of Harvard University Press, 1986.

List of Illustrations

General Index

Index of Spies

ACKNOWLEDGMENTS

I want to thank the staff of the William L. Clements Library at the University of Michigan for its assistance, especially John C. Dann, J. Kevin Graffagnino, Brian Leigh Dunnigan, Barbara DeWolf, Janet Bloom, Clayton Lewis, Cheney Schopieray, and Donald Wilcox. I also want to thank Katherine Ludwig at the David Library of the American Revolution in Washington Crossing, Pennsylvania, John C. Van Horne at the Library Company of Philadelphia, and Dan Rolph at the Historical Society of Pennsylvania.

I have benefited from the expertise of Gregory J. W. Urwin of Temple University, John L. Bell, Todd Braisted, R. Grant Gilmore III, Don Hagist, Ron Wetteroth, and Nancy Wilson, who have answered my many questions.

I want to thank Daniele L. Thomas Easton and Jacques de Trentinian for their assistance with French spies.

I especially want to thank Thomas Fleming, who provided guidance when I first started to write and has always been a source of encouragement. I appreciated the encouragement and assistance from Dan Kinamen and Bill Ochester of the American Revolution Round Table of Philadelphia.

I want to thank my editor, Ron Silverman, who has been a great help in getting this manuscript to its final form, Trudi Gershenov for her cover design, my editor, Lucinda Bartley, and also my publisher, Bruce H. Franklin.

I also would like to thank Ida Marie Nagy, Jennifer Ann Nagy, and Lisa Marie Nagy for their assistance, extreme patience, and encouragement.